ONCE UPON A TIME
IN THE WEST . . .
COUNTRY

About the Author

TV and radio comedian Tony Hawks regularly pops up on shows like *Have I Got News for You*, *QI*, *Just A Minute* and *I'm Sorry I Haven't A Clue*. He is the bestselling author of five books including *Round Ireland with a Fridge* and *Playing the Moldovans at Tennis* which was shortlisted for the Samuel Johnson Prize and Bollinger Everyman Wodehouse Prize. His books have sold over 1 million copies around the world. He now lives in Devon with his partner, Fran and their son.

ONCE UPON A TIME IN THE WEST . . . COUNTRY

TONY HAWKS

HODDER

First published in Great Britain in 2015
by Hodder & Stoughton
An Hachette UK company

First published in paperback in 2016

2

A CIP catalogue record for this title is available from the British Library

Paperback ISBN 978 1 444 79480 9
EBook ISBN 978 1 444 79479 3

Typeset in Sabon MT by Hewer Text UK Ltd, Edinburgh

Printed and bound by CPI Group (UK) Ltd, Croydon, CR0 4YY

Hodder & Stoughton policy is to use papers that are natural, renewable
and recyclable products and made from wood grown in sustainable
forests. The logging and manufacturing processes are expected to
conform to the environmental regulations of the country of origin.

Hodder & Stoughton Ltd
Carmelite House
50 Victoria Embankment
London EC4Y 0DZ

www.hodder.co.uk

For Fran

Contents

Prologue

I woke suddenly, not sure where I was. Strange – a fan fixed to the ceiling above my head was gently turning. I looked around me. The surroundings were unfamiliar; a spacious, plain, impersonal room. Ah yes, we were in a hotel. Abroad somewhere. Yes, I remember, the Philippines. Puerto Princesa, to be precise.

This town had been a little disappointing and, like quite a few of the places we'd visited before, was not as picturesque as it had appeared in the tourist guides. Perversely, holidays often end up feeling like hard work and this one had been no exception. Stifling heat and stomach bugs had further marred the enjoyment of touristic excursions that had already begun to feel voyeuristic and superficial. Three weeks into our trip and Fran was still struggling to find a connection with her roots and we were both looking forward to getting back home.

It would probably have been much more fun had we met up with Fran's mother and her friends who were holidaying in the country at the same time, but the proposed rendezvous in the capital city of the island of Palawan had not taken place, for complicated logistical reasons that I didn't fully understand. Spending time with them could have brought a more personal perspective to the days. Fran's mum Yolanda, or Yollie, as she liked to be called, could almost be called a Londoner these days, but she'd been born in the Philippines and had come to England in the 1960s seeking work, where she'd met Fran's English father and produced a beautiful daughter. The same beautiful daughter who was lying next to me on the hotel bed.

I checked the time. 3.09 a.m. I wondered if I should wake Fran. I had something to tell her, but I knew how much harder she found it to get back to sleep than I did, so I reconsidered.

The bedclothes rustled as she began to toss and turn. Maybe I *should* tell her. Had it been a dream? A voice in my head? A message from the subconscious, perhaps?

Another toss. Another turn. She seemed to be almost awake. Finally, I decided I would tell her.

'Fran?' I offered tentatively.

'Yes?' she replied sleepily. 'What is it?'

'I've had an epiphany.'

'Oh no! Shall we call a doctor?'

'No – an epiphany. A thought. A realisation. A revelation of truth.'

'Oh, right.'

Fran heaved at the covers and turned away.

'Tell me in the morning,' she said.

No sense of occasion, that girl.

1

A Change Is as Good as a Rest

How had I come to be sharing my life with a kind, gentle and loving person such as Fran?

Ah, now that is the kind of question it is customary for the author to offer up in stories like these. The authorial voice is required to be a modest one, for fear of alienating the reader. He doesn't want to appear a cocky bugger. He ought to be writing things like 'I don't deserve Fran'. But that wouldn't be true. I *do* deserve her. I'm an OK chap. I would be as bold as to say that I'm really quite a reasonable catch. Bucking the trend of many in my profession, I am not morose or moody, instead I'm jolly and fun-loving. I am over six foot, not bad looking, I lead a relatively stress-free life and, if I may borrow a rather ignoble term often used in singles ads, I'm financially solvent. I'm far from perfect, but I make a pretty good fist of being kind, as much as I can. And so does Fran. So that makes us well suited. Opposites only tend to attract when there are demons at play, and we both hoped that they had all been exorcised years before.

I'm not really a believer in fate, but it could so easily be argued that Fran and I are *meant* to be together. On 1 July

2010, I went along to the ceremony for the Samuel Johnson Prize for Non-fiction. Ten years previously, my book *Playing the Moldovans at Tennis* had been one of the five books that made the shortlist, and every subsequent year I had been invited as a special guest. This year I hadn't intended to go. I was single and had been unable to identify a suitable consort as my chaperone, but on the evening of the event the invitation on the kitchen worktop stared up at me, as if to ask what was so attractive about a dull evening at home. On the spur of the moment, I changed my mind, got ready, and headed for the door.

As I sat, suitably suited, on the busy, hot London underground, I convinced myself that it would not take me long to bump into someone I knew at the drinks reception. However, half an hour into the proceedings I discovered a more painful truth. I found myself still milling around a large reception area, glass of white wine in one hand, canapé in the other, with eyes darting around the room, urgently seeking out a familiar face. Surely someone from my publishers would be here? Or another author whom I'd met along the way? Even one of the organisers from one of the previous years. But no, I could not spot a single soul with whom I could dock conversationally, and I remained stuck in an embarrassing social wilderness. The guests looked smart, bright, engaged, and switched on. The men wore clothes that I took to be trendy, which probably weren't, and the ladies wore lovely summer dresses, fussed about their appearances and petted their hair. This was the London literary circle? Probably, because circles were what they had automatically formed themselves into, huddling together to discuss what they'd read recently and what they hoped to read next – leaving me on the outside, surplus to requirements, like a book they seemed to have no interest in reading. Something by Andy McNab.

Being a pleasant summer's evening, many of the guests had sat down at tables outside on a spacious terrace, and on one of my sad, acquaintance-foraging circuits I did see a couple of TV presenters who had once interviewed me, but they were seated and deep in conversation. My eye was drawn quickly to an Asian-looking lady at the head of one of these tables. She stood out from the crowd. Yes, she was exceptionally pretty, but there was a freshness about her too – almost as if she didn't belong here in this competitive atmosphere, but perhaps, I imagined, laughing and playing with children in a playgroup. She sparkled. Such a shame that she would now glance up and see this sorry bloke milling about on his own, looking lost. If I could only have been at her table now, sitting next to her, giving her the benefit of my enormous charm – which was currently going horribly to waste.

'Hello Ian!' I bellowed, at last spotting a new arrival who was known to me.

'Hello Tony!' Ian replied, looking – to my great relief – rather pleased to see me, 'You know Victoria, don't you?'

'Yes, we've met before.'

I shook hands with Ian and Victoria Hislop. Ian and I had met in the 1990s when I'd appeared a few times on the BBC TV topical comedy show *Have I Got News for You*.

'I'm so pleased to see you,' I said, 'I didn't bring anyone and I've been feeling like a lemon for the last twenty minutes, wandering around on my own. Do you mind if I latch onto you?'

'Not at all,' said Ian, my social saviour. 'Latch away.'

At that moment we were ushered into a seated auditorium, where we were told the prize-giving ceremony would begin shortly.

'Let me get you guys a drink,' I said.

'OK, we'll go through, and we'll save a seat for you.'

When I returned minutes later, walking with great care as I struggled with three glasses of wine, Ian and Victoria turned, waved and indicated the vacant seat alongside them. To my astonishment, next to that empty chair sat the beautiful girl from earlier. An adrenalin rush. My heartbeat skipped with excitement.

'Calm down, Tony,' I said to myself. 'She's bound to have a boyfriend.'

I'd learned to give myself this kind of emergency pep talk. Getting one's hopes up too high had been a regular failing of mine when it came to the opposite sex. Lowering expectations, I had since found, moderated the pain upon rejection. Marginally.

Perhaps unwisely, I allowed my hopes to rise again as I squeezed my way up the aisle towards Ian and Victoria and noticed that there was a female sitting on the other side of the lady of my interest.

'Aha! Good, no boyfriend,' I thought.

I was at it again. How could I jump to that conclusion? The boyfriend could have myriad reasons for not being there. He might be working late, or be on an overseas trip, or he may even be one of the authors sitting on stage hoping that he was about to be presented with the Samuel Johnson Prize for Non-fiction. As I got closer to my seat, I became very nervous. I would have to be careful not to spill the drinks. I was a clumsy man even when sober and, because you sip more often when you haven't got anyone to talk to, I'd been consuming wine faster than usual. But no, it didn't happen. I didn't make a fool of myself and spill wine all over the girl I wanted to impress. Instead, I calmly passed the drinks to a grateful Ian and Victoria and sat down, desperately trying to come up with a decent opening line to initiate a conversation with the girl beside me. To my delight, it wasn't necessary.

'You must be Tony,' she said, with a heart-melting smile.

'Yes. Yes, I am.'

What a lucky break. She knew who I was. Perhaps her colleagues had spotted me and had been telling her about my books. She could even be a fan. This would make things so much easier. I wouldn't have to impress her or prove myself in these opening exchanges because to some extent, the groundwork would have already been done.

'How did you know that I'm Tony?' I enquired.

'I tried to sit in your chair and Ian said that it was Tony's seat. So that must be you.'

Ah. It was Ian whom she knew, not me. Never mind, I wasn't complaining. This was a first for me. At last, compensation for all those times I'd longed for pretty girls to be allocated seats next to me on planes, coaches or trains, only to be presented with a fat bloke with body odour. There looked to be three hundred people or so at this event. That I should end up randomly being seated next to the person I most wanted to meet was finally my reward for having lived a relatively good life free from any involvement with international drug rings.

Whilst we waited for the formal proceedings to begin, I

did what any self-respecting single male would do in a situation like this. I completely ignored the people who had kindly come to my rescue. I had no need for Ian and Victoria. They had served their purpose and should now drink their wines alone. I had more important business afoot. A foot away, in fact.

The object of my excited attention turned out to be called Fran. She was a mature student completing a PhD in biomedical imaging. Blimey, a bit too brainy for me, I thought. She told me about her passion for books and literature, and I remember spurting some rubbish about how I felt science, one day, would be able to measure the force of love. Anyway, whatever happened – and it's something of a white-wine blur – things went well, because at the end of the evening we exchanged email addresses, and a courtship followed in which I was charmed not just by her obvious beauty, but by her giggles, her gentleness, compassion, astuteness and most impressively of all, her determination and desire to grow and improve herself as a person. It wasn't a whirlwind romance because it was more measured – more of a 'strong breeze romance' – and within a year we had dated, made love, holidayed and moved in together.

I keep Ian posted of each landmark.

***

What I had eventually said to Fran over breakfast at our hotel in Puerto Princesa, on the penultimate day of our trip, was this:

'We no longer need to live in London.'

'What?'

Fran was relatively unsurprised by this, being used to the randomness of my thoughts.

'We no longer need to live in London.'

'That's what woke you in the middle of the night?'

'Yes. I had it all worked out. You're finishing your PhD soon. I can write wherever I am, and I have to travel round the country for various shows anyway, so I'd just be doing that from a different starting point, that's all. There's nothing holding us to the capital anymore.'

'Where were you thinking of moving?'

'I don't know. At three a.m. this morning, the South West was in my head.'

'Perhaps that was your inner voice. I read this article a while back saying that we should try to listen to our inner voices.'

'So, what do you think? Should we move? What does *your* inner voice say?'

'Mine says I should have another breakfast pastry.'

* * *

My mind was particularly active as we sped down the A303 towards Devon. Actually, those of you who know the A303 will realise that very little speeding is done on that road. There are sections where this is possible, but with this particular road the Department for Transport prefer to offer greater variety, and there are plenty of opportunities to take a rest from speed to practise dawdling, queueing, and steering the car through meandering hilly sections.

The reason for our visit to Devon was twofold. Shortly after the Philippines trip, friends had asked me to make an appearance at a small village in the southern reaches of the county, and we'd decided that we could make this trip the beginning of a house-hunting process that might take months, maybe even years. It might not be Devon where we settled, but it seemed as good a place as any to start. Neither of us had any particular connection with the area, but we'd always loved our visits to our friends Kevin and Donna and had stayed with them on quite a few occasions, just as we would this time. However, this visit would be a little different. We would take a couple of days to scour the area, to see if it could provide the change that we had discussed over a breakfast on the other side of the world.

By the time the road was leading us through Salisbury Plain, the nature of 'change' was preoccupying my mind. There has been plenty of evidence to show that a lot of us don't like it very much, and I reckoned this was mainly because of fear. Fear of loss of face, fear of loss of control, fear of what will come next, fear of our competence to cope, fear that change will bring more work, and fear that everything will be different. It seemed to me that the only kind of change most of us like is the stuff that gets handed back to us in the supermarket after we've handed over our twenty pound note.

Be the change you want to see in the world.

Such had been the message from Gandhi, the indomitable and yet benign freedom fighter from Gujarat – a phrase that was always ready and waiting in the wings to shine a spotlight on one's hypocrisy. What this phrase meant was that if you wanted peace in the world, then it was no good getting angry about that unjust parking ticket. It meant that if you wanted better education for your kids, then you'd better start taking time out to teach them; and it meant that if you wanted to see the planet's resources preserved for future generations, then you might need to do a tad more than buy one energy-saving light bulb.

At least that was my interpretation of what Gandhi had meant. As it happens, there is no reliable documentary evidence that Gandhi actually uttered the words 'Be the change you want to see in the world' in the first place. It's far more likely that he said, 'Blimey, that doughnut looks nice.' The closest verifiable remark we have from Gandhi on the subject of change is this:

If we could change ourselves, the tendencies in the world would also change. As a man changes his own nature, so does the attitude of the world change towards him ... We need not wait to see what others do.

But let's face it, 'Be the change you want to see in the world' is snappier, which is probably why someone who sought a simpler world had paraphrased the little man's words.

'Look! Stonehenge!' said Fran.

She wasn't hallucinating. This is where it is, just off the road to the right as you go west. It was built more than four thousand years ago by pagans who wanted to prove that although they couldn't get the internet, they were still extremely good at lugging around exceptionally heavy stones. They also wanted to confuse academics and create accidents on the A303 as drivers looked across to admire a big and seemingly pointless arrangement of rocks. When I first drove past the stones, a quarter of a century earlier, I remember thinking how small they actually seemed. Somehow I had conjured up an image of them making a huge statement on the landscape, when they're really rather modest. Not that I've ever seen them up close. I should have done it years ago, when they weren't fenced off and you could clamber all over them and have some fun. Now it's a UNESCO World Heritage Site, fun is out of the question. Sites of significance require us to be sombre and serious, and ball games are generally not encouraged. Shame, some of the stones would make excellent goalposts.

As we moved from Wiltshire into Somerset, acre after acre of green fields spread like a quilt either side of the long spear of tarmac ahead of us. London was beginning to feel like a distant memory. In these parts there were trees instead of people, and nature had the tenacity to stand up and really get in your face. Gazing almost dream-like through the windscreen at the changing landscape, I felt different. More relaxed. More in tune with the philosophy of Gandhi. For a moment I felt like we were kindred spirits. I wasn't so dissimilar to him – but for the gluttony, lust, height difference, and lack of any major convictions. Like him, I was someone who positively embraced change.

Or did I? I began to run things through in my mind. I'd lived in the same house for twenty-three years, I'd driven the same car for twelve, I'd had cereal and toast for breakfast for as long as I can remember, and I still deposited and withdrew money from the same crappy, corrupt, greedy bank that I'd signed up with as a student. Could this be the reason why I was now driving west? Was it time to shake things up?

Upon our return from the Philippines we'd had many a conversation about this, not all of which had been easy.

Shortly after Fran had moved in with me, she'd asked me about my neighbours. I had been forced to admit that I only knew the ones on either side of me, and that my sole social engagement with them had been limited to conversations about fences or clarification on what days the bins were going to be collected. Fran thought this was a shame, and I had agreed, but I'd pointed out that this was simply what it was like in London.

'Are you sure?' Fran had questioned.

'What do you mean?'

'Well, what do you *do* about it? How hard did you work to get to know your other neighbours? Isn't it down to you?'

Fran was right. Her gentle honesty had been one of the many qualities that had drawn me to her, and had motivated me to pursue the path to our current position in society – where we could refer to each other as 'partners'. It's a funny word, 'partner', suggesting that one might need to be a partner *in* something. A partner in crime. A partner in business. A partner in bridge.

What were Fran and I partners in?

Well, *life* I suppose.

Which made her question 'Isn't it down to you?' so incisive. It had served as a reminder of how my life had begun to lose its way. Could it be possible that my path to a life of truth and integrity had become as circuitous as the road that was currently inching us towards Devon?

If so, I wasn't ready to admit it yet, so when Fran's question first landed, capitulation was not an acceptable option. I manipulated the discussion towards an area where I felt I would be more able to occupy higher moral ground.

'There are more important issues at play in the world than whether neighbours talk to each other,' I stated, with the bombast of a headmaster on his first day in a new school – desperate to assert authority. 'There'll be nearly nine billion people on the planet in 2050 and if people keep "consuming" at the rate we're doing now, then we'll need two and a half planets to provide the required resources. All our leaders do is bang on about growth. Growth, growth, growth. When are we going to accept the fact that we're fully grown?'

'That's all well and good. But what do you actually *do* other than provide rhetoric on this subject?'

'Oh, I think I do my bit,' I said, 'I . . .'

My sentence stopped there, halted by the realisation that my 'bit' was so small that, had I announced what it actually *was*, it would have seemed pathetic. Ridiculous even. All I could have offered up was that I occasionally cycled to places, I didn't buy battery eggs or the cheapest chicken in the supermarket, and I had voted Green in the European elections.

Remembering that conversation as I carefully negotiated the car through the winding roads that led us from Somerset to Devon across the Blackdown Hills, a rather wrong-footing thought struck me. Here I was – this man who complained regularly about mankind's overconsumption and denigration of the earth's resources – sitting at the wheel of my carbon-emitting car. All I really had to contribute to the subject was hot air. I had no excuse for living the way I did, because I knew better. My niggling appetite for the truth about how we'd all made the world the way it was had seen to that. And it had led me to become something that I'd never wanted to be. I had become someone who preached one thing and did another. I had become a hypocrite.

Maybe it was that startling realisation that had highlighted to me that a change was needed.

* * *

'Are you planning on making anymore daft bets?' asked a jolly, rather tousled lady in the front row.

I was in the midst of a question-and-answer session following a successful screening of the film I'd made of my book *Playing the Moldovans at Tennis*.[1]

Making the film had been a gargantuan task, and I'd been greatly relieved to find that it had been well received by audiences. After a short run in Picturehouse cinemas, I was now clawing in funds by turning up at screenings wherever there'd be an enthusiastic audience. Like Scoriton Village Hall. The venue's lack of glamour was amply compensated by its cosiness and friendly atmosphere, and I was delighted to find the bucolic audience in a distinctly good mood. I gave the lady who'd asked the question a straight answer.

'No,' I replied firmly, 'my days of doing bets on a whim and then writing about them are over. I need to have a good reason now.'

'I've got a bet for you,' the same lady chirped up with gusto, as if she hadn't heard what I'd just said.

'I told you, I've retired from bets—'

1   www.moldovansmovie.com

'I bet you can't walk from coast to coast in Devon with my pet pig Dave.'

A big laugh. In order to keep the audience on my side, I couldn't be too dismissive.

'It's an interesting idea, certainly. I promise to give it some thought. But perhaps another question now . . .'

* * *

I hadn't planned on giving it any thought, so I was rather surprised in the morning when I found myself, well, giving it some thought. A hazy mist was lifting over distant Dartmoor as I addressed the issue at breakfast with Kevin and Donna.

'You know, I woke in the night thinking about Dave the Pig,' I said, 'and although I dismissed it at the time, I think it could be rather fun. Do either of you know who that lady was?'

Kevin and Donna, who'd both been to the screening, shook their heads.

'It won't be a problem finding her,' said Donna. 'We'll just ask around in the village. Someone is bound to know her.'

'Found any houses to look at?' asked Kevin, changing the subject – perhaps to steer it away from the downright ridiculous.

I'd met Kevin a few years before, in Paraguay of all places. Both of us had travelled there as supporters of the World Land Trust. We were on a trip to see how land purchased by this excellent charity had prevented the expansion of cattle ranchers and energy companies, and protected the biodiversity and natural habitat of the region. After landing in Asunción, we'd flown on a petite five-seater plane to the remote northern part of the country and had made a further journey by boat upriver to reach the lodge that was to be our base camp. Over the coming days Kevin had protected me from mosquitoes by acting as a decoy – being bitten himself by every one of the available pests.

During the trip we'd also shared many a late-night conversation about the challenges facing the planet as the population continued to rise. It had been that trip, and those conversations, that had started to alert me to what we humans are doing to the planet – the planet we sometimes refer to as being 'our planet'. *Our* planet. Perhaps our propensity to view it this way had been the cause of the problem.

'We've found a few interesting properties to look at, so today is our "check out Devon" day,' said Fran.

'I don't think you'll be disappointed,' said Donna.

Donna was not wrong. Beautiful spots are bountiful in Devon. We were amazed at the feeling of space. Gaps in the hedgerows provided vistas that stretched before us as far as the eye could see, with only the odd farm building to remind us that people actually lived here. We'd always thought of England as being a country that was brimming over with people. Our escapes from London had taken us to the Surrey Hills or Sussex Downs, but we'd never felt far from a road or a development of houses.

Devon was a revelation. It has a population of about 1.1 million in an area of 670,343 hectares, but almost half of these people live in the urban areas of Plymouth, Exeter and Torbay. The remaining 55 per cent share just over

650,000 hectares, which is 1.32 hectares each. If you've no idea as to the size of a hectare (like me, until I looked it up), I can tell you that it's about two and a half acres or, if you're still none the wiser, about one and a half football pitches.

'It reminds me of the hills near the Pyrenees in France,' I said to Fran, on one of the many occasions when we'd had to stop the car to get out and breathe in the beauty.

A decade before, I'd bought a house for renovation not far from Pau, with the intention of providing myself with a bolthole where I could escape to write, play the piano, and generally swan around in shorts.[2]

Fran loved it, particularly the views that it afforded us. However, we both knew that neither of us wanted to live in France. We both felt that we would have been culturally at sea, not having shared the same experiences as those all around us. Different schools, different pop stars, and different politicians had made their mark on us – plus there was the added problem of having to ask people to repeat everything three times. Worst of all, the French don't have a radio programme called *Seulement une Minute*, so I wouldn't pick up much work either. No, France was not on the agenda for the new life, but both Fran and I had said that if we could find a house in England that shared anything like that view, then we'd jump at it. The odds were heavily stacked against it though, not least because England is short on mountain ranges.

There was another factor that was going to make this search difficult – the fact that I am such a sun worshipper. When the sun is good enough to shine in the UK, as it does

2   Only the 'shorts' part of it had really gone to plan.

18

with a consistent inconsistency, then I can become quite upset if I can't be in it. It seems silly, even immature, but oddly it's something of which I'm rather proud. That's why buying a house with a garden that faced north would be out of the question. So, that left us simply requiring a house with a breathtaking view, and with a garden that faced south. Not much to ask.

The three houses we did eventually view, late that afternoon, weren't right, and we both knew it the moment we walked in through the front doors. They felt too plush for us, too upmarket, too 'look how well we've done'. The poor estate agent[3] did his best to talk them up, but he must have seen that we weren't excited and that this particular outing was not going to produce any commission.

The problem was that if you wanted a big garden with views, then it seemed that you had to buy a grand house, and we wanted something modest. We knew that it wouldn't be easy – perhaps even impossible – to find what we were after.

'If it takes eighteen months to find the right place, then let's take eighteen months,' I said, as we went to bed after a delicious meal with our hosts.

'Yes, we're not in a hurry,' said Fran.

'Goodnight.'

'Goodnight.'

At 4 a.m. on the Sunday morning I was down in Kevin and Donna's kitchen trawling the internet again. I'd been struck at an odd hour by a new thought. Could it be that we had been searching for a property in the wrong price range?

3   Very nearly an oxymoron.

'Where have you been?' asked a sleepy Fran, as I tried unsuccessfully to slip back into bed without waking her.

'I've been online. I was wondering if we were looking at houses for too much money?'

'Huh?'

'Well, so far we've based our search on what we think we'll sell our London house for. That means we're looking at grand properties. Maybe we need to be more modest.'

'Hmm. Find anything interesting?'

'One or two.'

'Maybe I should take a look.'

And with those words Fran slipped out of bed and headed down to the kitchen.

Kevin and Donna were hosting a couple of very odd house guests.

***

Sunday's house search was more encouraging, but only marginally so. Fran's 'middle of the night' internet session had produced an extensive list of properties and although we didn't have any appointments to view them, we found that wandering around outside and peering through the odd window provided enough information to enable us to reject them. But we liked what we saw much more than on the previous day, and it was pleasing to know that if we could find somewhere in this price bracket then we'd have money to spare for any renovations or changes that might be required. But we had still drawn a blank. We'd soon be on the road back to London with tails, if not between our legs, then certainly not wagging.

'One more to go,' I said, as the car crawled up a steep and narrow hill towards another little village, and probably our tenth viewing of the day.

'I don't hold out much hope for this,' said Fran, reading from one of the sheets she'd printed out that morning. 'It's a cottage. It'll be quaint and tiny, no doubt.'

'Another head-bumper,' I added, with some resignation.

At six feet three, I'm taller than I seem on the radio, and I fall foul of the fact that in the nineteenth century people were considerably smaller, and couldn't reach high enough to build a ceiling at a reasonable height. High ceilings were for the nobility, who were well-connected enough to have access to ladders. They invested in this extra elevation so they could cater for gentlemen in extravagant hats and ladies with unreasonably lofty hairdos.

Cherry Cottage looked pleasant enough, but it didn't arouse our interest greatly when it first came into view. It was a long, pretty building, looking like it had started out as two cottages that had now been knocked into one. It was a little nearer the road than we would have liked, but we hadn't passed another car getting here so we had every reason to believe that speeding cars were as common as a politician's apology. It wasn't until we peered over the side gate and into the back garden that our hearts began to race. What we saw was about a quarter of an acre of well-tended garden with a small pond – charming but not particularly special. However, it was what lay beyond it that took our breath away. What a view. We were looking out at English countryside at its best. The land beyond the garden fell away before rising again the other side of the valley, pre-senting a spreadsheet of fields, paddocks, woods and hedgerows, all combining to create a green patchwork of varying hues that soothed the eye and calmed the senses. Not spectacular, but just simply beautiful. Absolutely beautiful.

'This is it!' I said to myself.

I knew it straight away. I just hoped that Fran liked it. If she didn't, then this search for a house was going to take a long, long time – because we'd clearly be looking for different things.

'I love it!' said Fran. 'It's magical.'

Good, we were on the same wavelength.

'Wait a minute, where's that sun?' I said, in a moment of panic.

Sod's law it could be facing in the completely wrong direction, and that would be a deal breaker for me. I looked up at the cloudy sky. The sun, although not shining, was attempting to break through and I could make out where it was, and where it was heading.

'The garden's south-facing!' I called out, at a slightly inappropriate volume.

'Great,' said Fran, no doubt relieved that this rather needless criterion had been met.

I rang the bell in the hope that the owners would be home and I could persuade them to show us around, and a pleasant grey-haired lady in her sixties opened the door. I explained how we were heading back to London in an hour or so and that we loved the house and could she possibly permit us to come and take a look.

'Goodness, the place is a mess,' said the lady. 'Could you come back in an hour? The pub is five minutes from here and it does nice coffee.'

'Perfect, we'll pop there then,' I said, wondering whether such an accommodating response would have greeted cold-calling house hunters in London. 'So sorry to descend on you like this. Thanks so much.'

A pub within walking distance. Another big plus. All of the houses we'd viewed on the previous day had felt rather remote. This house was performing a kind of conjuring trick. From the front it was a modest cottage that was very much in the midst of a village, and yet the view from the rear suggested that it might be in the heart of a rural wilderness.

As we walked through the village, which was pleasant but not so picturesque and quaint that it would be a target for Londoners who wanted second homes for weekend use – another bonus – we discussed excitedly the prospects of this house becoming our new home. The house that we'd not even seen inside yet. Fran's only concern was that she had wanted a bigger garden so we could begin growing our own food. Not that either of us had any experience of this, so how much land would be required was simply guesswork.

'Hang on, this might be the answer,' I said as we drew parallel with the Parish Council notice board.

A sign had caught my eye:

ALLOTMENT AVAILABLE NEXT TO
VILLAGE HALL
£15 A YEAR

'We could get an allotment.' I said. 'Let's ring the number and see if it's still available.'

A phone call later and we had done the most extraordinary thing. The lady I had spoken to on the phone had explained that the poster had only just gone up and that she expected there to be a lot of interest in the allotment and that if we wanted it then we should move quickly. I made an executive decision and told her that we'd take it, even though we hadn't even looked inside the house that had spawned our interest in it. Could this be a sign that we were *meant* to get this house?[4]

'Well, if we don't get the house, at least we'll have an allotment,' I announced proudly.

'Yes, and we'll be able to drive three and a half hours to do some weeding.'

'It would be a long way back if we forgot the shovel and fork, certainly.'

* * *

Following our quick refreshment in the friendly local pub, where every head had turned to look at us as we'd walked in through the door, we found ourselves back outside the house. It felt like we were eager students who had enrolled on an extra-curricular course – in house buying. The lady answered the door, introduced herself as Brenda, and conducted a thorough tour. The house turned out to be idiosyncratic in layout, the victim no doubt of a string of

---

4   It's never been really clear who is in charge of this stuff. It's nice that there might be someone in charge that cares about this kind of stuff. But if it is also them that organises tornadoes, droughts, landslides and floods, then I wish they'd desist.

makeshift 'improvements' that had happened over the years. The bedrooms upstairs were in a line – meaning that you had to walk through one to get to another. Like many a rugby player, the house was wide and shallow. Headroom was an issue, and I had to be alert to avoid beams on the ground floor.

But we loved it. We loved it because of what you could see out of the window. That seemed to be enough. Everything else we assumed could be sorted out in the future. Even when we shared a cup of tea with Brenda and attempted to ask all the questions that needed asking, all the time we kept turning and looking at the view. That view.

By the time we'd completed the drive back to London, we'd decided on every alteration we could make to the house, and we went to sleep dreaming of waking up there. In the morning I rang the estate agent, leaving it till 10.30 a.m. so I didn't look too keen, and made an offer that was duly accepted.

Good. We now had something to go with the allotment.

2

Accepting Your Fête

I won't pretend that selling the London house hadn't left me with some wobbly moments. Occasionally it felt like we were casting ourselves adrift and sailing off into the unknown. Fran had been born and raised in London and had never lived anywhere else, and it had been the city that had sustained me in my career and social life for the last thirty years. Now we were both turning our backs on it. Sure, it was only a train journey away, but we were putting a firework up the posterior of our lives and it was no use pretending otherwise.

Unlike Fran, I'd moved houses several times before. I knew that when you pull your car up outside the empty shell that will be your new residence, keys in your hands for the first time, there's a nervous feeling that you'll open the door, walk in, and not like it anymore.

'You OK?' I said to Fran, as I put the key in the lock.

She nodded. Perhaps the silence concealed the nerves.

We'd seen the house a couple of times more when we'd been near Devon on other business, and we'd popped in to share a cup of tea with Brenda and ask all the questions that we should have asked before we bought it. Like what kind of heating system does it have, or does it have mains drainage or a septic tank? We learned that Brenda was separated from her husband and she now needed a smaller house, but Fran and I took it as a very good sign that she wanted to stay in the same village and had bought a house further down the road. We would be neighbours, and for the next few months we could torment Brenda with questions about how things worked, and where various switches were located.

I took a deep breath as I turned the key in the front door lock. I threw open the door and we walked in. We looked around us and both smiled. Even without furniture, pictures, mirrors, books, magazines, and kitchen paraphernalia – it felt like home.

I let out a huge sigh of relief.

* * *

The months leading up to the move had been tough, but I wouldn't have described them as stressful, even though they do say that moving house is one of the most stressful things in life. My question is this. Who are the *they* that say this? Is it the same *they* that say that our bodies are 70 per cent water? Because if it's that lot, then I'm not sure that I trust them. I just had a bit of a check and, even after a glass of water, I seem to be far too solid to be nearly three-quarters water. I'm pretty certain that my knees aren't water at all.

Could this 'fact' come from the same *they* who tell us that we only use 10 per cent of our brain's capacity? Well, frankly, how can we trust a statistic that comes from anyone who is openly admitting that they didn't use 90 per cent of their brain in producing it? I want my statistics to come from those who are using a minimum of 62 per cent of their brains. And not from people who have those spongy damp brains that are 70 per cent water either.

Our move had been tiring, but it hadn't taxed our nerves too greatly. Packing had been a royal pain in the arse, of course, but it produced some good moments too. Objects, clothes and photographs were discovered that brought fond memories flooding back. Objects, clothes and photographs were also thrown out, and this delivered a cathartic healing, as well as presenting the local charity shop with a number of challenges.

'Thank you,' said the meek volunteer as I deposited another box containing a mix of shoes, jumpers, framed photos and prints, DVDs, CDs, and outdated audio gear. I didn't deserve a 'thank you'. I wasn't donating, I was off-loading, and by rights I ought to have been giving them a tenner to take it from me.

The good thing about unpacking is that it's quicker and easier than packing, and far more rewarding. Packing slowly strips a house of its soul, whereas unpacking breathes life into your home with each painting you hang, and each lamp you set in place. Within a matter of hours you can begin to feel that the job is almost done, forgetting that you don't know how anything in the house works and that you probably won't know how to run a hot bath for another three weeks.

On that first night we went to bed elated having created an environment that already felt like home. Like thousands before us, we had done it. We had moved from the city to the country. Now we just needed to find out if we would be accepted by everyone else who called this corner of Devon home.

'We'll introduce ourselves to the neighbours in the morning,' I said, as we lay on a bed that I'd just spent a disappointingly long time assembling.

'Yes. I hope they're nice,' said Fran.

'Me, too.'

It took me a while to get to sleep that night. Maybe it was the quiet. No distant hum of traffic. No occasional distant siren. Just the odd sound produced by unidentified wildlife. A wailing fox? A bird of prey? A badger? Fran's last thought had unsettled me. One of the attractions of our new home had been that we had neighbours within shouting distance. But what if we ended up shouting at each other? What if we were flanked by the neighbours from hell? What if, after all our time and trouble, we were to find our hopes of living in a peaceful community dashed on day one? Nothing in the estate agent's particulars had said that both sets of neighbours weren't unpleasant, small-minded bigots who complained at the drop of a hat and threw litter over the fence. They knew their jobs these estate agents, and that was exactly the kind of thing they might deliberately omit. Sneaky. No wonder nobody liked them much.

'Are you OK?' said Fran. 'You're very fidgety.'

'I'm fine. Just finding it tricky to fall asleep. I'm excited.'

'Me, too.'

'Sleep well.'

'You, too.'

* * *

As we stood at the door, I looked at Fran and smiled, trying not to reveal my concerns, before taking a deep breath and ringing the bell.

Ding Dong.

Good. A nice old-fashioned bell ring. Not the kind that psychopaths with dangerous dogs would have. Surely?

The door opened and before us stood a tall, strong-looking man in his sixties, and we introduced ourselves as the new neighbours.

'Oh, hello,' he said in a gentle voice. 'Come on in.'

Soon we were taking tea in Ken and Lin's small conservatory and enjoying the wonderful view from a marginally different angle. The conversation, if a little stilted at first, soon began to flow. Ken's gentle Devonian brogue was a product of this very village, where he had been born and raised. He was a retired builder, who had actually built the house in which we were now sitting. He'd worked on it at weekends when most would have been resting from the tiring paid work of Monday to Friday. His equally gentle, but considerably smaller, wife Lin was also a local but she had suffered the major upheaval of moving here from a few miles away. They had one son who lived with his partner in a neighbouring village, and who came every Sunday for lunch. Apparently he liked to go out with Ken on 'tractor runs'. I didn't ask what a tractor run was, because I didn't want to appear like a clueless 'townie' who knew nothing of country ways. Better that they discover the truth in the coming months rather than reveal all at the outset.

As we sipped our tea and ate rather too many of the tempting chocolate biscuits neatly spread out on the floral plate before us, it soon became clear that we had one set of lovely neighbours.

'Don't forget,' said Ken, as a parting shot while we waved goodbye from the end of their path twenty minutes later, 'if you need any help with anything at all – just call.'

'I will,' I replied.

I meant it. Poor Ken didn't know what was to come.

We repeated the same ritual with our neighbours the other side, making this day a veritable festival of tea and chocolate biscuits. Tony and Edna were very similar to Ken and Lin in many respects, just older. Tony, now in his eighties was also born and raised in the village, and his wife Edna had also suffered the disruption of uprooting herself from a nearby village, travelling literally thousands of yards to begin a new life here. Tony spoke proudly about his veg patch, and we left clutching courgettes and marrows wondering what the difference was between the two.[1]

'Well, we have two sets of lovely neighbours,' I said to Fran, as we got home, taking good care not to put the kettle on and accidentally have some more tea and chocolate biscuits.

'Yes. I wonder what the rest of the village is like,' said Fran.

'We should find that out at the village fête. It's coming soon enough.'

We'd seen the posters and the bunting as we'd followed the removal van into the village. Bunting. Nothing seemed

1   It's a size thing, I think. Of course, I could tell you if I just typed 'what's the difference between a courgette and a marrow?' – but I thought you might like to do that yourself. I don't want to spoil your fun.

to represent the move from urban to rural more succinctly. I imagined that there were black and white pictures from fifty or sixty years ago that would not have looked much different to the current decorations around the village. It made me wonder for a moment whether our move here was actually a progressive move? Were we gentle pioneers exploring a simpler, more honest way of living, or were we simply trying to go back in time?

* * *

I settled on a lime and coconut cake. I'm not sure what drew me to it, probably just the way the recipe and the instructions were laid out in the book. It looked easy. The usual set of criteria for choosing which cake to make didn't really apply in this case, since I wasn't going to eat it.

Unbeknownst to me, Fran had 'volunteered' me to bake a cake when one of the 'fête committee' members had called round to our house asking us to donate books and buy raffle tickets. We were now a few weeks into our new life here and at the end of the arduous but ultimately satisfying period of unpacking and creating order in our new home, which we couldn't have done without neighbour Ken. He'd helped me carry furniture from room to room, he'd fitted the washing machine, and he'd lent me countless tools (and then showed me how they worked when I'd got stuck). Fran looked on in wonder as I mounted shelves the wrong way up, and erected bookcases that fell down (pulling sections of the wall with them). Each time Ken happily rectified the situation in a kindly, avuncular way – and all the time I kidded myself that I was a man who could get things done without recourse to handymen and professionals. However, I made no such claims in the culinary department.

'But I've never cooked a cake before,' I protested to Fran, when she explained to me about my future baking commitments.

'It's easy,' said Fran. 'We want to make a good impression and show willing, don't we? I'm doing one. You should do one, too. Just follow the instructions in the recipe book.'

Indeed, this is what a lot of cooking is: following instructions. However, the cook must be careful not to deliver the line of the Nazi war criminal serving up their fare to a guest:

'I was only following instructions.'

I'm not comparing cake preparation with death camps. There are significant differences – not least the amount of eggs and sugar in each – but hidden within the respective processes there is a certain amount of obedience required. The truly creative, rebel cake-maker has the potential to make a name for him or herself, but the experimentation will almost certainly require a number of failures along the way. No such luxury for me. I had fête committee members to please, and I wanted this cake to be OK. Not brilliant. Not outstanding. Not sumptuous. Just OK.

The next two hours saw me doing all sorts of things I'd really only ever witnessed from a careful distance in the past. When cakes had been made by my mother, I had learned that close observation could lead to being hauled in as an assistant, or 'sous chef'. Now here I was, doing all of it myself. It seemed to involve an inordinate amount of whisking, measuring, and adding sugar. Boy, so *much* sugar.

33

No pun intended here, but there was something distinctly unsavoury about tipping a huge measure of sugar into a bowl and then mixing it in. Why had no one ever told me that cakes had this much sugar in them?

I laboured on, frustrated by the size of the task, thinking to myself, is this what people have to do, *every* time they make a cake? Finally, having concentrated hard for well over ninety minutes, and not having experienced any disasters, I reached the easy bit. I put my unbaked cake into the oven, sat in the garden for an hour, and 'hey presto', I'd made myself an OK cake.

'What do you think?' I asked Fran, holding the finished product under her nose.

'It looks OK.'

Hurrah.

***

The day of the fête, 13 July 2013, was a very hot day in Britain. After a series of rather hopeless summers, the UK was experiencing a heatwave that many were comparing to the one we'd had in 1976. The British, playfully lambasted by foreigners as being a nation who discuss the weather conditions relentlessly, were reverting to type. The general verdict, as gleaned from short exchanges on the streets and in shops, was that it was currently *too hot*.

It's not so much that the British discuss the weather, it's that they complain about it. To them, the weather is like Tim Henman or Andy Murray. There's always something wrong with it. It's never quite right. In the case of Tim Henman, he was *too nice*, and Andy Murray – well, he wasn't nice enough (although winning the Olympics and Wimbledon has possibly now placed him above this criticism).

'That'll be one pound each,' said one of the four elderly men who were manning the trestle table at the entrance to the field where the fête was being held.

Four men seemed a lot for this role, but I assumed they were there for security. Significant sums of money could change hands at this location and any potential burglar would be deterred by the possibility of four octogenarians shouting 'Oi!' as they ran off with their sack of pound coins. Unfortunately for the village, the sack would be lighter than all had hoped. The third man told us that numbers were down this year.

'It's too hot,' explained Man 2.

'Martha told me that on the news they said it's going to be thirty-two degrees today,' announced Man 3 proudly, 'and they said five hundred people would die today because of the heat. That's why she's not coming to the fête.'

Suddenly everything changed. What was supposed to be a leisurely afternoon had become a dangerous sport. Would we survive?

I clutched my 'OK' cake to my heart and walked past the men, hoping that they weren't St Peter and three gatekeepers, and that this fête wasn't my fate. The image of a gravestone flashed before me.

HERE LIES TONY HAWKS
WHO COLLAPSED
DURING HIS FIFTH GO ON THE COCONUT SHY
IT WAS HIS OWN FAULT
HE *WOULD* LIVE LIFE ON THE EDGE

We climbed a short incline and entered the main field, where an array of different stalls awaited us. Despite what the old man had said, a healthy number of people had taken their lives into their hands, and were happily milling about. They'd even risked their children, too, such was their reckless addiction to this English summer tradition. Bunting abounded, enthusiastic volunteers manned stalls, and the rest of us wandered about with an insouciant aimlessness.

I found myself feeling a little nervous. Was it because I wasn't sure how my cake would be received? Or was it because these kinds of events were always an opportunity to let yourself down badly? After all, I had a painful memory from a village fête. A scar even.

As an eighteen-year-old I'd been invited by some friends to attend a village fête just outside Lewes in Sussex. It had been a beautiful summer's day (a reasonable temperature with fewer deaths predicted) and after only a short meander around the fête's stalls we'd ended up in the beer tent, where I'd been bought a pint of some real ale or other, no doubt with a ridiculous name like Spruggles or Chattlespeare. A teacher from my school had introduced me to the local vicar, who clearly relished the opportunity to welcome one of the younger attendees at a function that traditionally attracted an older clientele. The conversation, at least from my end, had not been an easy one.

Talking to clergymen isn't easy, especially for young men who think about little outside the realm of sinning. As I stared at his clerical dog collar, I became acutely aware of how regularly I devoted time to the consideration of having sex before marriage. Should I confess this to him, or should I continue with the inconsequential exchange on which we had both now embarked? In the event, a wasp intervened and the question became irrelevant.

I've always been afraid of wasps, having experienced an extremely painful sting as a ten-year-old. Now, just as I was about to answer the vicar's question about what A levels I was taking, there was a sudden swoop down by this amber assailant, and I began to panic. I swung at the wasp with my free hand, but to no avail. The air-strike continued unabated, and when my attacker moved in towards my face, I lost all sense of reason and control.

Instinctively, I pushed out with both arms in the direction of this invasive flash of yellow and black. A second later the wasp was gone, and so was all hope of continuing the polite conversation with the vicar. Quite unintentionally, I had, with some considerable force, thrown a pint of real ale full into his face. He frowned, brushed down his clerical shirt, and with Spruggles (or Chattlespeare) still dripping from his nose, he headed off for the relative safety of a group of older ladies. To this day, I feel sure that he has never spoken to a group of teenagers again, and that the incident may even have rocked his very faith itself. After all, why would a loving God have allowed such a thing to happen?

Just as this painful memory was threatening to overwhelm me, a voice restored a sense of reality.

'That looks like a very nice cake!'

It was the voice of Karen, the village fête committee member whose house call had instigated this gastronomic, sugary delight. Karen beckoned us over to the cake stall, took my cake with a perfunctory thank you, and unceremoniously labelled it at £2.50. She did exactly the same with Fran's cake, which immediately sold to a family of four who had been eyeing everything else on display. Mine, it seemed, had a less obvious quality. It was more for the connoisseur. It was a niche cake and would have to wait to find its buyer.

Free of the responsibility of not dropping my cake, only now did I begin to survey the scene around me in any detail. The small field was dotted with stalls, all actively manned by eager volunteers. One thing seemed to unify them – the requirement of the punter to cough up some money if they wanted to play anything. This seemed a little churlish. After all, hadn't we already bought raffle tickets, donated books and cakes, and paid an admission fee? Since I didn't yet know where the profits of this event were going to go, I was beginning to resent paying a pound to try and throw some hoops, or take a shy at a coconut. It wasn't as if the prizes were that appealing.

But then they never are. To me, this is the mystery of the British funfair or fête. Here's the deal on offer, at least as far as I can fathom:

You give me £1 for the privilege of trying to do something that is almost impossible to do, with the incentive of winning something that you don't want, and probably isn't even worth £1 anyway.

It wasn't an offer I couldn't refuse, and despite the plaintive calls of eager volunteers for me to participate, I made polite refusals and headed for the bric-a-brac stall. Here, I redeemed myself by buying an antique douche pan for £2. I couldn't resist it. I didn't mind that I'd spend the rest of the fête carrying what looked like a portable toilet around with me, a bargain is a bargain, and I'd be laughing if there was an overly long queue for the portaloos.

A five-piece band started up, playing a kind of easy-listening jazz, and made up of what looked like four teenage lads and one of their dads. Fran and I sat on some deckchairs that had been placed before the little tent they were performing in. They were doing a good job, and we applauded politely after each song, something that seemed to embarrass them slightly. When they took a break, I turned to Fran.

'We're not meeting very many people, are we?'

'Not really. You kind of need to know people a bit already at events like this. There's nothing really enabling people to mix together. At the moment, anyway.'

'Does seem that way.'

'You carrying a portable toilet around with you may not be helping. Shall we go?'

'Yes, I think so. It's too hot. No point in risking our lives any further.'

As we walked home, I wondered if I'd been spoiled by the fêtes I had attended in France.[2] Over there, the village fête centres around a meal for the villagers. Yes, you paid for it, but it was good value and at least you got something back for your money, and it created a wonderful opportunity for everyone to get together, share stories and put on weight.

'I think that fête could benefit from some innovative ideas,' I said to Fran, as we settled into the comfy chairs of our relatively cool living room.

---

2   They ought to know better than us how to do it – *fête* is a French word after all. (I know, by this logic, that the French ought to be worse at enjoying le 'weekend' or finding le 'parking' spaces, but who knows, maybe that is the case?)

'Well, you should get yourself on the village fête committee then.'

'What?'

'You heard.'

Darn it. Fran had a point. Instead of being gently critical, maybe I needed to get involved. But did I really want to get *that* involved with village life? I swiftly changed the subject.

'I hope my cake sold. I'm not sure she put it in the best position to catch someone's eye.'

I looked up to see that Fran had fallen asleep in her chair.

Goodness, I thought, I must be getting dull.

3

Slugging It Out

With the house in an ordered kind of disorder, we turned our attention to the garden. It was our intention to develop this, especially since we'd been told that the allotment we had sought to reserve was not available for another year after all. Since the sun continued to defy the clouds and reign supreme, the time couldn't have been more opportune for gardening. We'd inherited a well-kept garden with lots of flowers and shrubs, none of which we could identify by name. I was now being punished for all the times I'd turned off the radio the moment *Gardeners' Question Time* had come on. As a younger city dweller, I'd simply had no interest.

I'd been duped into believing that I was a natural consumer. Other people grew and made things – I consumed them. That was the order of things, and to some extent the global economy depended on people like me to keep the wheels of capitalism turning. Food and goods are mass-produced and shipped around the globe for us to buy and consume. The endless drive for profit and growth conspires to have us purchasing electronic goods manufactured in the

Far East so that the man in the local repair shop can tell us, once it has developed an inevitable fault, that he can't help us and we should throw it away.

All the while, career politicians continue to explain how the economy would be plunged into recession if consumers weren't out in the High Street buying, buying, buying. No mention of what cost there may be to the environment, or even to our very souls (if you buy crap, don't you *feel* crap?). Buying new stuff mattered, and it mattered big time because if it didn't keep on happening – relentlessly – then the world's brittle economic system was going to collapse.

To my mind, it was going to collapse anyway, it was just a question of when and how. The optimist in me wondered if there could be a slow transition to a 'better way of managing ourselves', the pessimist knew the possibility of real suffering and wars over resources were more likely.

So – what to do? Well, clearly the answer was for me and Fran to cultivate some crops in the three raised beds that were already in the garden. We were going to change the world by changing what was happening in that soil. It was a noble plan, and one we took seriously given the enormous global responsibility that rested upon our shoulders.

Just a shame we knew sod all about gardening.

* * *

Our quest began in the nursery. We were lucky enough to have one close by (the kind that dealt in plants rather than fledgling humans), so while Fran prepared lunch I drove down there to begin this epic and heroic quest. An initial foray before we took it on together.

I walked past greenhouses containing a host of plants and flowers that I couldn't begin to name, and into the small shop that was in the corner of the nursery's plot. Behind the counter, a meek-looking man awaited me, like a character in a TV sketch show waiting for the action to begin.

I said hello – quickly getting the niceties out of the way – and then began to subject him to a barrage of questions.

What soil do we need?

How much water?

When do we plant?

Where do we plant?

Do we need to put it in a greenhouse?

When do you water it?

How much do you water it?

Is it best to wear tracksuit bottoms?

Are platform shoes a no-no?

Nursery Man answered each of my questions with great patience and diligence, but by the time I'd finished, his expression had changed from buoyant and dynamic to brow-beaten and deflated, as if someone had hit him quite hard in the stomach. Knowing that I'd return with Fran at a later date, I then scoured the shelves and returned with the rather pathetic haul of one tray of lettuce seedlings. As I faced Nursery Man over the counter, I realised that this wouldn't represent a fair remuneration for what I'd just inflicted on the fellow. I quickly grabbed some gardening gloves for Fran. The man looked at me with an element of incredulity.

'We'll use them for gardening,' I said, as he put the cash in the till.

He needed reassurance.

When I got home, Fran had left the kitchen and was eagerly awaiting me near the raised beds.

'Well,' she said, 'how did you get on?'

'I bought a tray of lettuce seedlings and . . .'

'And what?'

'And some spares in case you lose those,' I said, pointing to the gardening gloves she was wearing, that I'd bought her two weeks ago but had forgotten about.

'Did he explain what to do with the seedlings?'

'He did.'

'And?'

I opened my mouth with the intention of relaying the wealth of information that Nursery Man had imparted, but suddenly I realised that I couldn't remember a word of it. My brain can only cope with limited information in one hit. This is why, when I'm in the car and I pull over to ask directions, I can never really remember beyond 'go to the end of this road and turn left at the lights'. Instead of absorbing the ensuing data, I am distracted by inconsequential matters relating to my roadside guide. I am unable to hear 'take the third exit at the roundabout', because I am too busy wondering whether the speaker's receding hairline will result in complete baldness within two years. I don't hear 'after the Shell garage make a left', because I'm wondering whether the woman beside him is his wife, lover, sister, or care worker. In brief, I have a short attention span. In fact, my attention span is so short that I can't be arsed to finish this line of thought. So let's move on.

What I *could* remember from my encounter at the nursery was that the lettuces I'd purchased weren't ready for putting in our raised beds yet. They needed 'bringing on' a little – or some such term – so I watered them and placed them in the greenhouse that we had inherited, which up until now had become a storage deposit for boxes and items that didn't yet have a home in the house. I noted that none of these boxes had grown particularly well and I hoped this wasn't an omen.

It might as well have been. By dusk, my lettuces were as good as dead. Unbeknownst to me, my gentle watering had been at best, ineffectual (most of the water simply evaporates in the sun), and at worst, downright harmful (the droplets of water settle on the leaves and act like lenses that concentrate the sunlight and cause damage). Putting them in the green-house on a hot day meant that I had quite literally fried them. I'd jumped from growing to cooking far too quickly.

'What we need to do,' said Fran, as she surveyed the tray of shrivelled brown leaves that I had created within a matter of hours of becoming their custodian, 'is to go on a gar-dening course.'

It was difficult to argue with her. But worth a quick go.

'Do you really think that's necessary? It was just bad luck that I forgot nearly everything that the man told me. I'm beginning to remember it all now.'

I'd made better arguments.

'I'll go online and find a course for us,' said Fran, turning and heading for the house.

I was left holding the dead lettuces. Now, what should I do with them? Didn't Nursery Man say something about com-posting? He did, yes – just at the point when I was noticing his grey hairs and trying to hazard a guess at his age.

I buried the lettuces.

A quiet ceremony, with no guests and just a short speech from me. If I remember rightly it was:

'Sorry.'

Or something along those lines.

* * *

Devon has main roads, of course it does. But it also has 10,000 miles of narrow country lanes. 10,000 miles. Think of 1,000 miles, and multiply it by ten, and then you'll get some sense of what we're talking about here. (Or 100 miles multiplied by one hundred will also do the trick.) Some of these lanes are thousands of years old, built as the principal routes between villages, and they still provide important links between rural hamlets. Flanked by hedgerows, they are like mini nature reserves packed with wildlife. They are also bloody annoying.

Once again the Devonian sun (it's the same as the other one apparently, although locals will tell you it's more shy) blazed down upon us as we set off for our day-long organic gardening course. The drive would have been incident-free had it not been for our imprudent decision to seek the assistance of the new addition to our family – the sat nav.

I'd always taken a Luddite approach to this technology, claiming that it was counter-intuitive to rely on satellites orbiting hundreds of miles above us to locate addresses here on earth. However, Fran had requested that we get one now that we were in a completely new environment and, displaying a measure of both spinelessness[1] and

---

1   I didn't have the balls to defend my arguments.

astuteness[2], I had made the necessary purchase.

The danger with the sat nav is that you tend to shun the map, relying solely on a complicated piece of gadgetry. This is foolish. Maps are terrific things that were created by good, hard-working people who, like me, didn't have the faintest idea how a satellite worked. Maps gave you a sense of where you were in the world and, best of all, they didn't talk to you. Soon I came to realise that our sat nav had become possessed by an annoying, opinionated lady, who had no manners and who spoke too loud. Worse still, she continually interrupted me when I was talking and she would keep repeating herself. She also insisted on taking us on routes based on the shortest distance as the crow flies, which made absolutely no sense in terms of size of road or the speed that can be achieved on it.

It was for this reason that we were now driving up a section of Devon's aforementioned 10,000-mile labyrinthine network of lanes. Even though we were driving a Smart car – a hangover from city life – this lane was barely wide enough for us, and yet was supposed to accommodate two-way traffic. What would happen if we allowed our speed to get up to anything beyond a dawdle and if we happened to meet someone coming the other way reckless enough to do the same? It didn't bear consideration.

'We'll be all right,' I said. 'It's early on a Sunday morning and there won't be any traffic about.'

Of course, I shouldn't have uttered the words. I should have known full well that I would be punished immediately

2 Successful relationships are about giving in to what the other person wants. The other person then calls it compromise.

by the malevolent God who listens out for this kind of benign and yet overconfident statement.

No sooner had the words passed my lips, than the inevitable happened. *Sod* – let's give this God a name – hadn't just orchestrated us to meet a car coming the other way, but had arranged a kind of vehicular nemesis for us. The man who was now slamming on his brakes opposite us was an elderly man who was going to have a distinctive and not altogether reasonable approach to this chance encounter. Sod had pre-ordained a man who didn't view us as two cars meeting in a lane but as 'opponents' meeting in an important struggle for moral supremacy. So there we were, facing a sensible and clean hatchback (probably a Honda, Hyundai, or something Japanese beginning with 'H') containing an elderly couple, looking at us like we were aliens.

'What happens now?' said Fran, naively.

'Well, as I understand it, the etiquette in these situations is that the car closest to a wider bit of lane reverses there.'

'And who is that?'

'It's them. I've been keeping a lookout for passing points and they seem to be every few hundred yards or so, and we passed one quite a long way back. If he goes in reverse, I bet there's a passing point a few yards away.'

'OK,' said Fran, 'but I'm not sure that they see it that way.'

Ahead of us, the elderly man was gesturing for us to go back. It was a very firm kind of gesturing. The kind of gesturing the military might use when signalling to the enemy. The kind of gesturing that might just get your back up if you were a driver who was already irritated that the wretched satellite navigation system had dumped you in this lane in the first place.

'Oh dear, we've got one here,' I said. 'The important thing is to stand firm.'

As calmly as I could, I mirrored the same gesture that was being offered to me, quite possibly with less conviction (based on the fact that this was not the most important thing in the world to me).[3]

The driver quite simply repeated his gesture, as if I had done nothing. Worse still, his co-pilot, an old lady with a sternness of expression probably nurtured from years of alerting children to the presence of signs saying 'No ball games', offered up her own version of the gesture.

'Don't they realise that they only have to go a few yards back and this will all be sorted?' I moaned.

'I don't think so,' said Fran, astutely.

'Well, they'll just *have* to realise.'

I repeated my gesture, this time, I hoped, with a soupçon of menace. All this succeeded in doing was getting the lady in the car to raise her hand and make her gesture bigger, with more of a flourish. Her action was imbued with a sense of superiority, like I was a poor, hungry, underpaid servant that she was now dismissing for stealing an apple.

'I think you're going to have to reverse,' said Fran.

'No way. I'm not going to give in,' I replied.

'They're quite old and this is a very narrow lane.'

'They only have to go a few yards.'

'I'm not sure that they're going to.'

'They'll have to.'

3 Yet.

'Reversing is quite hard for old people.'

'So is being reasonable, seemingly.'

Impasse. I glared at my two elderly adversaries and they glared back. Fran, an innocent civilian caught in the cross-fire, sighed. Seconds passed that felt like minutes. No one did anything. Momentary stalemate. Not an official cease-fire, but a definite cease in hostilities. Time for both sides to review combat strategy.

'I know,' I said, having a bright idea, 'let's pretend to be asleep.'

'Don't be ridiculous.'

'Just close our eyes and let them think we've drifted off.'

'Like they'll believe *that*!'

'Well what do *you* suggest?'

'I suggest we reverse.'

'You mean give in?'

'No. Not *give in*. Reverse.'

'Reversing is giving in.'

'No it isn't, it's going backwards.'

I looked up to see the man gesturing to me once again. Suddenly and with some emotion – none of which was positive – I slammed the car into reverse and began to hurl us backwards at an inappropriate speed. As if the recklessness of my actions somehow lessened the sense of defeat.

'Look out!' said Fran.

The side of the car was now being scratched by the adjacent hedgerow. I quickly braked.

'Oops.'

'We'll have to do this slower.'

'Yes.'

What followed was nothing short of humiliation.

Watched by my two smug antagonists, I now had to reverse at a snail's pace. The lane, in all its magnificent, narrow bendiness, demanded a measured, calm approach not consistent with my current mood. I wanted to do the driving equivalent of storming out of a building, but instead it felt like I was being forced to leave on my hands and knees.

'Look how close he is,' I said, pointing to the car before us, which advanced with glorious ease at exactly the same pace as my desperate and inelegant reversing.

'Ignore him, he'll just put you off.'

I returned to my thankless and degrading task, and continued inching us backwards, yard after arduous yard. Each inevitable brush with the hedgerow was received with a physical wince from Fran, and the hint of a smile from the old man, who was just a matter of feet away, rubbing metaphorical salt into a not so metaphorical wound. I tried so hard to avert my eyes from his, meaning that I had to keep my neck in a cricked and twisted position, providing a physical pain equivalent to that currently being suffered internally.

Four minutes and hundreds of yards later we arrived at a farm gate that provided the required space for our two cars to pass. As the shitty little Honda drove past, the driver had the gall to raise his hand in a patronising gesture of thanks. Fran put her hand on my knee to calm me and prevent me from shouting at an old man who was no longer in earshot, but also to reassure me that our world was intact, and that no one had been injured. Physically, anyway.

Thirty seconds later, we were level with the spot where the two cars had originally met. We continued another twenty yards, and there it was, the perfect widening of the road that could have been reached by our adversaries had they not been so unreasonable.

'I knew it!' I exclaimed. 'I bloody knew it!'

Fran's soothing hand gently dropped onto my knee again.

Over the next half mile, I did my best to calm myself down. It was just about working when a voice piped up, seemingly out of nowhere. It was the overly loud sat-nav woman.

'IN TWO HUNDRED YARDS, MAKE A U-TURN.'

'Aaaah!' I cried.

Fortunately Fran restrained me physically. Otherwise that sat nav would have joined the wildlife, ending its days lost somewhere in a hedgerow in deepest Devon.

* * *

Amazingly, we made it to the organic gardening course on time, in spite of the sat nav having initially delivered us to a nearby industrial estate. This is what sat navs do, rather than admit they are lost. It's a default setting. When things have all become a bit much for them, they take you to an industrial estate. For them, this is more acceptable than providing the driver with the truth.

'IN ONE HUNDRED AND FIFTY YARDS, PULL OVER AND LOOK AT A MAP. I DON'T KNOW WHERE WE ARE.'

Needless to say that the word 'sorry' is not programmed into any sat navs anywhere.

The gardening course was on a small organic farm, and kicked off with us all sitting round in a makeshift circle in a marquee drinking teas and coffees, as informally as middle-class English people who have never met each other before are able to do. There were six of us in total, three couples eyeing each other with a cautious guardedness. Was this English reserve, or the fact that it felt a little like we were all about to undergo some kind of test, or medical examination?

The lady in charge, Joa, had a nice style and sense of humour, and was reassuringly muddy. For me this is a sign that someone is either a good gardener, or that they like to drink an awful lot. Joa asked us all, couple by couple, to explain why we were there. Malcolm and Ann were just like us, novices with a newly acquired garden, and Geoff and Maureen were looking to brush up on their skills. When it was our turn to give our reasons for attending the course, I toyed with saying, 'To prevent the needless slaughter of further young lettuces.' I opted, however, for something more sensible.

'We're keen to grow stuff and we want to avoid chemicals if we can, and learn to be more at one with nature.'

There. What splendid human beings we were.

Joa went on to explain how she'd got into organic growing, as a young woman, after she'd been poisoned by Lindane and developed pleurisy. I wanted to put my hand up and ask what Lindane[4] was – and what pleurisy[5] was,

---

4   Lindane, also known as *gamma*-hexachlorocyclohexane, is an organochlorine chemical variant of hexachlorocyclohexane, which has been used both as an agricultural insecticide and as a pharmaceutical treatment for lice and scabies. There. Now you know. By the way, in humans, lindane affects the nervous system, liver and kidneys, and may be a carcinogen. It is unclear whether lindane is an endocrine disruptor. Especially to me.

5   Look it up yourself.

for that matter – but I thought this would give the impression that I was too ignorant to be on a course like this, and I thought it best to keep the truth suppressed.

Joa began passing on her green-fingered wisdom. It's all about soil. We couldn't just *take* from the soil, we had to put goodness back into it. A weed is just a flower in the wrong place. Composting was key. So too was controlling pests. We'd all develop new relationships with slugs.

Wise words, indeed. I, for one, was looking forward to the slugs bit.

We all enjoyed a fascinating morning, as we followed Joa around her organic plot and she took us through each of the stages of organic cultivation and answered our eager questions. At one point, whilst Joa was in the process of showing us how to bring seedlings on, she stopped and offered up a question for all of us.

'Do any of you know how to prick out?'

Now, I knew the answer to this. Of course I did. But I just wondered why it was being asked on a gardening course. Wasn't this one for a rugby club outing on a tour bus? I chose not to answer, just in case a demonstration was required.

'Let me show you,' said Joa, who seemed to be about to prove herself to be one hell of a woman.

'Prick out' turned out to be a pincer movement with the fingers – a neat way of moving the fledgling crop to a bigger container, before planting it in the raised bed. Soon Joa had us all gaily doing the prick-out thing – something I hadn't expected to happen when we'd all shared that first shy cup of tea in the morning.

By the end of the day, both Fran and I had filled our notebooks full of information. We felt confident enough to buy pea, runner bean and carrot seeds as we were assured that we weren't too late in the year for these. We bought some more lettuces, too, which I intended to treat more compassionately.

The planet might not be safe yet, but it had just taken a very important step in the right direction.

* * *

In the coming weeks, Fran took responsibility for the peas, beans and carrots, and I concentrated on my particular area of expertise – lettuces. The ones we'd purchased were infant 'Little Gems', and I had every expectation that this was exactly what they'd turn out to be when fully grown. Gems. And not so little, once I'd fed them with the organic plant food in which we'd invested.

Things went well, and the continued hot weather meant that I did a lot of watering in the early morning and at dusk. I found this very therapeutic and it enabled me to create a fatherly relationship with my little green babies. However, I knew that it wouldn't all be plain sailing. We had been given a very important speech about slugs on our course. Slugs liked to come out at night and if we didn't pay attention to this then our salads wouldn't be that appetising. All sorts of alternatives to chemical slug pellets had been suggested as a means of protection, one of which happened to be beer. It seemed illogical to put out free beer to keep things away, and I wasn't keen on any of the other methods either, so I favoured the approach of patrolling the patch physically after dark for half an hour each night. Hard work, yes, but I was up for it.

My first tour of duty, torch in hand, left me shocked. The slugs were already out in force. Each of my little apprentices had at least one small slug crawling upon it, eagerly a-munching. It's a mystery quite how these presumably stupid creatures (academically they achieve little) know within a matter of hours that these lettuces have been planted, but know it they do. Somehow the word must go around:

Here, have you heard that the new idiot in the village has stuck some Little Gems in?

Yummy! Let's get over there.

But how do they do that without mouths? Or ears? Or noses to smell with? It's uncanny.

Each time I discovered a slug, I responded with an audible 'Gotcha!' and picked them off with my gloved hand. Harmless though they are, slugs are not attractive to touch and the big ones recoil upon being picked up, giving the impression that they're wrapping themselves around your finger. I'm not overly squeamish, but I was grateful for the gloves, the extra pair purchased at the nursery now coming in very handy. Once nabbed, I placed each slug into a large carton of salty water. I assumed that this killed them quickly and humanely, but I hadn't bothered to check, probably because slugs are both ugly and a nuisance and therefore one shouldn't need to worry oneself too much over the method in which they are dispatched. Ethically very shaky ground.

Poor old slugs. They're so slimy and ugly that it's even difficult to write these words – 'poor old slugs'. Many years ago, I made an appearance on a TV panel game where we comedians were asked what we thought animals or creatures might be thinking. I suggested that slugs were saying to themselves, 'Euurggh. This is no kind of a life.' The laugh from the audience suggested that we assume that slugs are miserable. They may be having a wonderful time, but compared to dolphins, they're piss-poor at showing it.

The Latin name for a slug is:

Limax (-acis) m/f – a slug.

Yes, the Romans had slugs too. The creators of Latin had made a mistake, though, when they'd allocated a male and female ending to the noun. It has since been revealed that these creatures are hermaphrodites. This doesn't mean that they cross-dress, but it does imply that they have both male and female reproductive organs. I've often wondered whether this means they can have sex with themselves. If so, one imagines there would be very little sympathy for slug 'single parents'. It would be difficult to argue with the line: 'Well, they've only got themselves to blame.'

Biologists, however, assure us that slugs can't have sex with themselves, and they're probably right. Slugs would look a lot happier and more spritely if they only needed consent for a shag from themselves. Instead they have to go to all that trouble of finding a partner for sex. Admittedly, it's made easier by the fact that it doesn't matter whether it's a male or female that they do it with. In that sense, they're very much like pop stars in the late sixties and early seventies.[6]

I collected and mercilessly killed twelve slugs on that first night. Their offence? Trying to survive by eating *my* lettuces. This, I'm afraid, is the rather depressing aspect of

6   But often with better taste in music.

growing anything. Unintentionally, you're providing food for other life forms, and they cannot stop themselves from seeking it out in order to survive. These organisms are so dim-witted that they cannot understand the nature of ownership. To them, it's not obvious that this is *my* lettuce because *I've* bought it and *I've* planted it. It's no good reasoning with them either. So we found ourselves locked in a battle for survival, being fought in the lettuce trenches. Pleasingly, it was a battle where the stakes weren't quite so high for me. Even if I lost, I could always buy a Mars bar in a shop.

One gardening hint that I picked up on the growers' course was that it's a good idea to wee on your compost heap from time to time. Apparently, it's an excellent 'activator' for the compost because it's full of nitrogen, although I would have thought that would depend on what you'd been drinking the night before. I'm not sure how much nitrogen there is in Pinot Grigio, but I'd need to check. There are other benefits, too. No need to flush the loo, thus freeing up more water for those occasions when multiple flushing is required for that stubborn floater that just won't disappear down the pan. I've never liked those. Unwanted calling cards that say: 'Feel free to contact me if you ever want a consultation on the optimum diet for turd buoyancy'.

So, knowing that what I was doing was environmentally sound, it was with a great sense of righteousness that I marched down through the garden one day and lifted the lid to the compost bin, unzipped my trousers and hoisted my vast member[7] into the opening – as you do.

---

7   Some artistic licence at work here.

I began to pee, watching proudly as the stream of urine headed towards the detritus of Fran's worthy culinary activities. All the evidence was there of how healthily we had eaten since our arrival here. Lemon skins, pea pods, apple cores, corn husks and the rejected bits from numerous salads, all basked beneath the warm flow of liquid gold that I was providing for the ease of their decomposition. I looked up at the cherished view that encompassed the horizon and I allowed myself to slip into a pleasant reverie. Just how well had we done in moving here?

What happened next was quite extraordinary, and it pains me even now to recount it. I do so only to help other males who are reading this and may have access to the potentially dangerous combination of a penis and a compost heap. The odds against what happened next may be staggeringly high, but they could happen again. So be warned.

As I gazed into the reassuring and life-affirming distance, my gentle reflections were interrupted with a breathtaking rudeness.

'AAAAAH!' I screamed.

Suddenly there was an excruciating pain in the end of my penis. I looked down to see a wasp had settled on the end of my right-honourable member, and off it now flew, no doubt with the wasp equivalent of a smug grin on its face.

'JESUS CHRIST ALMIGHTY!' I cried out. 'THE BUGGER HAS STUNG ME!'

I panicked. I turned and charged back towards the house, wincing with pain and belting out expletives as I went. Any neighbours gardening within a square-mile radius would have stopped and wondered, 'Now what was that noise, and what could have caused it?' They wouldn't have guessed the terrible truth. Hearing these disturbing sounds, Fran appeared from the kitchen.

'What is it?'

'A WASP HAS STUNG THE END OF MY KNOB!'

I didn't wait for a response, feeling fairly sure that Fran wouldn't have been able to find the right words to provide adequate comfort, and I dashed passed her and up the stairs.

'What are you doing?'

'I'M GOING TO RUN A BATH! AAAH!'

Everything I said and did for the next few minutes was accompanied by an 'AAAH!' as my penis throbbed in response to the spiteful wasp's venom. Pain, unwanted and excruciating pain, was accompanied by an equally unwelcome cohort – fear. As the bath filled, my mind raced with all the hideous possibilities that might result from this incident. Would I ever be able to pee again without it hurting? Would erections be heady things of the past? Would my knob simply fall off? Then there was the swelling. I could virtually see this happening before my own eyes as I sat, rigid, wincing, fear-stricken, in the tepid bath water. Erotic thoughts or feelings of desire couldn't have been further from my mind, and yet my penis was swelling. I had a swelling penis for all the wrong reasons. Surely the worst kind of swelling penis.

Fran popped her head into the bathroom.

'How is it?' she asked, timidly.

'Look,' I said, pointing to it, 'it's swelling up.'

'Oh dear. Should we go to casualty?'

'Not yet. Let's see what happens. Maybe research it online and see if there's anything I should be doing.'

'OK.'

The odd thing is that I couldn't quite disconnect the comic side of my brain. Bizarrely, it occurred to me that a trip to casualty would give me a chance to weave an old joke into a natural situation.

TONY: 'I've been stung by a wasp, have you got anything for it?'

DOCTOR: 'Whereabouts is it?'

TONY: 'I don't know, it could be miles away by now.'

Not worth a twenty-minute drive and a two-hour wait staring at people who had fallen off things.

Fifteen minutes later, I was sitting in the kitchen, greatly relieved that the pain was now easing off. Fran's internet search had revealed little, other than the fact that some ancient cultures had used wasp stings for penis enlargement. Surely a foolish quick fix? It had certainly worked for me, but it hardly encouraged amorous thoughts. It was an excellent way of creating a big, pointless penis at short notice, so I guess I could take solace in that useful information gained.

It wasn't until several days later that the soreness and last vestiges of the swelling disappeared completely. My body was back to normal. Not a temple maybe, but akin to a small church, at least in so far as it had a fully functioning organ.

Amen to that.

4

Harnessing Skills

One morning, when I popped round to Ken's to ask for his help with something, I eased into the question slowly and began by telling him about my problems with the slugs.

'Our son Andrew entered a snail in a snail race once,' he said, going off on a rather surprising tangent, 'and he had the idea of removing its shell to lighten its load.'

Ken then waited, his eyes imploring me to enquire further.

'And how did it perform?' I asked.

'It was sluggish.'

Ken beamed broadly, pleased at having had the occasion to work this joke into a conversation. The opportunity probably didn't come up that often.

'I walked into that,' I conceded. 'Very good.'

Ken beamed all the more. I had a go at changing his cheerful demeanour.

'I don't suppose you could help me shift my grand piano?' I asked.

'Where to?'

'Just from one room to another. Should be fairly straight-forward, although we may have to remove the legs.'

Instead of this question puncturing his high spirits, Ken responded as jovially as ever.

'No problem. Shall I pop over this afternoon?'

'Yes, please.'

Well done, Ken. So far, he was following instructions to the letter from the text book *How To Be the Perfect Neighbour*.

To be fair, the job was no more complicated than I'd made out. Having changed my mind about which room I preferred to play the piano in, I now wanted it moved into our living room from the 'adjacent studio/office' (as it had been described in the estate agent's particulars). I'd allowed one hour to complete the job before I would need to leave for a meeting with a local councillor about buses. I'd noticed that the ones that came in and out of our village were nearly always empty, and I wondered why. Later that afternoon I would have some answers.

I was well prepared for the job. I'd watched my piano being moved several times before by teams of two men, and I was pretty sure I could remember the procedure. Admittedly, Ken and I didn't have a special grand piano removal trolley, but I had a plan to overcome that. The wooden floor was shiny and flat between the two rooms, so I figured we could drag the piano between them on cushions and sheets. All we needed to do was remove the three legs.

Ken arrived, beaming with enthusiasm, and we set about our task. Disappointingly, we went off-script almost imme-diately. Instead of engaging in piano removal, we found ourselves scratching our heads, Stan Laurel-style. We just couldn't fathom how to remove the legs without the help of a third person. In the end, Ken went back to his house to fetch a car jack – but unfortunately for me, he didn't do this until we'd already tipped up the piano and removed one of the legs. This meant that I had to take the weight of one corner of the piano until Ken made it back.

'How are you getting on, darling?' said Fran, as she popped her head in.

'Oh, not so bad,' I said. 'Just waiting on Ken, who's fetching something.'

'Great. I'm just nipping out to yoga. See you later. Good luck.'

It seemed an awfully long time before Ken re-entered carrying the new equipment, but it may have been only a few minutes. As I looked at Ken readying the jack, I couldn't see a place on the piano where it was going to have any real effect. Then it dawned on me.

'I remember now,' I said. 'We lower this corner, where we've removed the leg, down onto the cushions. Then we tip the piano to remove the other two legs.'

'So we don't need the jack?'

'I don't think so.'

It was galling to think that I had supported the piano for all that time without any sensible reason. Ken, who had now supplied the room with gear more normally seen alongside beaten-up cars in greasy garage forecourts than around pianos in Parisian conservatoires, lined up the cushions and then joined me on the corner of the piano, and we began to lower it down. The further down we got, the greater the weight. As we neared the floor, it became apparent the cushions weren't aligned properly.

'I've got the weight,' said Ken. 'Quickly, move the cushions into place.'

I jumped into action, whilst my retired neighbour held a fair proportion of the entire weight of this 800-pound piano – roughly the equivalent of me, four and a half times. As I observed the strain on his entire body, a horrible thought struck me. What if he had a coronary? Being responsible for the death of the man next door wouldn't be the best way to establish myself in the locality. I would also have a piano stuck at this dreadful angle and it would be very difficult to play. Worse still, every time I played it, I'd be reminded of my dead neighbour.

Fortunately I was able to slide the cushions quickly into the correct position and Ken and I were able to complete the lowering without incident. The end of the piano keyboard was now resting on the cushions, with one leg successfully removed.

'There!' I declared.

The problem was that this had taken us twenty-five minutes instead of two, and we'd need to speed up this process if I was going to make my appointment.

'Now what?' asked Ken.

We both continued to look at the piano – no longer a musical instrument, but instead a giant puzzle. Bewilderment reigned. Utterly. Dictatorially. It had all seemed so straightforward when I'd watched other people doing it.

'I think I know,' offered Ken, his tone of voice suggesting that he'd had a brainwave. 'From this position I think we need to lay the cushions in a line and then hoist the piano so it's lying along them on its side. Then we'll be able to remove the other two legs.'

'That's it!' I said, with great relief. 'Let's do it!'

This is where we learned that not having the correct equipment was indeed a huge disadvantage. Normally, at this stage the piano would rest on its side on a specially designed piano trolley, not cushions just lifted off a sofa. Unfortunately for us, these cushions slipped and moved on the smooth and shiny wooden floor, and we soon had an 800-pound piano resting half on and half off them. The piano didn't balance as it would have done on a flat trolley either, so I had to hold it in position whilst Ken circled it, assessing whether it would get damaged if we dragged it through from room to room as it was.

'Before we remove the other legs,' he finally declared, 'I think we need to get more cushions under it.'

'How do we do that?'

'I think we can get the jack under it enough to wedge a few more cushions in.'

And so, a further fifteen minutes were lost making use of the car jack and getting the piano in the best position for dragging it along the floor. The first leg came off easily enough. The second one started to prove a problem. Ken twisted hard. Nothing. Something may have gone wrong with the thread. He tried again. Still nothing. He took a deep breath and exerted the kind of pressure that a builder exerts when the whole job depends on it. He started to turn blue. Panicky thoughts about coronaries returned. Ken let out a huge gasp of breath.

'Bugger!'

The leg hadn't shifted. We both looked at it.

Stalemate.

I let a reasonable amount of time pass,[1] before asking the obvious question.

'What are we going to do?'

Ken repeated the Stan Laurel head-scratch.

'Maybe,' he said, 'maybe I could shift it using an oil filter band.'

'A what?'

'It's a tool I use for removing oil filters on tractors.'

Oh my. In our novel approach to piano removal we'd now moved from cars to tractors. We were getting further and further away from the Paris conservatoire.

Bereft of any ideas of my own, I had no option but to declare that this was a good one, regardless of nagging doubts to the contrary.

'Good idea, Ken. I'll hold the piano here. How long do you think you'll be?'

'Well, I've got to find the tool, but I shouldn't be longer than ten minutes.'

Twenty minutes later I was still supporting my grand piano. I'd had ample time to assess what we'd achieved. In just under an hour we had put the piano on its side, removed two of its legs and established that we couldn't remove the third. Ken was currently lost in some shed or another searching for tractor tools. I now realised that I had absolutely no chance of making my appointment with the councillor to discuss buses. Momentarily supporting the weight of the piano with my back, I fished in my pocket for my mobile phone and called the town councillor. With only one bar of signal on the phone, I knew that the line wouldn't be a good one.

1   10 seconds.

'Hello, it's Tony Hawks here,' I began, sounding strained as a result of the weight on my back. 'You know we're supposed to be meeting at four? Yes, well I have a slight problem . . . I'm currently supporting a piano that has a leg on it that won't come off . . .'

'You're *where*?' I heard from the other end of the line.

The situation wasn't helped by a poor signal on the phone.

'I'm waiting on my neighbour, who's fetching this tool we need. I can't move from the piano till he gets back.'

'You're at your neighbour's, playing the piano?'

'No, I—'

The line went dead. Curses. The one bar of signal had buggered off. Where does it go when that happens, I wondered? And why does it come back again? Does it drift off in the wind? Whatever the reason, the councillor was now left thinking that me playing the piano to my neighbour was more important than honouring our appointment. I stood there, disappointed, a piano at my shoulder. Alone. Trapped. Once again I had been undone by my own misplaced confidence. I'd thought I knew how two men could move a piano, and I'd thought it would be easy. How wrong I'd been.

Finally Ken returned brandishing an odd-looking tool unlike any I had seen before. It somehow resembled a cross between a screwdriver and a scythe.

'Sorry, Tony,' he said, as he let himself in, 'it was a bit trickier to find than I was hoping.'

What followed was crunch time. If Ken, with this new and unfamiliar tool, failed to remove the leg, there would be nothing for it but to give up and call in the professionals.

Ken strained as he pulled on the tool. He went blue again – for the third time in one afternoon. This time, though, his final gasp was exultant.

'Gah! Dunnit!'

Heroically, Ken had loosened the leg, and now it could be unscrewed.

I'm not going to begin to say that the rest of the procedure went smoothly. We dragged the piano between rooms easily enough, but lifting the piano to get the legs back on tested us once again and we were unable to manage without recourse to the car jack. I've since looked at YouTube clips of pianos being dismantled and moved with relative ease and without a car jack in sight, but for some reason Ken and I couldn't have managed without it.

So much for it taking less than an hour. We were still toiling away when Fran made it back from yoga.

'Why are you both purple?' she asked.

I dodged the answer and suggested, not without a sense of urgency, that she make us both some tea.

A little later, poor Ken went home exhausted.

I left a nice bottle of wine on his doorstep that night.

* * *

The summer continued to be the kind that made the front pages of the newspapers.

PHEW! WHAT A SCORCHER!

This sort of headline had always puzzled me. The weather was not news. Whilst a correspondent might be required to bring us the latest on missing planes or the latest conflict in the Middle East, we didn't need the newspapers to tell us what was happening bang outside our front doors. Was it hot yesterday? I hadn't noticed. Thank goodness for that alert newspaper reporter.

Whenever it's hot, I want to swim. Devon's beaches were only forty minutes away, but we'd discovered that they weren't Britain's best-kept secret. August brought hordes of holidaymakers, who selfishly got into cars and formed themselves into traffic jams, doubling the journey time for us. They made the beach experience uncomfortable and sometimes disagreeable. I've always much preferred being on a beach in a foreign country, where the conversations of the families on adjacent towels remain a mysterious burble of exotic sounds. Raised Italian voices, or instructions called to a child in French or Spanish, were a positive part of the experience, mainly because they had no meaning. On a beach in my own country I am drawn into the family conflict, however hard I try to shut it out.

'DARREN! GIVE THE BUCKET BACK TO YOUR SISTER!' shouts an irate dad.

I immediately check on Darren's location, observe the tears of the sister, and wonder how the situation will become resolved.

'NO, YOU CAN'T HAVE A BLOODY ICE CREAM! YOU HAD FOUR YESTERDAY!' shouts a despairing mum.

'Yes,' I inwardly concur, 'four does seem an awful lot. The mother seems to have a point.'

Thus my beach experience is ruined.

Which is why I came up with my idea.

'Fran doesn't think it will work,' I said to Ken, as we chatted over the fence.

'Well, I don't see why it shouldn't,' he said, supportively.

'I'm tempted to give it a try.'

'I'll help you, if you need a hand.'

'Thanks, Ken.'

'I've got a good name for it.'

'What's that?'

'You can call it the Hawks Harness.'

'Excellent idea.'

I'm no inventor, but I felt I was onto something with this. The trouble with small swimming pools is that if you want to do any meaningful swimming – the kind that keeps you fit and healthy – then you reach the end of the pool after only a few strokes. It can end up feeling like you're doing more turning than swimming. What better idea than a harness that ties around your waist and attaches by rope to a pole at the rear of the pool? Essentially a swimming machine, in the same way that you have a running machine. You simply swim on the spot. If Ken thought it could work, then it couldn't be crazy. This man was rebuilding a tractor. He'd built the house he was living in. He knew what tool would remove a stubborn leg of a piano and, better still, what that tool was called. Ken knew what was possible and what wasn't.

'Trust me,' I said to Fran, as I made the online payment for the plastic pool. 'This will work.'

* * *

The pool arrived a week later, a few days after some of Fran's family had come to stay: Ted, her dad, and her half-brother

Oli and sister Monica, who were ten and thirteen respectively. And her nan. Nan was in her mid- to late eighties (there was some familial dispute as to her definite age, no doubt caused by her own bogus claims to be younger than she actually was), but she was in good physical health. Mentally, she hadn't fared so well in the last couple of years. Her memory was definitely on the wane, and she regularly told you the same thing over and over again. On her previous visit to see us in London, before we'd moved, she'd informed me about fifty times that she loved travel. The exact words she uttered on each occasion, never with any variation, are indelibly stamped on my brain.

'I love travel, me. Ed, my husband, he used to come home sometimes and say to me "Do you want to go for a spin in the car?" and do you know? he didn't need to ask twice. I love travel, me.'

She'd also told me forty times how she'd felt about moving.

'I never wanted to move to Eastbourne.'

And thirty-five times how she managed her children financially.

'I always took good care to treat my children equally. If I gave to one, then I always gave to the other.'

Some days I just couldn't stop myself from being mischievous.

'Nan, I've been wondering lately how you feel about travel?'

'Oh, I love travel, me. Ed, my husband, he used to come home sometimes and say to me "Do you want to go for a spin in the car?" and do you know? he didn't need to ask twice. I love travel, me.'

'How about your children? Did you give more to one than the others?'

'No. I always took good care to treat my children equally. If I gave to one, then I always gave to the other.'

I'd usually be belted by Fran before I could ask her how she felt about the move to Eastbourne.

As I unpacked the pool and spread it out in the garden, Nan went momentarily off-script.

'What are you doing?'

'I'm going to inflate this pool, fill it with water, and then try out the Hawks Harness.'

'I see.'

Poor Nan. She spent most of her day pretending to 'see' what she clearly didn't 'see', and had no way of differentiating between what was straightforward information, and what was downright confusing. However, on this occasion, given that no one in the family had grasped the concept of the Hawks Harness (only Ken and I had so far shown the intellectual capacity), then she could hardly be expected to 'see'. She claimed that she did though, which made her unique in the house.

If 'seeing' meant 'watching', then she was excelling. She had great fun observing me as I stretched out the blue plastic onto the lawn, attached the hosepipe, and began filling the pool. I had not gone top of the range. I'd spent about £90 on a circular kids' pool, twelve feet in diameter. It would be enough to establish whether my idea would work. As Nan and I watched the pool filling with water, I could see sceptical faces inside the house, observing from the kitchen window.

Swimming pools, even tiny ones, take a long time to fill.

By the time the water had reached the required level, I was so magnificently aware that Nan liked to travel, that she treated her children equally, and that she hadn't wanted to move to Eastbourne, that only a combination of family loyalty and a lack of suitable implements had prevented me from hoisting her in to see if she floated.

'That's very good,' she said, coming off-script again when the pool was full.

If only she'd been correct. It wasn't really very good at all. Like all non-professionals, in my eagerness to accomplish the task in hand, I'd only skimmed through the instructions. A glance at them had confirmed to me what I'd expected. They were poorly written, and stated only the obvious. Yes, there had been a line in there about ensuring the pool was placed on level ground, but the garden was only on a tiny slope, and that couldn't be a problem, surely?

A tiny slope, it was now becoming apparent, was enough. At the end of the pool that was on the lower end of the gradient, water was now trickling over the side. Nan was watching this and smiling, as if it was a nice water feature. As if its creation had been the very reason I'd performed this laborious task in the first place. I rushed inside to get my harness and rope. The pool was now emptying itself, and at an alarming rate. I had only a small window to test the efficacy of the Hawks Harness. Ken had lent me a weightlifter's belt that we had both surmised would be perfect for the job. It took me ten minutes to find it, and a further ten minutes to locate the rope.

Fran's brother and sister chuckled and sniggered, as I chased around the house in swimming trunks and anxious search mode. I could see their point of view. People in swimming trunks belong by pools or on beaches. The moment they begin doing anything else of a domestic nature away from the waterside environment, they look like perverts. OK, attaching myself to a harness and rope and climbing into a kids' paddling pool that was rapidly emptying itself of water wouldn't make me look any less of a pervert, but I considered it a good enough reason to run around the house in a state close to nudity.

A single rain cloud had now spitefully come out of nowhere and arranged itself overhead. It began to empty itself, quite liberally, as if the maiden outing of the Hawks Harness had no divine backing. I rushed outside and fixed up a stepladder so I could attach the rope to a nearby tree. I glanced down and saw four giggling faces at the kitchen window, and Nan smiling and giving me the thumbs up.

The rope in place, I was ready to trial the Hawks Harness. The single cloud had now been joined by cumuli cronies, and together they were providing heavy rain as I clambered over the pool's sagging sides. I soon found myself standing in a few feet of water. The pool had emptied much quicker than it had filled. The water now barely came up to my knees. Given that each second saw more water lost, my initial hope of attempting the stroke of front crawl was now out of the question, given that there was nowhere near enough water for the downward strokes of the arms. I still held out some hope that the breaststroke could work, though. I quickly got down into the swimming position.

Ah.

Not good.

I was like a beached whale. I had run aground. Pride, more than anything, made me attempt to swim the breaststroke, but too much of my body weight was pressing against the bottom of the pool for any forward momentum to be achieved. From the kitchen, Fran and her family looked on, as a man attached by a rope to a tree tried his best to do the breaststroke, lying in a few feet of water. Judging by the noises I could hear, this was a source of some amusement for them.

At dinner that night, Nan quietly asked me what I'd been doing previously in the pool. Laughter erupted, causing food to shoot out of several mouths. It was almost as if my earlier behaviour had been silly.

It's not easy being a genuine innovator.

* * *

'How'd it go?' asked Ken, the following morning, as I chatted to him whilst he tinkered with his tractor.

'Not that well,' I replied, with a measure of understatement. 'The pool definitely needs to be on the flat.'

'Does it?'

'Yes, it very quickly emptied itself completely.'

'Haven't you got a flatter bit of ground at the bottom of the garden?'

'Yes.'

'Well, shall we have a go at trying it there then?'

I was impressed. Ken seemed even keener than I was to see the experiment with the Hawks Harness carried out successfully, quite possibly because he hadn't suffered the previous day's humiliation.

'I'll pop over in the afternoon and give you a hand.'

My neighbour, like me, had the pioneering spirit.

Fran's ten-year-old brother Oli helped with the preparation of the land. I believed him still to be a Harness sceptic, but levelling ground was obviously more fun than preparing food, and this was the only other activity that was on offer to him. This odd mix of workers soon had a circle of land close to our rear fence ready for the second attempt with the pool. After a couple of hours' hard labour, we sat back and watched as the pool filled with water again. Ken reiterated his confidence that the harness would work, but made a suggestion for an improvement.

'I've been thinking,' he said. 'If you add a chest expander – you know, like body builders use – between the rope and the harness, that will provide a bit of give and stop you being pulled backwards too sharply, after you take a strong stroke that pulls you forward.'

'I've got one in a box I haven't unpacked yet,' I replied.

'Shall we try it?'

'What have we got to lose?' I asked.

A beat.

'A chest expander,' said Ken.

'And my pride,' I added.

Ken then popped back home for tea, on the understanding that I would fetch him for the successful unveiling of the Hawks Harness once the pool was fully filled.

That fine summer evening saw six adults (Ken had brought his wife Lin) and two children gathered by a low-grade, bottom-of-the-range, above-ground, inflatable swimming pool. Two of the onlookers were excited. The rest were ready for a good old belly laugh. With Ken's assistance, I tied the weightlifting belt around my waist, and reached down for the chest expander and began to attach it.

Big laughs. Mocking noises of derision. Stolid, resilient, unflappable Ken – a picture of concentration like a top golfer's caddy – fetched the rope from the tall post that he'd attached earlier to the back fence. He had done this so that the rope could be angled down from a sufficient height for my legs not to become entangled in it, as I swam. To the others, this attention to detail was reason for yet more juvenile giggling, but I wasn't allowing this atmosphere of jovial cynicism to dent my spirits. This would only serve to make the moment more precious, when the Hawks Harness did what it said on the (not-yet-available) label.

For the second time in twenty-four hours, I clambered into the pool. Behind me, a chest expander dangled and a rope trailed. The frivolous audience applauded mockingly in feigned deference to a special moment. I raised my hand.

'Ladies and gentlemen, thank you for coming here today to see the first experiment with the Hawks Harness.'

'Second experiment!' called Fran's dad. 'What about yesterday?'

'OK, second experiment,' I conceded, 'but the first one in a pool that isn't rapidly emptying itself.'

Renewed applause.

'I shall now lower myself into the water,' I said proudly, lowering my swimming goggles to cover my eyes, 'and we shall see if the Hawks Harness is the success that Ken and I think it will be, or the hopeless failure that the rest of you are wishing for.'

Laughs and more applause.

I let myself fold down into the shallow pool and I felt the chill of the water prick my skin. The initial signs were good. My arms seemed to have enough water beneath them to affect a swimming stroke. There was no point in delaying, so I stretched out my feet behind me and set off, launching into my best crawl. To my amazement (I hadn't been as confident as I'd been making out), one stroke followed another in the same way as normal. I kicked with my feet and pulled with my arms and yet I was being held in the same position. There was no jolting, no discomfort. I swam for a full minute. Each time my head turned to breathe, my goggles framed the stunned faces of the surrounding witnesses. I experienced a totally new feeling. Elation whilst submerged in water. For a second, I knew the joy of the Channel swimmer and the Olympic gold medallist. No point in smiling into water, but that's what I felt like doing.

After enough time had passed for there to be no doubt that the Hawks Harness had enabled me to swim on the spot effectively and normally, I ceased swimming, drew in my knees, lowered my feet and let myself rise triumphantly from the water, like Britannia from the waves.

'Yes!' I shouted euphorically. 'It works!'

'What does?' said Nan, who had presumably, not for a single moment, had any idea what it was that she'd just been witnessing.

'Oh, no!' said Fran. 'It works. This means he'll be trying to get me to do it.'

Oli jumped into the pool, eager to go next. Fran's dad took photos. I looked at Ken, who was smiling, arm proudly around his wife.

Triumph.

We were inventors, not piano removers.

5

Mister Chairman

When you move to an entirely new area, where you know nobody at all, you need to be a little proactive in order to move your social circle beyond your immediate neighbours. One method I have always used over the years is to join the local tennis club. OK, you're not going to meet the crowd from the wrong side of the tracks, but you'll soon know, whether you want to or not, the doctors, solicitors and architects in the area. And one eccentric. And one bossy committee member who will tell you off for wearing training shoes with the wrong kind of soles. These are the rules.

Despite our distinctly rural location, our neighbouring village had a tennis club with three courts, two of which had floodlights. (Don't let the floodlights give you the wrong impression – the clubhouse was a hut with no changing rooms or toilet facilities.) I found the name of the club coach in the local monthly parish magazine, rang her, arranged a hit, and when she saw that I hit a half-decent ball, I soon had the men's team captain on the phone.

'Would you consider playing for the men's team?' he asked.

I hesitated . . .

* * *

There was good reason for my hesitation. When I'd first moved to London a quarter of a century earlier, I had pretty much followed the same procedure outlined above, and I'd agreed to play for the Globe Lawn Tennis Club men's team in Belsize Park. Soon I became involved in a seemingly never-ending string of rather tedious matches, all of which appeared to be 'vitally important' in the eyes of our captain – who clearly didn't have enough going on in his life.

After several years of this, I reached breaking point one day and decided to retire. The occasion was a damp evening when I was sitting in my hundredth wooden clubhouse, eating disappointing cheese-and-pickle sandwiches and drinking stewed tea, desperately trying to make conversation with a group of men with whom I'd spent the past three hours hacking bald tennis balls around drab hard courts wedged between middle-class suburban houses, and with whom the only common ground was a willingness to subject ourselves to this social torture. For the hundredth time, I'd been asked how our team were doing this season, and for the hundredth time I'd replied that I wasn't even sure what division our team were in.

I don't know why I'd never bothered to find out – perhaps I was concerned that to do so would exhibit a dangerous level of commitment that could be spotted by my team-mates. The remotest display of enthusiasm could be reported to other team captains in the club who were always on the lookout for players in the many available leagues. The summer mixed-doubles league. The winter men's. The summer men's. The winter mixed. And let's not forget the cup matches too. The summer men's cup. The winter mixed cup. The winter men's cup. The mixed summer cup.

As if all this wasn't bad enough, it was pointed out to me one day by some team captain or another that I was allowed to drop down and play one match per season in the second team too. This generated a new batch of fixtures that required fabricated excuses in order for me to avoid more monotonous tennis and, worse still, the agonising post-match teas with their excruciating tête-à-têtes about missed volleys and banter about our prospective relegation from this division, the identity of which had never been known to me in the first place.

Finally I'd cracked. No more weakness.

NO MORE MATCHES.

A friend asked me why I'd packed it up.

'Because I don't think I ever really enjoyed it.'

'And it took you all these years to work that out?'

'I guess so.'

I was a slow learner. But most of all, I was crap at saying no. Periodically, I am asked to give a talk quite some distance from home, at an inappropriate venue to an undesirable audience, with little or no money on offer. I still struggle with the 'N' word until a conversation with Fran brings me to my senses.

'But didn't you *pay* to play in those matches?' my friend asked.

'Err. Yes.'

It was true, and it simply compounded the madness of it all. The protocol was that you had to give the team captain a match fee. This was to cover the cost of the balls, and the post-match refreshments. We were, to all intents and purposes, the *opposite* of professional tennis players. Instead of being remunerated, we had to pay for the privilege of representing our club. And there were no bonuses for winning either. Not even an extra cupcake.

So that's why I hesitated when the men's team captain called.

He assumed that I hadn't heard the question properly.

'Would you consider playing for the men's team?' he repeated.

'Err . . . Um . . .'

'It's an important game. We need to avoid relegation.'

'Err . . . OK. Yes.'

What did I *mean* – 'yes'? What was I *thinking* about? The answer was no. An unequivocal 'no'.

'Why didn't you just say "no"?' said Fran, over dinner that night.

'I don't know,' I replied, 'perhaps things are different now. The last time I played in a match was years and years ago. Things must have changed.'

* * *

I found myself sitting in a wooden clubhouse with seven other middle-aged rural tennis players, tucking into crisps, supermarket quiche, and cheese-and-pickle sandwiches. Laborious conversation stuttered and faltered. The man to my right, the opposing team captain, congratulated me on our narrow victory and asked me how we'd done so far this season. I replied that I didn't know what division we were in.

Forty-five minutes later, I was handing our captain the five pounds match fee.

'You will play again next week, Tony?'

'Err . . . it's just that—'

'It's an important match versus the division table toppers.'

'Umm, I, er—'

'We need you.'

'Oh. Right. OK. Same time, same place?'

'No, next week we're away. It's quite a long drive, so can you meet us here an hour earlier?'

'OK.'

I played five more matches for the team, before it became more agonising to answer Fran's questions about why I kept agreeing to play, than it was to explain to the captain that I'd had enough. I broke the news to the team captain, which he took with a surprising, and ever so slightly disappointing, *bonhomie*.

My unsatisfactory, unheralded, and spectacularly unprofessional competitive tennis career had come to an end. Three words best described the feeling.

Hoo – fucking – ray.

* * *

'Perhaps we need to get more involved in village life,' said Fran, looking up from the parish magazine that had just been pushed through our door.

We were taking breakfast at the table in the garden. Oh, what a joy this is. Were I ever to be convicted of a terrible crime (wrongfully) and slammed away in solitary confinement, then this would be one of the pictures that I would conjure up in my head to help make it bearable. The morning sun, warm but not yet hot, gentle and comforting on the skin, kindling the anticipation of a day coming to life. The methodical culinary journey through juice, fruit, cereals, egg, toast, and tea, leading to a satisfied stretching of the legs and a wish that if the stomach weren't so limiting then one could simply do it all again.

'Involved in village life in what way?' I asked.

'Take a look at this.'

Fran handed me the parish magazine, which wasn't a magazine at all but a small booklet, although no one called it that. This was the second edition we'd received. Fran had read the first one from cover to cover, whereas I'd just thumbed through it and looked at the small ads at the back. I noted that one handyman had included in his ad that 'no job was too small'. I'd been tempted to call him and explain that I'd dropped my Biro, and ask him if he could give me a quote to come round and pick it up for me. In another ad someone had been trying to sell a lawnmower. After the price and the phone number they'd written the words 'No timewasters'. This intrigued me. What exactly *was* a time-waster? Was *I* a timewaster?

Clearly I was, because I was currently allotting time to the consideration of whether I was a timewaster or not. Hardly a good use of time. Did this mean that I was barred from making enquiries about the purchase of this lawnmower?

I knew, however, that this was not what the advertiser meant. What they wished to communicate was that they didn't want anyone to phone them up and ask questions about this lawnmower, unless the caller was genuinely interested in purchasing it. One wonders what kind of person would choose to ask a string of questions about a piece of garden machinery that *didn't* interest them. The type who would simply feign interest for their own amusement. Whoever these people might be, and I suspect that there can't be many, I doubt that they are put off by the words 'No timewasters'. Surely these words would act like magnets to them? If you happened to be one of these peculiar individuals, wouldn't it be much more fun to waste the time of someone who had formerly announced that they didn't want their time wasted, rather than someone who was more relaxed about their time? Anyway, enough about that. I don't want to waste your time.

I looked at the piece in the magazine to which Fran had directed me. It explained that the village hall was in something of a crisis. No reason was given why, but apparently the entire committee had resigned, and nobody had put themselves forward to replace them. Unless a new committee was found, then the village hall would end up being locked permanently.

'Are you thinking that you should stand for the committee?' I asked Fran.

'No, I was wondering whether *you* should.'

I had never been on a committee in my life. The very word sent shivers down my spine. It conjured up images of grey people, sitting around grey tables on grey days, discussing what particular shade of grey to paint the walls.

Committees were flair-free zones. Bastions of boredom. Forums for elongated discussion rather than instant action. An 'Emergency Committee' was an oxymoron. Like Rasputin or Caligula, I wasn't a committee man. (The comparison ends here.)

'I'm not sure that I'm the stuff of committees,' I said.

'Me neither.'

The short discussion was halted as we looked out across the valley to the green hills that formed our morning tableau. The beauty soothed. It bathed us in goodness. Maybe that's why I returned to the subject with more generosity of spirit.

'It would be a shame if the village lost the hall,' I said.

'I agree,' said Fran.

Metaphorically, we were standing on a sea cliff, wondering whether we should jump into the waters below. I peered over the edge.

'I guess you've got to have a committee to get things done.'

Fran looked over too.

'Yes, someone has to do this kind of stuff or it just doesn't get done.'

Several minutes later we had joined hands and jumped.

We'd decided that we would both put ourselves forward. Neither of us admitted it, but mixed up in our good intentions there'd been the less noble element of 'if I'm going to suffer this, then you should too'.

'How do we let them know?' I asked.

'There's an Annual General Meeting coming up, where volunteers for a new committee need to make themselves known, otherwise the hall will close.'

'And when's that?'

'Next Tuesday.'

'Right.'

A thought occurred to me.

'Do you actually know what happens up at the village hall?'

'No, but it says here,' said Fran, finger delving into the parish magazine, 'that there's a new Zumba class starting there on Monday night.'

'Ah yes, I've seen posters around the village for that. You should go along. It's important that we see what kind of stuff currently happens there and how well-attended it is. It's very fortuitous that there's an opportunity for one of us to do so before the AGM.'

'I can't go.'

'Why not?'

'I told you. I'm going to London on Monday. To hand in the corrections to my PhD.'

'Oh, no. That's a shame.'

'You could go.'

'What?'

'You could go to Zumba.'

'I can't. It's a ladies thing.'

'No, it isn't. It's a health and fitness thing. You'll be good at it.'

'Oh, I don't know. I'm not sure that it'll be my thing.'

'Right. And what *is* your thing?'

This was an unfair question from Fran. In life, one needs only a list of things that *aren't* your thing – like ironing, queuing in airport security or Prime Minister's Question Time. Not a list of things that *are*. Fran should know that.

'It's dance,' said Fran. 'You like dancing. You'll be good at it.'

* * *

So it was, that in the interests of research, it fell upon me to go to the Monday-night Zumba class. By this time I'd made enough enquiries to know that I would be attending a kind of fitness/dance class that drew on Latin-American rhythms. A glance at Wikipedia had informed me that Zumba was created by Alberto 'Beto' Perez in Colombia during the 1990s. I guess when he'd first made it all up he figured it was only a question of time before it made it to a small village hall in Devon. He would no doubt be delighted to know that the great Tony Hawks was now going to give it a go.

I wasn't overly nervous. I'd done aerobics classes in the past and I'd been skilful enough to learn some of the moves. In my first aerobics class, when I had been outnumbered ten to one by women (this is not compulsory, but seems to be the standard ratio), I had been completely thrown off-guard when the instructor bellowed 'Grapevine!' and everyone in the class set off on a kind of wiggly shimmy to the left or right. (How they knew which way to go still remains a mystery.)

Initially, my attempts at 'grapevining' had been, at best, embarrassing and, at worst, dangerous. Setting off in the wrong direction with flailing limbs causes painful collisions and does not endear you to other Lycra-clad participants, who are already deeply suspicious of you because of your slightly grubby tracksuit bottoms. Wishing to avert future humiliation, I'd practised the 'grapevine' at home and, though I say so myself, I'd become pretty adept at it, only letting myself down occasionally in classes when I launched into it in the wrong direction.

The village hall interior, like its exterior, was unremarkable. Exactly what you'd expect from such an edifice. Wooden floorboards, large windows, a rather unattractive low suspended ceiling, and a kitchen at the far end, the other side of a serving hatch. I'd arrived at the village hall at 7.25 p.m. for the 7.30 p.m. start, well kitted out in a tracksuit (not slightly grubby anymore, due to just another one of Fran's many positive influences in my life) and with a towel and bottle of water. This impressive display of preparedness may have given a false impression of competence to those waiting inside the hall, who were, of course, all women. The recognised ten to one ratio had been respected. Ten women of different shapes, sizes and ages were milling around, limbering up or chatting, as a super-fit-looking instructor fiddled with a ghetto blaster. I felt a flutter of nerves, but reassured myself.

'I'll be all right,' I said to myself. 'I can grapevine.'

Besides, I thought, at least it's a new class, so we're all in this together. There would be a fair chance that most of the others would be as much in the dark as me when it came to the finer points of 'Zumbaring', or however they liked to describe it.

I made a base camp in the corner of the hall, putting my accessories on a windowsill, and I began gentle limbering movements. Then I took a deep breath and made the bold step of striding across the room to announce myself to the instructor – the presence of a man in proceedings seeming to create something of an edge to the atmosphere. Or was that me being paranoid? Or vain even?

'Hello, I'm Tony!' I said, as I arrived in front of the teacher, like a small child pushed forward by an overzealous parent at an audition for a show. 'I'm here to represent the male sex.'

It seemed like a good idea to open with a gentle bit of humour, but as soon as I'd said it, I realised that it sounded naff.

'Hi, Tony, I'm Sandra,' replied our tutor, 'have you done Zumba before?'

'No.'

'Are you reasonably fit?'

'Yes, I think so.'

'Great. Well, it may take you a while to find out what's going on, as we've been doing this for twelve weeks down at the neighbouring village hall.'

A cold shiver.

'What?'

'We've lost the use of that village hall – which is why we've moved up here. The others know the moves pretty well, so you may be a little at sea for a while.'

Shit. This wasn't good. Not good at all.

'Maybe find a place at the back, so you can follow what's going on.'

And with those words, she clapped her hands and summoned everyone into starting positions with a hugely enthusiastic:

'OK, girls. Let's go!'

Normally I don't respond to such a call, but I recognised my place as an 'honorary girl' and carefully positioned myself in the extreme back right-hand corner of the hall, which seemed to be the most private place I could find, short of being in the storage cupboard.

The first song began, unrecognisable, but driven by a strong, pulsating Latin rhythm. Sandra counted to four and then suddenly everyone was off. Instructions were barked and the 'girls' duly followed. They clearly knew what they were doing. For them, it was like practising a dance routine that they'd been rehearsing for months. For me, the experience was different. It was like being thrown into a room where . . . well, where ladies were practising a dance routine that they'd been rehearsing for months.

I had no clue what was coming, or what to do once it had arrived. The moves seemed to run for eight bars of the music. This gave me enough time to sort out my direction and begin to make some pathetic attempt at the move that was being done by everyone else in the room. However, just at the very moment when I'd begun to establish what was required for that move, Sandra would bark instructions for another. The process would then repeat. There appeared to be about five moves for the entire song, and each time they repeated, I was able to make a better fist of getting them right. But then the track finished. Sandra looked at me and smiled.

'Well done, Tony, not bad!'

For the second track, I made going in the right direction my main priority. The session for the lady to my left was being made more testing by the need to keep an eye out for the idiot to her right. Suddenly a huge sweeping move to the right was required, bringing me into direct contact with the outer wall of the village hall – which I could now confirm, was very well-constructed. Worse still, it meant that all the ladies in the room were facing me, and they could see that I was not even beginning to do any of the things that were required of me. Now in the spotlight, I just guessed at what I should be doing, and flailed some arms and legs in a kind of medley of every move that had happened thus far. At the end of the song, and with the patience of a careworker, Sandra smiled at me encouragingly.

I was now getting very hot. I drank some water and decided that the tracksuit bottoms would have to come off. I'd booked for the full hour of torture, so I might as well be comfortably attired. Besides, I thought I looked pretty good in shorts.

As the next song raged into life, something alarming began to happen. It became clear that the elastic had gone in the waistband of the shorts and that what had been holding them up before had been the elastic in the waist of the tracksuit bottoms. Any jolty movement from me now meant that my shorts started to fall down. I clutched at them with one hand, but Sandra was constantly calling for us to wave our arms about. I tried, but to let go for too long was risky. Shorts around the ankles, in front of a group of women at my first village hall event, was unthinkable. Better to fail even more hopelessly than before with each move, than to tarnish my reputation for years to come.

At the end of that track, I rushed quickly over to my base camp and put my tracksuit bottoms back on. Sandra glanced in my direction, perhaps thinking that I was leaving.

'You all right, Tony?'

'Yes. Yes, thanks. Just putting my tracksuit bottoms back on.'

The same ones that she, and everyone else, had observed me removing three minutes earlier.

'You're doing well,' she said.

Sandra was a fine dancer, a good teacher, but an absolutely fabulous bullshitter. If I was *doing well*, then just how low could her expectations of me have been at the start? I was only *doing well* because I hadn't killed anyone or napalmed the building.

The same pattern continued throughout the next forty minutes – that of learning a move, only to have it immediately switched to another. I watched the clock with the same foolish devotion of the bored factory worker. Time, of course, passes more slowly when monitored. The agony is prolonged.

What was most upsetting was that Sandra seemed to be utilising every dance movement known to man *except* the grapevine. My chance to shine was being denied. It wasn't until the very last song, when the clock was reading 8.26, that Sandra suddenly called 'Grapevine!'

Brilliant! At last! I thought, and I leapt into that move like a shot – with all the gusto and all the enthusiasm I could muster. I knew what I was doing at last.

There was a problem though.

I went left and the rest of the class went right.

'Sorry!' I blurted out, as I kicked the lady next to me quite hard on the shin.

She looked away, either lost in her dancing, or in her fury. I had dealt her quite a blow, but she did not even break stride. Adrenalin was carrying her through.

'Well done, ladies! A great class!' announced Sandra at 8.30 on the dot.

The gaggle of ladies applauded. The solitary man hung his head. He tried to seek out the lady he had kicked to make another attempt at an apology, but she was in a huddle with another group, no doubt bad-mouthing him.

The man went home alone, rubbing an elbow that was now hurting, following an earlier collision with a solid wall. He had a bath. He went to bed.

He wouldn't be doing Zumba again in a hurry.

* * *

He was back at the village hall again all too soon, though, twenty-four hours not being enough time for the scars to have healed. The Zumba elbow was still sore too.

I had never been to an AGM before. I'd happily, and somewhat irresponsibly, lived in a world where the running of things was done by others. My life had been one in which I'd been happy to complain and criticise where necessary, whilst ensuring that I never became involved in any of the processes that had led to the decisions or policies that I disliked. That was about to change.

Fran and I got to the hall at 7.02 p.m. About twenty-five people were already seated in a semicircle in front of the table that presumably contained the vestiges of the outgoing committee. Village life seemed to be well-represented, from the grubby to the well-turned-out, but there were no children. Or young people. Surprisingly, they had chosen other activities ahead of sitting in a hall on a summer's evening, listening to their elders discussing how it might best be managed. Even the youngsters who might have been interested could have a more stimulating experience playing the computer game 'AGM', in which the chairman can be zapped if he gets someone's name wrong, or fails to point out the fire exits.

Heads turned to see who it was that had turned up two minutes late. We lived less than five minutes' walk away, so not being on time wasn't impressive, but both Fran and I are good at faffing.[1]

The meeting kicked off the moment our arses touched the hard chairs, almost as if this was the cue for the grey-haired outgoing chairman to begin. What followed was not top-quality entertainment. He was only a few minutes into his speech, outlining the improvements that the previous committee had made to the hall, when my mind started to wander. His voice became a monotone backdrop to myriad thoughts about sea walks, jobs that needed doing around the house and whether the oil needed changing on the car.

I tuned in occasionally, just for long enough to learn that a three-phase electrical renovation was recommended, but most of the time I surrendered to my mind's indiscriminate meanderings. It was like being back at school. No engagement. Oh, how I remembered that feeling that one should sit down, shut up, and listen. There was nothing to draw you in, or prick your interest, and so the creative mind used to rebel and play truant.

Are you listening, boy?

The honest answer was no.

---

1   I actually suffer from a condition that has no official name, but it's a *fear of being early*. If it looks like I'm well ahead of the game and might arrive ten minutes before required, I begin some other needless task that will then cause me to run late. There is no known cure.

No, I'm not listening, because nobody asked me if I wanted to do this, and actually I don't – because I find it dull.

But that was an invitation to punishment. So we lied.

Yes, sir.

And upon this system we build the fabric of our society.

Half an hour into the meeting, there was a rare moment of audience participation. Those present were asked to vote on whether the village hall should adopt the new constitution that had apparently just been explained to us. (I was on horseback in the Andes at the time.) It must have made good sense since everyone in the room, including Fran, raised their hands. I raised mine too, simultaneously exercising and, given my ignorance of what I was now approving, abusing my democratic rights.

With the new constitution in place, two of the three men behind the table then announced that they were resigning and that a new committee was needed. The other man, the treasurer, said that he was prepared to stay on for one year. No real explanation was offered as to how and why this situation existed, but all we'd been told was that there had been a clash of personalities and that this was why fresh faces were needed for the committee. Untainted by the past. The moment that Fran and I had come to seize had arrived. The now ex-chairman asked if there were any people present who were prepared to form the new committee. I raised my hand.

For a moment, Fran seemed to hesitate. Was she going to betray me? To my relief, I saw her slowly put her hand up too. Those present turned and looked. A buzz of conversation echoed around the hall. I looked around to see that there were three other volunteers, two grey-haired ladies in their sixties and Brenda – the former owner of our house. The ex-chairman counted the hands and asked for each of the volunteers to be seconded. Seconders were not hard to find, and I got the feeling that there was immense relief that anyone was prepared to take on this task. It was announced that this was enough for a new committee to be formed and the AGM, wonderful spectacle that it had been, came to a close.

History had been made.

There was a part of me that kept thinking – could it really be done like this? You could simply put up your hand and that was enough to get you on a committee? Were there no votes? No declarations of policy? Was this how rural Britain operated?

The new committee were ushered to the front table, whilst everyone else slowly dispersed from the hall, chattering excitedly. Perhaps it wasn't quite our village's equivalent of a new pope being elected, but it was still reason for a good old gossip. To the relative noisy soundtrack of an emptying hall, the new committee (all of retirement age but for me and Fran) were introduced to each other and then asked to sign a document that was witnessed by the outgoing chairman. We were then instructed to have our first meeting, and we were invited to sit down around a table.

I felt rather unnerved at this point. The way sportsmen feel when they've won a big trophy, but without the elation. I was experiencing the 'Ah, this has actually happened' moment. As we gathered around the table, the new committee eyed each other in turn. The looks weren't suspicious, but they could have been interpreted so by any onlooker who didn't know what was going on. Introductions were made, followed by hasty judgements. There was Rose, apparently strong and confident. Ann, sweet-looking and timelessly dressed. Brenda, whom I already knew, well-dressed and genial as ever; and Mary and David, a smiling and assured couple. Then there was Fran. I knew her. I'd slept with her. Good. Always good to have slept with at least one person on any committee on which one sits. It's the British way.

We all sat down and David, the incumbent treasurer from the previous committee, showed himself to be the only one who had the vaguest idea of the protocol.

'I suppose the first thing we'll need to do is elect a chairman,' he said.

'And how do we do that?' I asked.

'Well, we'll need to see if anyone will volunteer for the position and if so, if anyone will second them. I don't want to do it, but is anyone happy to be chairman?'

Chairman? Who would make a good chairman, I thought? I was pondering this baffling point in my head, when I received a dig in the ribs.

'Put your hand up!' muttered Brenda between her teeth, presumably having made a judgement that I was good chairman material, based on the authoritative way in which I had viewed her house.

The jab was sharp and sudden enough to cause me to obey without thinking. Only when my arm was aloft did I realise that I was now volunteering for the position of chairman of the village hall. Before I had a chance to drop my hand, Rose chimed in.

'Great. I'll second Tony,' she said, her hand aloft now alongside mine.

'Excellent, that's it. That's decided then,' said David, who proceeded to jot something down on a piece of official-looking paper.

Was that it? Was that all it took? A jab in the ribs, an arm aloft and everything was done and dusted? Seemingly so.

I flushed. Strangely, I was experiencing a sudden and entirely unexpected rush of adrenalin, as it dawned on me that for the first time in my life I found myself in a position of authority. Albeit only seconds into the job though I was, it felt strangely invigorating. I found myself thinking about power. I was the Chairman. OK, I wasn't Chairman Mao – presumably I had an altogether different remit – but I had power.

My creative mind ran amok, allowing me to indulge in absurd fantasy. It told me to stop and think of all that authority! Boy, the changes I could wreak upon these people. For a moment I was Napoleon, Gaddafi and Hussein, Assad, Stalin, Hitler, Pol Pot – the only difference being that, rather than torturing, maiming and slaughtering, I would be deciding whether we undertook a three-phase electrical renovation.

In that moment, I understood what drives men to seek power. It was intoxicating. It was all-consuming. It was seductive. And, in my case, unfeasibly stupid.

'L . . . l . . . let's get the me . . . m . . . m . . . mee . . . meeting underway,' said David, falteringly.

It now became apparent that David had a slight stutter. He'd spoken smoothly before, but perhaps now the realisation of who was holding the position of chairman was making him nervous. A horrible thought occurred to me. What if he *knew*?

What if he knew that in 1988 I had written and performed (as one third of the trio that were Morris Minor and the Majors) the Number 4 hit 'Stutter Rap'.[2] Rather insensitively, and with a brash disrespect for political correctness, the lyric had outlined the difficulty of the stutterer when faced with the task of rapping.

My life was so well-planned
Survivin' and a-jivin' in a funk band
'Cos rapping it's my bread and butter
But it's hard to rap when you're born with a stutter

What if David *knew*? What if he'd harboured a 25-year grudge against me and that this entire 'village hall crisis' was a sham, fabricated so that I could be inveigled into becoming chairman and then slowly be driven to suicide by the weight of petty and yet overwhelming bureaucratic tasks?

Time would tell.

'W . . . w . . . what should we call you?' asked David.

'What do you mean?' I replied.

'Well, should we refer to you as Mister Chairman?'

Oh yes, it was coming back to me now. This was the protocol for committees, wasn't it? The chairman suddenly loses his or her first name and becomes mister or madam, gaining the new surname 'Chairman'.

---

2 The modern jazzier version can be heard here – www.tonyhawks. bandcamp.com – and at least it's doing some good. All proceeds from downloads are going to my care centre in Moldova for kids with cerebral palsy.

'Mister Chairman?' I said. 'That sounds a bit weird.'

'It's normal.'

'Does anyone mind if we go with *Tony*?'

The first radical seed had been planted. Outrageous. Suggesting that we call someone by their own name, rather than a silly made-up one.

'I think that's a good idea,' said Brenda.

The others looked on nervously but then, as if struck by a thunderbolt of good sense, they all began nodding. Before we knew it, we had unanimous approval. This seemed to be rather a nice committee.

Of course, Napoleon, Gaddafi and Hussein, Assad, Stalin, Hitler and Pol Pot would never have done such a thing and allowed their apparatchiks to be on first-name terms – to become friends, instead of subordinates – but mine was going to be a benign rule. I had never sought out this office, but now that it was mine, I was going to use it to make the world a better place.

'OK, so what happens now?' I said, demonstrating enormous authority.

'We need to appoint a secretary,' said Rose.

'Well, are you willing to do it?' I asked.

There was sensible logic behind this offer. Rose had thought that we needed a secretary and therefore Rose should *be* the secretary. It was borrowed from the sensible logic of children – a kind of 'he who smelt it, dealt it' approach.

The remaining committee looked at Rose. She raised her eyebrows.

'Well, I suppose I *could* do it,' she said.

'Excellent,' I said, getting into the swing of things. 'You can be secretary then.'

It felt like I was a team captain and we were picking sides in the school playground.

'What about a vice-chairman?' asked Brenda.

'Good idea,' I said, 'can you do it?'

'Well, I suppose I could,' said Brenda.

I was on a roll. Why had I not been in government before? I was a natural.

'Right, I think that's all the positions filled,' I announced. 'Shall we make a date for a proper meeting next week?'

'Yes, and I'll write an agenda for it,' said Rose.

'Good.'

'And I'll prepare a treasurer's report,' said David.

'Splendid. Everyone all right for Thursday night at 6.30 p.m.?'

Nods followed. No London-style consulting of agendas, or negotiation on the time slot, so that it could be 'squeezed in' between other meetings. Here in Britain's rural countryside we all seemed to be frighteningly available.

'Well done, everyone,' I said, 'I look forward to Thursday night.'

'We're a great team,' said Rose.

We were indeed. OK, we hadn't done anything yet, but that is always the high point for any government or organisation. This was our 'Obama moment'. We were popular for two reasons. We were different to what had gone before, and we hadn't done anything yet.

It would be all downhill from here.

6

The R Word

The seventh of August was another scorching day. It was the kind of heat you expect when you alight from a plane in a far-off, exotic location; the kind of heat that hits you, as you walk onto the aircraft steps and cannot help but exclaim, 'Wow!' – such is the contrast to the dreary, cloudy mediocrity that you'd just left behind. Now we had it all on our doorstep. No need to fly anywhere. Devon was a holiday paradise with few shortcomings.

Everything seemed right with the world. OK, snippets of the global news accidentally reached my ears via the odd radio dotted around the place, so I knew that all was not well everywhere. However, Devon remained blissfully devoid of drones, landmines, terrorists, freedom fighters, corrupt dictators, human rights abusers, food shortages, contaminated water, power shortages, and disease.

'I am,' I said to myself, 'a lucky, lucky bastard.'

Fran was not so lucky this morning, though, complaining of feeling unwell. We had recently registered with the doctor in the neighbouring village, so I called up and made an almost instantaneous appointment – something that in

London might have taken a few days to achieve, following a conversation not unlike this:

'I'd like to make an appointment with the doctor, as I'm not feeling very well.'

'The first appointment I have is in a week's time, at four p.m. on Thursday.'

'But I might be better by then. Or dead.'

'In which case, make sure you have someone cancel the appointment for you.'

I shouldn't moan. It's incredible that we even have a National Health Service. I grew up taking it for granted. It had been all I'd known and it seemed a sensible way to do things. If you felt unwell, you went to see someone and they helped you. They didn't ask you for money or demand to see insurance paperwork. It seemed normal and remarkably civilised. It was only after reaching the age when I started to travel that I learned this was not necessarily the natural order of things. There were places in the world where doctors would leave their citizens in all kinds of discomfort until they were sure they could perform the operation that they deemed most important – the location and removal of money from their patients' bank accounts.

'I am,' I said to myself, in the comfortable, clean environment of the surgery waiting room, 'a lucky, lucky bastard.'

A copy of *Devon Life* and a host of other kindly magazines stared up at me from the coffee table, but I was content simply to sit and wait, occasionally eyeing other patients and having an inward guess at the reason for their visit. Fran had been gone less than five minutes, when she appeared in the corridor.

'Tony, you'd better come,' she said.

'What?'

'Just come.'

Fran turned and headed back into Room 4. I followed her down the short corridor, my mind beginning to fill with fears. Was this going to be the announcement of some earth-shattering news? A terminal illness? An amputation?

I entered the room and was immediately greeted by a pleasant-looking lady doctor of about Fran's age. She was smiling. Good. That was comforting. Doctors don't smile when they announce terminal illnesses. It's not something they learn in their formal training, but it's a little thing they pick up along the way.

'Congratulations,' the doctor said, 'Fran is pregnant. You're going to be a father.'

Blimey.

So that's it? Pregnant.

Blimey.

OK, I'll be honest. This had been at the back of my mind. Fran and I had stopped using contraception a few months previously, and in that sense we had been 'planning' to start a family. However, we hadn't bothered to work out when Fran would be at her most fertile, and I hadn't cut down on hot baths, or done anything to facilitate the production of top-quality sperm. All we'd done was halted the deliberate prevention of pregnancy. In truth, probably neither of us was quite ready for this news. Especially me. I was definitely in shock.

'I think I need to sit down,' I said, rather like a feeble geriatric.

I hugged Fran, and held her hand as the doctor talked us

through what happened next. I didn't listen properly. For the moment, I felt I knew enough. Fran would get tubby, and then a baby would pop out roughly nine months from now. I'd get to grips with the technical side at a later date. My mind was currently preoccupied with what we'd be losing rather than gaining.

Freedom.

I felt a little faint. Sick even. Probably morning sickness. Here I was, just past fifty, finally about to embark on doing what almost every single one of my contemporaries had nearly completed – raising a family. Why these feelings of trepidation? Why not joy? That was what you were *supposed* to feel, weren't you?

'You must be thrilled!' said the doctor.

'Oh, I am,' I said, failing to display any sign of such an emotion. 'We're both thrilled.'

Fran smiled, a twinkle in her eye. I could tell that she wasn't as afraid as I was. I'd spent much of my life avoiding it, but now there was no escaping it. The R word.

Responsibility.

This was the word that was written on the bullets that would soon emerge from the barrel of the shotgun down which I was now staring. The doctor was saying something about midwives and appointments, but I could barely hear her above the deafening sound of the R word.

Responsibility.

Even though I was clearly grown up, I'd never been *a* grown-up. OK, I was no longer what most people consider to be a young man. But that's not the point. I felt like one, and I lived like one. I'd never had a 'proper job'. Most mornings I got up when my body was ready, and consequently, on those rare occasions when the alarm needed to go on, I always needed to remind myself how to set it. If I wanted to go somewhere, most of the time I just went there. Adventure was not off-limits. Risks (I preferred calculated ones) could be taken.

I was routine-free, often taking a kind of perverse delight in not knowing when and where the next paid job would materialise. I owned stuff, but I was prepared to lose it. I jumped in the air with the expectation that I would land on my feet, and if I landed on my arse, then I accepted the helping hand that always seemed to be offered. I didn't want for much, and what I had, I liked. The only thing that was missing in life was ... was ... was, well, responsibility.

Perhaps I'd yearned for it without knowing. Maybe the very thing that scared me now was what I actually *needed*. The reality was that I had sown my seeds, and therefore roots were bound to grow. Maybe this was just supposed to happen and that up until now, for reasons that an expensive psychoanalyst might be able to figure out, I'd simply spent my life avoiding it? Or could it simply be that we all move at different speeds, and that I just happened to be ready twenty years later than most people, that's all?

Either way, on the seventh of August in the thirteenth year of this millennium, I became a grown-up.

As we left the surgery I looked down the corridor. On the far wall there was one of those eye-test charts with letters arranged in varying sizes. I could only see one letter.

R.

* * *

'How are you feeling?' I said to Fran, as I drove her to her first hospital appointment, a fortnight after the revelation of the 'thrilling' news.

'Fine. Just fine.'

Fran appeared to be having a relatively easy time of it. Apart from those initial feelings of discomfort that had prompted the first doctor's appointment, she was now only experiencing tiredness. No throwing-up in the mornings. Not bad, given the enormous physiological changes taking place in her body. To me, it felt like Fran was living a science-fiction story similar to that in the movie *Alien*. She had another body growing inside hers. Quite extraordinary, except for the fact that it was so commonplace. And yet it felt so weird – another body growing inside hers . . .

Maybe I would have been less incredulous if I'd known more about the biology. My extensive ignorance on this subject (which I made a good fist of concealing from Fran) was entirely my own fault. In the past, whenever the subject of childbirth had arisen, I had zoned out. Words like labour, contractions, placenta, Caesarean and umbilical cord had all been signals for me to extricate myself from a conversation where I had neither any interest, nor anything meaningful to contribute.

There was an irony here, though. For all the time I'd spent pursuing female bodies over the years, I'd been comprehensively uninformed when it came to what was actually contained within them. Having been to a boys' grammar school, where sex education had been non-existent, I'd been reduced to garnering any information regarding the workings of the female body through playground banter and occasional access to pornographic magazines. The vagina, according to teenage lads, had been created as a play area – a source of potential pleasure, not unlike a football pitch or table-tennis table (although ideally hosting very different activities). The pivotal role it had played in us boys actually *being there* in the first place, didn't seem to concern us. We were, as Mr Mainwaring might have accurately described us, stupid boys.

However, it was an embarrassment that over the years my knowledge had not really advanced measurably. Yes, I knew (or thought I knew) what bits of a woman to touch in order to elicit the pleasure that I hoped would then enable my sexual needs to be sated. But I would never have picked the female body as my specialist subject on *Celebrity Mastermind*.[1]

'It's an odd word "midwife", isn't it?' I said to Fran, as we pulled into the hospital car park. 'Do you know what it means?'

'Not really. Doesn't the "mid" stand for "middle" because the midwife is a conduit between the child and mother?'

'Sounds logical. But why *wife*? That would mean that she's halfway to being your wife.'

This might have been a dangerous conversational area to negotiate had Fran not been so level-headed. I'd never asked Fran to marry me, and I had no intention of so doing, even though we were about to be bound together in the most binding of ways. However, this was not a bone of contention, and we'd discussed the matter and found ourselves to be in agreement.

---

1   Not that I'd done particularly well with the subject that I *did* pick. See: http://www.youtube.com/watch?v=6rQeY5s5oTM

I have nothing against marriage, and I respect all the diverse cultural reasons why people opt for it. Some want a celebration to mark their love and mutual commitment, others to follow a religious duty. Some want to make a social statement, and spend a pile of money and lose themselves in relentless organising, others want a good, old-fashioned piss-up. Some want legal recognition, others are simply following social protocol. Some want to placate their family, others to defy them. Some want to cherish a holy exchange of vows, others do it for the tax breaks. Whatever the reason, it happens. And it happens quite a lot.

For me, I've never wished my commitment to Fran to be a public affair. Nor have I ever wanted to enter into a promise that I might not be able to keep. Yes, it's true that couples can tinker with the marriage vows these days, but the culturally recognised and fundamental gist of marriage is that you're promising to stay with someone for the rest of your life. In the conventional Anglican wedding ceremony couples are asked to agree 'to have and to hold from this day forward, for better for worse, for richer for poorer, in sickness and in health, to love and to cherish, till death us do part'. It's very nice, and I'm sure that most people plan on keeping the promise when they make it. I'm sure my parents did. I'm sure Fran's parents did, too. The trouble is, they *didn't*. What they did instead was tear up the bit of paper on which the promise was written, and got divorced.

So I rather like the idea of a mid-wife or mid-husband. You make a commitment but it's tempered to suit a reality in which we are simply honest enough to admit that we don't *know* what the future holds, or how we're going to feel about someone in twenty-five years' time; especially if they've been sleeping with our best friend or keeping us locked up in a basement. I could go for the kind of commitment that is required in the mid-wife/mid-husband version of the wedding ceremony. It's much simpler and far more acceptable to agree 'to have and to hold from this day forward, for better for worse, for richer for poorer, in sickness and in health, to love and to cherish, *for as long as it seems like a good idea*.'

'Yep, I'm up for that.'

Fran recognised my loving commitment to her. I'd promised to do everything I could to make our relationship work in a loving space. I'd pledged to 'love' her till death did us part. The difference was that we had made the significant distinction between love and ownership. We'd decided that 'love' should be defined as 'wanting the other person to be happy'. As long as Fran was happy being with me, and I was happy being with her – and that we were prepared to work as hard as we possibly could ensuring that both our sets of needs were met – then we should stay together. If not, we should acknowledge the change in our relationship and get on with building a solid and loving friendship. Countless couples do it. They marry, they divorce, they become friends.[2]

My theory is that the divorcees who stay angry (and suffer as a result) do so because they bought into those initial marriage vows so comprehensively that they are left

---

2   They call this 'conscious uncoupling' now. Ironic that it was probably a coupling whilst barely conscious that kicked the whole thing off in the first place.

with a bitter taste in their mouths – 'You bastard/bitch, you said you'd never leave. You said you'd love me forever. You lied to me.'

Yes, the mid-wife/mid-husband idea works better.

When we met Maureen, our extremely jolly and convivial midwife, she put us right immediately on the meaning of her job description. Apparently, in Old English the word 'wife' (spelt 'wif' originally) meant 'woman', and 'mid' meant 'with'. So it means 'with woman'. That made sense. The midwife stayed *with* the *woman* and helped her deliver the child. In the NHS, though, she seemed mainly concerned with paperwork, for now at least. Form after form was completed, and Fran and I were handed a kind of idiot's guide to having a baby, although its writers had cleverly given it another name, *The Pregnancy and Baby Guide*. Pleasingly, Fran was declared 'low risk' and we were given a hospital appointment for a couple of months' time to go and have an ultrasound scan.

'You can make all the decisions of where and how to have the baby much further down the line,' said Maureen, as she showed us to the door. 'For now, just concentrate on eating well and resting.'

'I will,' I said.

A fairly poor attempt at a joke, but Maureen laughed generously. Most likely an act of compassion.

* * *

I had always feared that it would be something quite bereft of glamour. I had figured there would be no excitement. A forum where the mundane always trumped the inspired, where protocol trounced flair and where, to put it frankly, there would not be many laughs to be had. Now I was discovering that I had not been wrong. In fact, I had been spot-on.

The occasion was the first village hall committee meeting. We'd met in the hall itself, which looked very different from when there'd been a room full of ladies jumping around, mid-Zumba. Now just one table with a few chairs around it. It looked a little sad.

We had just ploughed our way through the exciting Apologies for Absence,[3] rejoiced in the treasurer's financial report, and now we were discussing the seismic question of who should be the signatories in the cheque book.

It was all quite riveting. (But only in the sense that a rivet is a short metal fastener with no exciting qualities.)

I'm not meaning to criticise. This kind of stuff is necessary. I had lived my life trying to escape it and, by and large, I'd made a pretty good fist of it. However, all forms of governance require some kind of system, some protocol, some conventions. Except dictatorship. Dictators can do as they please. They can insist on only their signature in the cheque book if they like. Or they can even dispense with the cheque book altogether, by just taking over the bank. But I wasn't at that level yet. Chairman Hawks would have to play by the rules a little longer.

'Item six on the agenda,' I announced, doing my best to sound absorbed. 'The question of where we place the rag box that the parish council has given us.'

---

3 It remains a mystery to me why an item like this remained on the agenda when, as in this case, no one had the decency not to turn up.

This was good stuff. One day I'd write a musical about it.

* * *

One of the many important things I'd learned at our first village hall meeting was that the Zumba class didn't count as a 'village hall event'. Sandra, the instructor, had hired the hall and was running her class for profit. What qualified as a 'village hall event' was one that the committee put on for the villagers, and from which any profit went into the treasurer's coffers.

Which is why Fran and I were going to be spending this Friday night at skittles.

Skittles is a variant of bowls or bowling. Originally, it would have been played in the open air on lawns, but people soon realised that it rains and gets dark outside so they developed a game that could be played inside. Tonight I was about to witness our village hall variant.

It's certainly not normal for most rural newcomers to go to their first village hall event as its chairman, but that was my privilege. Not that it made any difference when I got to the door. The man collecting the £3 entry fee, whom I was to learn later was Jonathan, a tip-top gardener (the mud beneath his fingernails was a clue that he wasn't a beautician), welcomed me jovially.

'Aha! A newcomer!' he said. 'We'll put you in the twinning team.'

Rose, the village hall committee secretary, quickly intervened:

'He's for the village hall team.'

'I thought he'd be good for "twinning" as they're short of players.'

'He ought to play for the village hall.'

'Why?'

'Because he's the chairman.'

A moment passed, and Jonathan exhaled and smiled cheekily.

'OK. I'll put him down for village hall. He just about qualifies.'

Ann, whom I already knew from our committee meeting (she'd been especially good on the issue of where to place the parish council's rag box), popped up from nowhere.

'Would you and Fran like to buy some raffle tickets?'

She led me to the windowsill with her eyes, where the prizes were proudly laid out. A small carton of Maltesers, another unidentifiable box of chocolates, some hand cream and a bottle of shampoo. Shampoo. How is it that shampoo always seems be a raffle prize at parochial events in the UK? Shampoo must be the most un-prize-like item you can have. Where can the excitement of winning come from? With chocolate one can look forward to the stimulation of eating the chocolate. With a small decorative item one might have a tingle of anticipation as you consider the moment that you place the item on your mantelpiece. But *shampoo*? What is the feeling when you win?

'Great, I can use this to wash my hair. But better still, this solves a huge problem because, as we all know, shampoo is almost impossible to get hold of in pharmacies and super-markets around the UK, and therefore this has saved me untold grief. Never mind that it's a shampoo for another kind of hair type to mine, I care little about the damage that it may cause to my follicles, because these minor reservations are trumped by the overwhelming feeling of exhilaration.'

I looked at the windowsill longingly.

'Give me five pounds' worth,' I said to Ann, in a moment of quite irresponsible recklessness.

'Certainly,' she said, tearing off a strip of tickets and raising an eyebrow – not realising just how much my hair was itching to be washed.

I thanked Ann and thrust the raffle tickets into my pocket, filled with a sense that tonight would be my night – the occasion when I finally won a raffle. I suspect that in my life to date I must have bought raffle tickets on more than a hundred occasions, but have never been the one at the end of the night who walked away with a spring in his step, clasping a bottle of VO5 or Pantene. Tonight, however, I could feel it in my bones. Inferius Prizus, the Greek god of piss-poor raffles, would atone for those terrible years of bad luck and disappointment.

I was pleased by what I saw before me. The hall was full. Forty or fifty people were happily milling about, drinking, chatting and organising the trestle tables and chairs that lined one of the walls. Along the opposing wall was a large art installation. A long strip of material had been laid lengthways in both sympathy and contrast to the harshness of the wall beyond it. At one end, some white grooves had been cut, representing birth, and at the other end, after one's eyes had traced the empty yards of flat and matted material that represented the monotonous routine of our daily lives, there stood nine upright objects, symbols of purgatory, death, or the afterlife.

'How do you like the skittle lane?' said Ann.

Ah. I must stop spending so much time in those modern-art galleries.

'It's lovely,' I said.

I'd never played skittles before, but like many of us, I'd been tenpin bowling, so there were no surprises in store. The thrust of this game is probably in our DNA, the earliest forms of bowling and ground billiards dating as far back as 3000 BC in Ancient Egypt.[4]

Skittles, played with nine pins, had remained popular as a pub game in alleys at the rear of pubs in the South West of England, whilst it had all but died out in the great metropolis of London, where people were too busy trading in money markets or forming gangs to have any time for such trifles. The village hall – my village hall – seemed the perfect setting for this ancient sport.

Rose ushered me and Fran to a table, and soon I was sharing a beer with Francis, a healthy-looking sixty-something, while Fran chatted with his wife. Francis was a former winner of 'best allotment in the village'. Roger joined us. It turned out he'd been a former allotment prize-winner too. I seemed to be surrounded by green-fingered horticulturists, who would have been appalled by my recent endeavours in the garden. (The pea plants had been optimistically tethered to a cane, but they had wilfully rejected the option of growing up it, favouring a form of shameful withering instead.) Around us, I noted that the atmosphere was warm

---

4   Many creationists who hold that God didn't actually get round to creating the world until a few thousand years ago, are no doubt impressed that skittles was one of the first things that man started to do with his time.

and convivial. The kitchen at the far end of the hall had now become a bar, and drinks were being served by Steve the postman, the son of Tony and Edna, our neighbours, and his chum Mark. All age groups seemed to be represented, from teenagers through to pensioners, all apparently from our village.

When we began playing the game of skittles itself, I learned that it was a great leveller. The athletic bowling of the eager teenager didn't necessarily reap anymore results than the timorous effort of the sweet old lady whose ball dropped out of her frail hand and fairly trickled down the track. Luck played a big part. Strength counted for nothing. The way the skittles scattered seemed to be random. Yes, skill and accuracy were rewarded occasionally, but the incompetent players were able to turn in an average score without letting their team down too much.

The nine skittles were repeatedly being knocked down by players and then eagerly put back up again by two young boys, who clearly relished this responsibility. Just to one side of where all this exhilarating action was taking place was a chalkboard that listed the names of the participating teams:

Church Mice
Fête
Twinning
Village Hall
WI

WI? What were the West Indies doing having a team here? And how had they managed to recruit so many white-haired old ladies to represent them?

I received a smattering of applause when I stepped up to the mat for the first time to bowl my balls. For those anticipating great things, there was only disappointment. It took three efforts to knock over only seven skittles and this resulted in some laughter, a little desultory (or sarcastic) applause, and one audible heckle of 'Rubbish!' from the corner of the room. I couldn't identify the perpetrator, but if I were able to do so before the night was out, I would ensure that they were 'dealt with'. We could not have the chairman being treated with such disrespect.

The chairman improved a little with his subsequent bowls, but this only served to make him unworthy of derision or celebration; an average player of the game, as unremarkable as the light-brown walls that surrounded him. Pleasingly though, an entertaining evening seemed to be had by all, chairman included, even though his team finished the evening in penultimate place.

But at least we were ahead of the West Indies.

'Never mind,' explained Ann, as we were all leaving, 'skittles happens once a month and it's a running score through till the spring. Plenty of time to make up ground.'

Good, I thought, that would give us the opportunity to make some key signings in the January transfer window, if necessary.

7

Brassica Massacre

'What's this called again?' I asked, as we drove into the hospital car park.

'It's the ten-week scan.'

'Ah yes, the one they also call the dating scan.'

I'd read about this in the idiot's guide to pregnancy and had been intrigued by its name. Surely, I figured, if you'd got to the point where a ten-week-old baby was growing inside one of the couple, then you had gone beyond 'dating'. It was nudging towards the point where an affirmative answer was necessary to the question that people ask courting couples: 'Is it serious?'

The NHS kicked in and did its stuff. I've never liked hospitals much (who does?) but this one was all right, and compared to many of the hospitals I'd visited in Moldova, it was absolutely marvellous. Soon we were sitting with a bubbly lady in front of an ultrasound machine.

'You're going to meet your baby now,' she announced.

I was nervous. However good-humoured the scan lady[1]

---

1 A sonographer, if you want to show off. I will, later in this chapter.

was, I knew that what she was doing was serious. She was making sure that the baby had a head, two arms, two legs, and the rest. She was checking to see whether it was one baby or two. Twins. I didn't want twins. Twice the noise, twice the poo and sick, and basically twice the aggravation.

She smeared jelly onto Fran's tummy and then started pushing around something resembling those gadgets that assistants use in supermarkets for scanning barcodes. Instead of finding out how much a can of beans cost, we were about to find out if we had a healthy foetus. Suddenly a horrific thought struck me. What if there had been serious implications resulting from the attack upon my penis by the compost heap that day? What if we now discovered that our baby was going to turn out to be half-human/half-wasp?

Much to our relief, Fran and I left the hospital having been told that she was expecting only one baby, and that it had no wings or orange-and-black abdomen. All was well. We'd been given a due date of 24 March and an appointment for a twenty-week scan. Until then, all the baby had to do was grow. Just like the seeds we had planted in our garden.

Well, with any luck, it would perform a little better than that.

***

Summer was giving way to autumn, as it did every year with irritating regularity. At least summer had been decent enough to put in a reasonable appearance this year. Years ago I'd met an American, now living in the UK.

'How long have you been over here?' I'd asked.

'Four summers. Or ten years.'

The light faded, the leaves began to fall and the temperature dropped. I no longer had the toughness to walk down the garden and indulge in my daily Hawks Harness workouts in the makeshift pool. I emptied it and put it in the shed. Although Fran never said as much, I felt she was relieved.

Outdoor activity decreased dramatically, but sadly not for my old nemesis, the slugs. They carried on eating, regardless of the shorter days and decidedly lower temperatures. Slugs, however, were not our only rivals in the 'Battle of the Back Garden'. We had already suffered a number of humiliating defeats. Our carrots had seemed to be growing rather well without any interference from bugs or slugs, until one morning I went down to water them, only to discover that the whole crop had been pulled out and eaten. Tony, our neighbour on the other side to Ken, peered over the fence, shaking his head as I looked down at the space where the carrots used to be.

'That'll be a badger,' he said, 'it had our lot too. The bugger waits till the carrots are big enough for him to eat, and then he swoops down and wolfs the lot in one night.'

Up until that moment, I'd quite liked badgers. They seemed rather attractive creatures and I tended to speak up for them in the debate about whether they should be culled or not. Now culling seemed too good for them. Too quick. Not enough suffering. That needed to be looked at.

We lost our cabbages, kale and broccoli to another foe. This came as a bitter blow, as we'd worked so hard on our defences. Following the advice that we'd picked up on our organic gardening course, we'd covered the brassica[2] with protective netting and I was fairly convinced that it was impenetrable. This is why I was confused when on each successive visit the leaves were increasingly more decimated. No slugs could be in there, so why the damage?

One evening, I lifted off all the netting and surveyed the bed that lay beneath it. It felt like I was looking down on an aerial photo of Manhattan after a nuclear attack. The remaining kale, cabbages and broccoli resembled the shells of buildings after a horrific and devastating strike. Then I saw the problem. A small and brilliantly disguised caterpillar crawling across what was left of one of the leaves. Upon closer inspection, I saw that every leaf in the bed had several of these hungry little larvae hiding away on its stems.

I had made a schoolboy error. Fran and I had been delighted to see butterflies flitting around the garden. Simply divine. Our spirits had been lifted on a summer afternoon by the sight of these delightful, fluttering dashes of colour. However, unbeknownst to us, they'd been up to no good. They'd laid their tiny, almost invisible, little eggs on our brassica. I had then compounded the problem by placing netting over the bed and trapping the caterpillars inside. Even if the little pests had wanted to get out and feed elsewhere, they couldn't. I had incarcerated them and given them no choice but to destroy our crop. There might have been tastier pickings elsewhere, but there was no escape from my secure unit.

2 *Brassica* is not, as I'd originally thought, a resort on a Greek island, but the name for the genus of plants in the mustard family.

Was it now time, I wondered, to follow the advice of W. C. Fields?

If at first you don't succeed, try, try again. Then quit. There's no point in being a damn fool about it.

Well, he did use the word 'try' twice.

There was always next year.

* * *

Ding Dong.

We'd acquired a reasonably sophisticated doorbell from the previous owners. I'd probably spent half my life living somewhere with a sign up next to the doorbell, saying: 'Please knock, doorbell not working'. Doorbells weren't important enough to fix. Knockers are for knocking. Knockers rock.

I made my way to the front door. We weren't expecting anyone this afternoon.

'It'll be a parcel,' I called to Fran. 'I'll get it.'

I opened the door to find a little boy looking up at me. Surely too young to be working for the Post Office. Furthermore, he was carrying no parcel.

'Excuse me,' the boy said politely, 'but there's a sheep in your garden.'

I was rather taken aback. I wanted to do a double take. A big, comedy double take. I wanted to say 'I beg your pardon?' in a taken-aback voice, a bit like a character in a sitcom.

'I beg your pardon?' I said, in a taken-aback voice.

There. Why not? It was my front door, and my right.

'There's a sheep in your back garden,' the boy repeated, confidently.

'I don't think there is.'

'There is. My mum's dog chased him in there.'

Two adults joined the boy at this point, and added weight to his argument. Apparently, the lady's dog had chased a sheep, and it had separated from the flock, run through the field at the back of our garden, gone through an open gate, doubled back up the lane, darted into Ken's garden and then squeezed through a gap in the fence and into ours.

'You'd better come and take a look,' I said to my visitors.

Fran looked a little puzzled, as I now led two adults and a child through the house and into the garden.

'Just going to deal with the sheep,' I said, setting her mind at rest.

Outside, we could hear a sheep making sheep noises,[3] but we could see no animal. The lady, who hurriedly introduced herself as Susie, was a little anxious because she knew that if anything happened to the sheep, then as owner of the dog she would take the rap and compensation would need to be paid to the farmer.

The man with her, in his early thirties, introduced himself as Sam. He had no connection beyond having been out walking and then becoming embroiled in the sheep debacle.

'The sheep is startled and frightened,' he said.

A noise from the bottom of the garden.

'It's behind the shed,' called the little boy/ace sheep hunter.

We made our way down to the shed, where we found the boy's statement to be spot-on. The anxious-looking animal had clambered to the top of a pile of soil and general garden debris and was now looking longingly back into the field

---

3   This is traditionally written as 'Baaaaa', but I can't bring myself.

from which it had originally escaped. It could see its brothers, sisters, friends, cousins, parents – or whoever the other sheep happened to be. They were clearly more preferable company for this sheep than the three adults and a child who were now hovering nervously behind it.

'Get it to jump over the fence!'

This new voice was neighbour Tony's. He had wandered around the back of his house and into the field, which actually belonged to him and that he rented to a tenant farmer.

'Get it to jump over the fence,' Tony repeated.

The sheep certainly looked like it wanted to jump, but it was hesitating like a swimmer at the end of the high board. It needed some encouragement.

'How do we get it to jump?' I asked.

'Kick it up the backside!' he called back.

Ah, the subtleties of country life.

My new acquaintances Susie and Sam now turned to me, as if I should do the kicking. The sheep was on my land, after all. It would have been rude to kick a sheep on someone else's patch. It seemed that this was my responsibility, even though I had been blameless in the process that had led to the sheep's presence here. I moved behind the sheep and took a step towards it. Then another. Soon I was within booting range.

I hesitated, a bit like a swimmer at the end of a high board. That made two of us now. The sheep and me. Anxious high divers. This wasn't easy. I needed to get myself into a new mental state for this action. I'd never kicked a sheep up the arse before. Nor indeed had I done anything else with a sheep's arse. Honest.

I stood there, unable to swing my foot into action. It was no good. The sheep looked too much like a sheep and not enough like a football. I felt too much like a city boy and not enough like a farmer. As far as I could recall, I'd never even touched a sheep before. How could I make a sharp kick up the backside my first contact with this kind of animal?

In the end I was spared the humiliation of having to explain to everyone that I couldn't do it. The sheep must have sensed that someone was about to kick it up the arse because it jumped. All on its own, the sheep made the leap to freedom. Perhaps it was an act of compassion. It sensed that someone was expected to kick it up the arse but couldn't do so, and it had taken pity. Either way, it was gone, and it was gambolling back to join the other sheep, as if nothing had happened.

'Thank goodness for that,' said Susie.

'Hooray!' said the little boy.

'Fancy staying for a cup of tea?' I suggested to the trio of unexpected guests.

'That's very kind,' said Susie, 'but we were late before this happened, so we'd better be off. Thanks so much for your help.'

'My pleasure. Your boy has excellent sheep-gathering skills.'

Sam stayed for tea. His story was fascinating. He lived the other side of the valley in a farm that he and four other friends had bought six months previously. They'd all met as volunteers, offering their labour in exchange for free food and accommodation on an organic and eco-friendly farm. Now they were setting up on their own, establishing a market garden growing vegetables and soft fruit, and delivering door to door in the local area. Their aim was to make a living on the land, but for the moment, all of them were doing other jobs part-time as well, just to ensure that they didn't go under.

'That sounds like a brilliant plan,' I said. 'Can we sign up for some of your veg deliveries?'

'Sure. Why don't you pop over for a tour of the farm?'

'We'd love that.'

The phone rang and even though Fran took the call, Sam took it as a cue to head off.

'Come and see us soon.'

'We will.'

By the time I'd seen Sam off, I returned to see Fran looking a little shaken.

'What is it?' I asked.

'They're coming in the morning.'

'Who are?'

'The Dartmoor National Park Authority.'

'What for?'

'To check on our property and see if they'll approve our planning application.'

'Right. So why are you looking so anxious?'

'Because of the trees. They'll see the trees.'

'Ah yes. The trees.'

* * *

Perhaps I should take a moment here to clarify this exchange a little. Fran and I had applied for permission to add an extension that would enable us to enlarge the kitchen, and make the most of the views over the garden and beyond. To do this work, we would need to cut down a big cherry tree that was in the way, and which happened to block out most of our afternoon and evening sun, too. We'd already had it checked out and we'd been told that it was at the end of its life, and that a fungus growing out of the side of it provided the proof.

However, various people had told us that the National Park Authority could be tricky customers and that they liked to throw their weight about, and should they choose to stick a preservation order on the tree, then that could scupper the whole plan. Fran and I had decided that the best thing to do was simply to cut the tree down ourselves, thus averting any issue. This phone call, therefore, had rather wrong-footed us.

'What time do they want to come?' I asked, not quite in a panic, but getting there.

'Nine a.m.'

'That doesn't give us much time,' I said, delivering the line with an urgency that made it sound like it belonged in a Hollywood thriller.

'What shall we do?'

'I'll call Ken.'

Fifteen minutes later, Ken was in our back garden with a chainsaw at the ready, and a spare one for me. This, ladies and gentlemen, is what all neighbours should be like – ready to drop everything and produce a chainsaw the moment you want a tree chopping down at short notice. I can only sympathise with those of you who have the kind of crap neighbours that might be out, or who don't own two chainsaws.

Cutting down a tree requires planning. It's important to ensure where the fallen tree will land after it has been cut. Ken made some measurements to ensure that we didn't destroy our greenhouse and began attaching a rope to one of the higher branches. It would be my job to hold onto the other end of this rope, once the cutting began. Following a flourish of Ken's arm on the pull cord, the chainsaw cranked noisily into action and was soon munching its way through the tree.

I looked on with mixed feelings. Cutting down this tree, dying though it was, seemed like an act of eco-vandalism. Trees, we'd all been constantly reminded in recent years, are good things. Cars, planes and consumer items are bad. Chainsaws are bad, too, especially when cutting down trees. They are quick and efficient, though. In less than two minutes, the fallen tree trunk laid across our back garden, testimony to man's massive technological advantage over nature. Perhaps the sight before me represented, in microcosm, what we humans had done to our planet. It is precisely because of the speed and ease with which man can transform the natural world around him that we may be standing at the precipice of an environmental catastrophe. We've just got *too good* at stuff.

All except me, that is. If left on my own, I probably couldn't even start a chainsaw. So there – I was doing my bit. Being crap at stuff is ecologically sound.

'Well done, Ken,' I said. 'Job done.'

'Not yet,' he replied, 'I'll lop the branches off and cut them into log sizes so you can use them in the log burner next year.'[4]

* * *

4   Face it. He's a much better neighbour than yours.

I didn't warm much to the lady from the National Park Planning Department, as I showed her round the house. She had that air about her, often displayed by people who perceive themselves to have power. It wasn't disdain, but it was well on the way. She didn't communicate with me as another human being, but as a subservient underling. She behaved as if my wish to build this extension was an irritation to her, forgetting the fact that if people like me didn't want to make changes to our houses, then there'd be no job for people like her to turn up and sullenly consider whether to grant permission or not.

What is unfortunate about this kind of situation is that one feels that it would be foolish to be anything other than especially accommodating to these types; the fear nestling at the back of your mind that if they didn't like you, they could invoke an ancient bye-law that not only prevented you from doing the work you wanted to do, but also meant you'd have to knock down part of what was already there. So, when they're bossy or surly, you smile obsequiously, reply politely, and offer them a totally undeserved cup of tea.

'So, why do you want this extension?' the lady asked, as she ungraciously nosed around our kitchen.

'Because it's so dark in here,' offered Fran hurriedly. 'The window is so small we have to turn the lights on in the day.'

This had indeed been the case – *before* we'd cut the tree down. However, today as Fran uttered these words the sun blazed through the window, dazzling our visitor and causing her to squint before she could answer. The idea that we now needed lights on during the day was patently absurd, and Fran was given a sharp look by our visitor which expressed as much.

'Can we go out the back?' she asked, choosing not to question the logic of Fran's remark.

'Of course,' I said, at my submissive best.

I was only too aware, as I led this lady out of the back door of the house, that the first thing she'd see would be a bloody great felled tree. I had already considered the things that I might say, as and when she commented, and had rejected the following:

'Blimey, how did that happen?'

'Helluva breeze last night, wasn't there?'

'That's always been like that.'

'We were lucky the lightning didn't strike the house.'

Unable to come up with a suitable line, I'd just left it and hoped that the inspiration would come to me when required. Now that moment had arrived.

Or had it? The planning officer looked at the fallen tree, made a mental note, and simply moved on. Maybe she didn't like trees. Perhaps she'd seen the fungus and recognised that it was already a dying tree? Or was she experienced enough to realise that a tree, once cut down, couldn't be put back up again? Revenge for dispatching the tree might be exacted further down the line in the planning process. Time would tell.

'How did it go?' asked Fran, once our unwelcome visitor had departed.

'I don't get a good feeling,' I replied.

* * *

As autumn set in, some unwelcome things started to happen. Firstly, the weather became wintry and with a distinct penchant for cold and damp. With a disappointing foresight, supermarkets started to stock 'Christmassy' items like mince pies and crackers. The assault had begun. It's the time of year when people cease to be people, but simply consumers who should be relentlessly targeted, wherever they are, and whatever they are doing. What should be a short, and fun, winter break is preceded by this wearisome, extended period in which we are urged to indulge in an unwarranted, ill-advised, and unwelcome spending spree.

Oh yes, and the days got unreasonably short too.

* * *

'It's a beautiful morning, isn't it!' announced our beaming sonographer.

Were we just being lucky, or were all NHS women working in childbirth unfeasibly jolly? Could they really be this happy, or do they go on acting courses, as well as the ones that teach them the difference between a perineum and a pelvis?

The occasion was the twenty-week scan, and the sonographer was checking that the baby was developing normally, and taking a peek at where the placenta was lying in Fran's uterus. There would shortly be the opportunity to see our baby on a screen,[5] and to make out its head, torso, little hands and little legs. This ought to have been exciting, but it wasn't – it was scary. How could one disguise the fact that this event was all about checking for abnormalities? They even called it the anomaly scan. Now was the time, far more than at the ten-week stage, when if there were any problems, they were likely to be spotted.

---

5   Showbiz beckoned. On TV already.

So there I sat, looking on anxiously as a deadly serious examination took place against a backdrop of the sonographer's extroverted and misplaced *bonhomie*. Fran seemed to cope better with this onslaught of bubbly banter than I did – I was far too intent on listening for a change in tone, a more serious expression, or an alteration in breathing. How would she react if she spotted something untoward? Surely the joviality would have to cease upon the discovery of bad news?

To my relief, it didn't need to.

'Everything is just as it should be,' she said, unable to deliver this excellent news with any increased level in chirpiness, having peaked, quite irresponsibly, already. 'I'll give you a nice little printout of what your baby looks like.'

Soon we were holding a picture of a very, very young baby. Twenty weeks old and, though I say so myself, looking remarkably intelligent.[6]

---

6   All parents want to have bright, intelligent children. Dog owners are the same with their dogs. 'Look, isn't she clever!' they say, when the dog brings them back a stick they've thrown – as if this is a measure of anything other than gross stupidity. I sense that this need for bright pets and intelligent offspring stems from our own insecurities. Rather cruelly, I've always enjoyed playing on this when around the parents of newborns or toddlers. Away from the parents, I will spend a little time with the child before returning to declare:

'Beautiful child.'

The parents beam.

'Very calm. Very much at peace.'

More smiles.

Then I deliver the sucker punch.

'Not very bright, though.'

Looks of horror.

I'd then leave it as long as I could, before revealing that I was only joking.

As Fran and I marvelled at this incredible sight, our ultra-sound hostess had time for one more question.

'Are you sure you don't want to know what sex the baby is?'

'We're sure,' I replied, 'we're going for a surprise. Besides, it's not one hundred per cent accurate, is it?'

'Not far off. Ninety-six per cent. Sometimes if the baby has excess wind and too much tummy fat, it obscures the view and it's hard to tell the gender accurately.'

Surely if the baby had excess wind and too much tummy fat, then it would have to be male? And an extremely precocious one at that. Some males can take up to thirty years before they do the farting and the beer gut thing, so a baby like this would be well ahead of the game.

No, Fran and I didn't want to know the sex. We'd decided on this without much debate. We were happy for technology to be there as a back-up in ensuring a safe birth, but we wanted nothing further from it. We'd find out the sex by taking a quick peek when the time was right. Just like Henry VIII had done, before storming out of the room in a huff when one of his dispensable wives had been guilty of providing him with a girl. Both he (and the country) had required a boy to be the next king and heir. Us? We'd be happy with whatever we got. As Ken had said to me, when we discussed the subject:

'As long as it's one of the three.'

8

Titch

It had been nagging away at me all through the summer, despite the many distractions I'd had. Why had we not heard anything? Surely the lady and her pet could be found?

Well, seemingly not. Despite a lot of effort, Dave the Pig – the subject of the challenge laid before me on the initial trip to Devon that had led to the house purchase – had remained at large. Kevin and Donna, who had organised the event where the challenge had been made, had advertised locally and emailed most of the audience who had attended, but no one seemed to know Dave's owner or the pig's whereabouts.

Dave the Pig had failed to leave my consciousness, largely because questions about whether I had anymore bets lined up were always asked whenever I gave any kind of live performance. When I mentioned the Dave the Pig challenge at a literary festival in Dartington, a lady put up her hand, claiming that she had actually *bred* the pig in question. She told an enthralled room that she had originally sold the pig to a gay couple, who found the pig too much for them, and that they had sold it to its present owner who, as far as she knew, lived in Torquay.

The net was closing in.

Irritated that I couldn't trace this pig, I emailed the *Judi Spiers Show* on Radio Devon, asking if I could come on and be interviewed about my current mini obsession. An invitation was duly offered and I trundled off to the studios in Exeter. However, after a lengthy discussion on pigs, Judi put out numerous appeals for listeners to call in and offer clues as to Dave's whereabouts, but none were forthcoming. The location of this wretched pig remained a mystery.

'Maybe you should ditch Dave and take one of those cute micro pigs from Pennywell Farm?' suggested Judi, as I left the building. 'They're adorable.'

'Micro pigs?'

'They breed them as pets. Taking one of them would be much easier.'

Easy had never been something I'd sought out. *Easy*, I'd found, often went hand in hand with *a bit dull*. However, in this case, when Judi had used the word *easier*, she had probably meant *possible*. One of the callers to the programme had explained that there is a reason why we use the word 'pig-headed' to describe stubbornness, and that when a pig decides it doesn't want to do something, it lets you and the world know. Unless Dave had been well-trained by its elusive owner, then the idea of me dragging a 250 pound dead weight all over England's third-largest county seemed to be a distant prospect, not to mention an activity that would be entirely devoid of any pleasure.

Not that I was in it for pleasure, particularly.

My new-found interest in Dave the Pig had been prompted by a phone call from Moldova.

'Tony, we need five thousand pounds or the building work will have to stop, and we will have to lay off the builders,' Diana had said.

And that had been enough to set my mind buzzing with ideas. Maybe I could do the Dave challenge and get people to sponsor me? On the one hand, it went against my natural inclination. I'd founded the children's care centre for kids with cerebral palsy using the royalties from my book *Playing the Moldovans at Tennis*, and I'd always intended it to be something that I would fund, rather than get involved in cajoling others to do the same. There seemed to be so many worthy causes out there, and only so many times one could call on people to dig into their pockets.

However, Diana, the charming, determined and kind-hearted Moldovan woman who was director of the centre, had put her heart and soul into making this initiative a success, and helping to transform the way disability was viewed in Moldova. Now the money was needed urgently in order to complete the building work on a new and bigger centre.

That's how I found myself driving to Pennywell Farm, with a bicycle in the back of the van. After hours of research on the internet, I'd come up with the ideal challenge:

CYCLING COAST TO COAST
WITH A MICRO PIG

Now, it does sound a little more impressive than was actually going to be the case. I was cunningly going to exploit the fact that Devon is unique in Britain in having two distinct coastlines (Cornwall's is continuous coast), thus keeping the mileage down to just over 100 miles. Secondly, I'd had the brainwave of using an electric bike. Devon's hills would almost certainly prove too much for an untrained cyclist, especially when carrying the paraphernalia for a three-day excursion for one human – and a pig.

Peter from AXcess Electric Bikes in Honiton was not how I'd imagined the owner of a bike shop. He was far from being someone you would expect to see clad in Lycra – his appearance was more that of a middle-aged academic. However, he knew his stuff and he had been most accommodating. When I'd explained the charitable nature of my quest, he'd immediately offered to lend me a bike for a week, and he'd kitted it out with panniers, and a basket on the front intended for the pig. He'd also suggested that I use a cord on the back, operated by a ratchet mechanism, which would keep the pig's carrier securely in place. He carefully explained how the ratchet system worked, and I took due note. Tricky little bugger, I thought, but important to keep the pig safe. Don't want it falling off as soon as I go over the first major bump.

* * *

'Here she is,' said Chris, 'she's the smallest one we've got. Her name is Titch. Lovely temperament. You won't want to give her back.'

I was standing with Pennywell's owner, a confident, avuncular man with a cheeky sense of fun and a speaking voice that suggested that he had received his education at some distance from an inner-city comprehensive. We were both peering over the side of a straw-filled pen, looking at three micro pigs jostling each other. Titch was considerably smaller than the others and looked delightful.

'Can I pick her up?'

'Of course.'

'She won't mind?'

'She's been picked up and cuddled for the past month. She loves it.'

Chris had been breeding these pigs for the last twenty years, and they were an important part of his unique business – a farm activity park – a kind of cross between a farm and a theme park, billed as a great day out for all the family. Mind you, show me a leisure facility that *doesn't* make such a claim. I think the reality is that most of these resort venues can't provide fun for *all* the family. They can only satisfy *some* of the family, leaving others bored, sulky, and itching to leave. Looking around me, though, I saw only smiling faces, as kids, their mums, dads and grandparents played with lambs, rabbits, guinea pigs, goats and pigs – a testament to the joy that animals can bring to us humans, even when not served with vegetables or wedged between slices of bread.

Chris had already explained to me over the phone that three-month-old Titch would not be remotely phased by being carried around on a bike.

'Just put her in a basket, cover her in blankets, and she'll go to sleep. As long as she's warm, she'll be happy.'

Naturally enough, I was concerned about how she might empty her bowels and bladder, but when I'd first enquired, Chris's email had been as direct as it was faintly reassuring.

If pig sleeps in her carrier, she will wait till morning to go to the toilet. If you feed her only in the morning, by evening she should have cleared out her surprises, or you could, of course, put a nappy on her if you are worried. She will need a little stroll before going to bed. If you have a spray of pee and pooh (hers) mixed with water and you spray that on the grass when you give her respite, she will feel more comfortable peeing and poohing there!! Of course, nappies are the bolt emergency situation!!

It was after receiving this email that it occurred to me that this trip could be viewed as the perfect training for fatherhood. Thinking that this would gain me valuable brownie points, I mentioned this to Fran, who looked at me, askance. (Never an easy face to do.)

'It's true,' I insisted, 'clearing up poo and wee, putting nappies on, getting it to sleep, carrying it about – perfect training. In fact, I could even carry her in one of those baby slings!'

That's how I'd found myself in Mothercare.

Mothercare is actually titled incorrectly. A quick look around the store revealed that there was absolutely nothing available for the care of mothers – you know, things that would be useful like chocolates, sedatives, or wine lists – but instead it was filled with products for infants. Quite why they had dismissed the name 'Babycare' is beyond me, but it's surprising how lax companies can be when they name their stores. The company Kwiksave didn't even bother with a routine spell check; Carphone Warehouse doesn't sell carphones and it's a shop, not a warehouse; and up until a few years ago, there was a High Street chain called Radio Rentals, where renting a radio was impossible.

And as for the number of times I've been served by gaunt assistants in Fat Face . . .

I asked the lady shop assistant where the baby slings were, and she led me to the other side of the store and showed me what was on offer.

'The things is, this is a bit different,' I explained. 'This one is for a baby pig.'

'Right,' she replied, without a hint of surprise, 'you'll want this one then.'

She gestured to one of the five that were on display and simply walked off, the mention of a pig leaving her quite unmoved. Perhaps she was so numbed by her job that nothing could really tease out a reaction from her.

I'd like to buy a baby harness, please, so I can throttle a goose.

Right, in that case you need the Henderson 450. It'll provide the strength required.

I didn't buy the baby sling, in spite of the shop assistant's confident recommendation, because I was still not certain that it would work with a pig. This particular purchase would have to wait until I'd done more research.

I was intending to buy nappies, but as I wandered around the shop I couldn't see them. I considered seeking the help of the same shop assistant, and to ask whether the standard nappy would stay attached to a baby pig, but I was unable to test her seemingly imperturbable nature, as she was now surrounded by a couple who were no doubt wasting her time with boring questions about humans. Instead, I beat a hasty retreat.

* * *

'Go on then, pick her up,' said Chris. 'If she's going to be your companion all week, you're going to have to get to know her.'

I leant over the side of the pen and with both hands I seized Titch and lifted her up, feeling something like King Kong must have felt as he plucked screaming women from the streets of Manhattan. Titch didn't scream though, but she did let out a mini squeak, which ceased the moment I held her close to my chest.

'Get your arm underneath her,' advised Chris. 'Pigs like to lie down and don't enjoy having any pressure on their coccyx.'

'Right,' I said, resisting the temptation to jest, saying that if she had a coccyx, then she must be a lady-boar from Bangkok.

Soon I was cuddling and stroking Titch. I could feel her warmth against my chest, and I could hear a gentle grunting that I assumed to be the pig equivalent of a cat's satisfied purr. She was simply adorable.

'Wow,' I said.

'I tell you,' said Chris, 'you won't want to give her back. But you'll have to because we won't sell her. She has such a good temperament that we want to keep her for breeding. Pigs like Titch are very special.'

'I think we're going to be very happy together,' I said, making the assumption that Titch would be as enamoured with me as I was with her.

'Put her down for now,' said Chris, 'we'll come back for her after we've completed all the paperwork.'

'Paperwork?'

'Defra[1] insist on it. I'm afraid young Titch is classed as livestock, and as such we'll have to complete movement orders for you.'

Forty-five minutes of agonising bureaucracy followed, in which we slowly completed the online forms. I was now officially a 'haulier', and I needed to have a movement order for each day of the trip, stating where Titch would start the day and where she would end it. Fortunately, I was prepared and had already lined up some accommodation along the way.

I'm not going to pretend that it hadn't been a source of some concern as to where Titch and I would sleep. Whilst I hadn't imagined that there are many hotels and guest houses that have a specific 'no pig' policy, it may well be something that is taken as a given.

So, armed with a dose of fragile optimism, I'd spent a day sending out emails to hotels, claiming that Titch was toilet-trained and that she would be 'no trouble at all'. (Well, pigs never are.) To my amazement, I'd received two positive responses from hotels in Ilfracombe and Tavistock offering complimentary bed and breakfast. Only in Great Torrington, which I'd scheduled to be the middle night of my trip, had sanity prevailed. Polite rejections only. For me and Titch, it was a case of Not So Great Torrington.

'I'll tell you what we'll do,' said Chris, who was turning out to be a great problem solver. 'We'll put down the address of any old hotel in Great Torrington for now, and then we'll just amend the online form when you know where you're actually going to be.'

---

1 Department for Environment, Food and Rural Affairs, also known as DEFRA or Defra.

'OK. Does this mean I'm ready to take Titch?'

'It certainly does. You just need this. You don't need to put it on Titch, but just keep it with you at all times.'

Chris handed me a tag that was supposed to be for Titch's ear, but was bigger than her ear itself. She was now officially a 'pig in movement'. She was now UK vn0497, though I decided to keep calling her 'Titch' as it rolled off the tongue so much better.

Titch made no fuss at all, as we lifted her into her little pet carrier and I escorted her off the premises. It's always amazed me how pets and animals cope so well with this method of being moved about. I'd be a jibbering wreck if someone bundled me into a box and started carrying me about the place.

I popped the carrier on the passenger seat of my car, wrapped the seatbelt around it, and headed off. Titch was off to explore pastures new. As I drove along, I began to think how remarkable it was that I actually had a pig on the seat beside me. I hadn't realised just how charming a creature one could be. OK, Titch was a baby, and a baby micro pig at that – and puppies and kittens are always much cuter than dogs and cats – but nonetheless, I was sensing that a pig could easily be man's best friend, just like a dog. Maybe that was because they were so clever. I'd read about experiments conducted by Penn State University between 1996 and 1998 in which pigs were taught to manoeuvre a modified joystick to move a cursor on a video monitor – and that they learned the task as quickly as chimpanzees.

So pigs could watch video and computer games? I wondered if Titch was a fan of *Tony Hawk's Pro Skater*, and that was why she was sitting so quietly? Perhaps she was delighted to have been abducted by her skateboarding hero.[2]

The other goods news about pigs is that they are much cleaner than the myth would have it. Yes, they're not averse to being caked in mud, but this is because they have no sweat glands[3] and they roll around in the mud to cool down. From my perspective, the best news is that they will not excrete anywhere near where they live, given the choice. To be fair, this is an area where they've got one over on me. I still use the upstairs toilet, thinking that relations would be soured with the neighbours if I went round and had a crap on their lawn. People can be so sensitive.

Pigs have had admirers is high places too. Winston Churchill once made a wry observation about them:

'A cat will look down to a man. A dog will look up to a man. But a pig will look you straight in the eye and see his equal.'

One can only assume that Winston had downed a few whiskies when he'd uttered this, after all, this is somewhat off-message when delivering a speech about the Middle East. Nevertheless, these words offered me an interesting insight as to what I might expect from Titch in the coming

2   Those of you who enjoy my confusion with Tony Hawk the skateboarder may enjoy this: http://www.tony-hawks.com/skateboarding.php

3   Remember this the next time you hear someone saying that they're 'sweating like a pig'. Pick them up on it. May I suggest that you begin your sentence: 'Well, that's just where you're wrong, my friend . . .' Thus, you will win their admiration, and they won't find you remotely annoying.

days. It was just going to be a shame that Titch, as my 'equal', wasn't going to do any of the pedalling.

* * *

'She's lovely!' cried Fran, as I let Titch out of her carrier and she began roaming our kitchen. 'She's so cute!'

She was indeed. She did seem a little disorientated, though, as I set her down. She immediately began exploring the place, nudging around with her nose, almost as if she was foraging for food. I took out a handful of the animal feed Chris had given me, and offered it to Titch, who gobbled it up with gusto. Thinking that this would lead to an inevitable need for her to have a poo, I lifted her into the garden, where she continued nudging away with her nose, this time at the lawn.

'Come on!' I called to her, after a few minutes had passed. 'Have a poo!'

This was probably a mistake. If Winston was right, and pigs are our equal, then shouting at them to have a dump isn't going to work. Admittedly, I've never had it done to me (I'm trying to think of the sequence of events that might lead to such a request), but I feel fairly sure that my bowels would contract rather than open in the face of vociferous goading. Of course, if I'd left Titch totally alone, then I wouldn't have known if she'd been or not, and I was keen to try and establish how she liked to manage things in the bottom department. Well, it would have to wait for now. She was far too interested in feigned foraging than satisfying my need to feel on top of her toilet habits.

In the evening ahead, Fran and I took turns at picking up

Titch and cuddling her, as this is what she seemed to like. She was a baby, after all, and our soothing embraces definitely comforted her. It was Saturday night, and I wasn't going to set off for my cycle ride until Tuesday. This time had been set aside for Titch to settle in, and for some experiments to find how she'd be comfortable travelling.

When bedtime came around, I popped Titch into her carrier with the lid removed – this was to be her sleeping quarters – and covered her with blankets. We decided to enclose her at one end of the kitchen, so that she didn't go on a foraging expedition around the shelves that were open at the foot of our kitchen island. We lifted down bags full of duvets and pillows and piled them up as a makeshift barrier.

'Goodnight, Titch,' I said, 'sleep well.'

She'd beaten me to it. She was already away with the fairies.

We awoke to something of a mess in the kitchen. It seemed we had been naive to think that our makeshift blockade would limit Titch to our designated area. She had simply bulldozed through our defences, spreading duvets and pillows around the floor. Piglets, it seemed, were strong little creatures. She'd had a little poo in the corner – this was made up of hard pellets like sheep dung, I was pleased to note – and there was a puddle of pee by the cooker. Titch, though, was nowhere to be seen. She hadn't returned to her pet carrier or 'bedroom'. I had a mini irrational panic that she had escaped. Then I spotted my rucksack by the radiator. That was odd – I hadn't left it there. I went over and looked inside, and there was Titch, fast asleep. She must have nosed the rucksack into that nice, comforting position by the warmth of the radiator, and crawled inside for a snug, cosy bed.

During the coming day, Titch seemed to settle in well. Perhaps her unrest during the night had been down to a strange environment and it had all been overwhelming for her. She had been used to snuggling up to other pigs at night, and now she had a new house and two strangers with which to familiarise herself. However, by teatime she'd been cuddled senseless by both me and Fran, and she seemed to be a happy little pig.

'I think I should try her in the bike now,' I declared with confidence.

'You may as well,' said Fran. 'The rain has stopped and she seems ready.'

I tried to lead Titch outside on the little harness that Chris had given me. Titch clearly didn't like the harness, nor did she like the idea of going in any direction that she hadn't decided on herself. After several minutes of grunts and squeaks, I gave up and carried her out to the bike. It made me realise just how impossible the initial bet – to walk round Devon with a full-sized pig called Dave – would have been.

To be fair, Chris hadn't given me the harness for walking, but to secure Titch to the basket on the bike, so that she couldn't make a leap for freedom whenever the fancy took her. I plumped up the basket's pillow and blankets and clipped her in. Then I mounted the bike and cautiously began cycling. At first, no problem. Titch seemed happy enough. It was only when we went around the first corner in the village that Titch started to become agitated. As the front wheel turned, the basket turned, too, and it tipped up.

Titch didn't like it. It clearly felt like she was being tipped out. She began squeaking.

When a pig squeaks, it seems to activate the same nerves in a human as a baby's cries. Something in the pitch, the sharpness of the sound and the frequency at which it's delivered, combined with the urgency and the volume, can make one begin to believe that the world is going to end if something isn't done, and isn't done quickly. Thankfully, the village was quiet and no one was around to witness what sounded like me slaughtering a pig on the street, but I quickly lent forward, unclipped Titch, and lifted her to my chest.

'There, there,' I said, stroking her, 'you'll be fine. You're just getting used to the bike, that's all.'

Fifteen minutes later, it was clear that my forecast – of Titch being 'fine' – had been as accurate as most of those emanating from the Met Office. Titch was not fine, and she clearly would not have listed 'being in a basket at the front of a bike while it goes round a corner' as one of her favourite pastimes. Her noisy protests prompted a young woman to come into her front garden to investigate. I recognised her as Kate, with whom we'd once exchanged brief pleasantries when she'd walked past our house with her dog and two-year-old daughter.

After she'd got over the shock and sheer enchantment of seeing a baby pig in a basket, I explained what I was about to undertake. Kate smiled, and her eyes lit up with what could have been delight, or disbelief. Or both.

'The trouble is that the basket isn't going to work,' I said, disconsolately. 'It moves too much when the bike corners.'

'Have you tried a baby sling?'

'I thought of that. But would it work?'

'Come on in, let's try.'

Life, as well as sometimes chucking shite at you, does deliver its fair share of serendipitous moments. Kate, it turned out, had up until very recently been running a business where she sold baby slings, and she still had plenty of samples in her house. She recommended the Asian design of the Moby, assuring me that it would cope ably with a pig. I paid Kate for it there and then – she was delighted to have made a sale simply on the strength of having gone into her front garden – and Titch and I cycled off in complete harmony.

Titch adored the sling. She loved being cuddled and feeling the warmth of another body next to hers.

As we continued on our test cycle, the village seemed to come to life and soon I was showing off Titch to everyone I passed. I was flagged down by fellow committee members, familiar faces whose names escaped me, and people I had never met before. All paid homage to Tony and Titch. Before I got home, I stopped at Ken's workshop, where he was tinkering with his Massey Ferguson (if you'll pardon the expression).

He emerged from beneath his tractor, grinning broadly as I unzipped my jacket to reveal Titch.

'You'd better not wear bicycle clips,' he said.

'Why not?'

'Well, if she has a wee, it'll need to trickle out somewhere.'

'Yes, good point, Ken. Hadn't thought of that. By the way, can you show me how this works.'

I pointed to the strap that Peter from the bike shop had

given me to keep the pet carrier on the back of the bike. Before the successful introduction of the baby sling, the idea had been for Titch to travel in the front basket in good weather, and to switch to the pet carrier on the back should the rain start to fall, as it surely would in mid- to late December. The trouble was, this strap was confusing to me.

'It's a ratchet strap,' said Ken, 'I'll show you how it works.' Peter had already given me a full and thorough demonstration of how it worked, but I had retained none of the information. Knowing that I wouldn't remember what Ken now told me either, I took out my smartphone and filmed his explanation. I watched it back, and felt rather chuffed that I'd had the foresight to do something quite so sensible.

'How does Titch like travelling like that?' said Ken, pointing to the sling.

I lifted the edge of it that was covering her eyes, and discovered that she was now fast asleep.

'Clearly she loves it,' I said triumphantly. 'Titch and I are ready.'

'*She* certainly is,' said Ken. 'By the way, are you going to smile on your trip?'

'I don't know. I should hope so. Why?'

'Because I've noticed that cyclists never smile.'

'Really?'

'Well, have you ever seen one smile?'

'I don't know – I've never really looked that closely.'

'You have a look next time you're out in the car. You'll see, cyclists never smile.'

'Well, when I'm cycling I'll try.'

'You do that.'

I just hoped I'd have something to smile about.

9

Too Young to Die

The first day couldn't have got off to a better start. After an excellent night's rest, I came downstairs to find Titch fast asleep in her pet carrier, no evidence of any accidents anywhere. I lifted her into the garden and watched with pride as she had a wee and a poo.

'Well done!' I announced, punching the air.

I could have sworn that Titch threw me a look as if to say, 'Leave it now, Tony. This is me crapping. It's not an Olympic event. I haven't just scored a winning goal in a cup final, I've had a poo, that's all. No need to remove your shirt, swing it round and around, and blow kisses to the heavens.'

Maybe I was reading too much into a quick glance from a small pig, but I resolved to change my ways. No more faeces festivity. Titch came into the house, ate the food I offered her, and drank the water. We seemed to be an excellent team now – ready to hit the road.

The bike, on the other hand, had other ideas. In the process of packing the bike with clothes and provisions, I managed to break both of the plastic zips in the panniers.

Using the stretchy bungee straps, I botched a way of keeping them closed, which by my standards was surprisingly effective. Worse news than two faulty zips awaited, though. I hadn't bothered to charge the bike up overnight, as I'd done less than a mile on it, but I'd made the mistake of leaving the key in the 'on' position. This seemed to have run the battery dry, because the 'pedal assist' system was not kicking in.

This was a worry, because I had a long cycle ahead of me, quite possibly with some very steep climbs. This was an extremely heavy bike, weighed down by a big battery and three days of stuff for one human and one small pig. The schedule today was to put the bike in the van and get a lift from Fran to Exeter station. Unfortunately, there was no through train to Ilfracombe, so I was going to have to take the train as far as Barnstaple and then cycle the fifteen miles to Ilfracombe. I'd allowed myself a leisurely morning and booked myself on the 13.25 train. This, I figured, would give me plenty of time to cycle to Ilfracombe before darkness fell. That was before the battery packed up.

I called Peter from AXcess Bikes and he kindly agreed to meet me at Exeter station and replace the battery, but his schedule meant that he couldn't get there before 2 p.m. This meant I'd now be on the 14.25 – with the result that I'd have only half an hour or so of daylight to reach Ilfracombe, and the unlit cycle paths wouldn't be an option. Titch and I would have to begin our cycle by sharing the roads with cars and lorries.

Things were further complicated after I did the Radio Devon interview. Once they found out about my revised challenge, the *Judi Spiers Show* had thought it would be fun if I spoke to them every morning at 9.45 a.m., and gave an update of how my journey was going. In homage to a previous trip I'd made in my life, they'd had a little jingle made specially – called 'Round Devon with a Pig'. I hoped that having these daily chats would raise awareness of what I was up to, and help me and Titch to raise money. I couldn't have guessed that there would be a potentially significant downside. A downside that might throw the whole expedition into jeopardy.

'Hi, Tony, it's Chris from Pennywell,' said the voice from down the phone line. 'You were excellent on the *Judi Spiers Show*. It has created a problem, though. Someone was listening from Trading Standards' animal health team. They've called me to say that I've got the wrong licence. Sorry about this, but can you call them straight away?'

'Ah. OK. Will do.'

I took the number and put the phone down. How could things have gone wrong so quickly? The high point of Titch's al fresco poo, though only half an hour ago, seemed a distant memory.

Soon I was speaking to a very helpful lady at Trading Standards. The good news was that she didn't seem to be a bureaucrat who took pleasure in blocking, preventing, or refusing, but instead she had an attitude whereby she genuinely seemed to want to help. The bad news was that Chris and I had filled out forms one week later than we should have done, which currently meant that Titch had to stay at my house for twenty-one days.

Charming though Titch was, this was going to slow things considerably, and make for a new start date of 11 January in the following year.

'There is a possible solution, though,' said the lady.

'What's that?' I asked, trying to keep a note of desperation out of my voice.

'You could apply for an Annual Exhibition licence. This would mean you and your pig could make multiple movements. However, you'll have to keep her in her pet carrier and she must not leave that carrier until you reach your destination.'

'What if she needs a wee or a poo?'

'That's not possible. It's illegal. Unless you spray any ground that your pig touches with Defra approved disinfectant. Also, you'd need to notify us of the exact location, so we could amend our records.'

'Of course,' I replied, adopting a timid, supplicatory tone that I've found to be helpful in dealing with bureaucrats in the past. 'Thank you so much for helping with this.'

'Right. I'll go back to Chris to arrange the correct licence. We do want to help you with this, as we are aware that you're doing this for charity.'

'Thank you so much.'

OK. Suddenly I needed 'Defra approved' disinfectant. And fast. The clock was ticking and I was due to leave in just over an hour.

'What will you do?' asked Fran.

'I'll call Ken,' I replied.

Somehow this had become my default position when there was any kind of practical problem. Call Ken.

The best thing about adopting this policy was that it nearly always worked.

'No problem, Tony,' he said, not at all put out by the sudden and random nature of my phone call, 'I'll jump in the van and go over to Terry at Drummonds Farm. They're bound to have some.'

Forty-five minutes later, he was standing at our front door, handing me two spray bottles containing a pink liquid.

'There,' he said, 'Defra approved disinfectant. Don't drink it all at once.'

'Thanks, Ken, you're a hero.'

'No problem.'

Titch looked on, oblivious to the problems that being classified as 'livestock' was causing. Why couldn't she just be classed a simple pet? I certainly had no intention of eating her. Not unless she was insubordinate. So this live-stock tag was unfair.

'Anything else I can do to help?' said Ken.

'Well, you couldn't just help me fix the pet carrier to the back of the bike? I'm struggling with that ratchet strap thingy.'

'No problem.'

Half an hour later the phone rang.

'Tony, it's Chris from Pennywell. Good news from Trading Standards. They've successfully unravelled all that needs to done for compliance regarding Animal Health and the associated Animal Disease Control Welfare measures.'

'Have I got the certificate I need?'

'Yes.'

'So Titch and I can leave?'

'Yes.'

Phew.

* * *

I was a little jealous as we said goodbye. Fran seemed to linger longer in the hug with Titch than in the one with me. When she said 'Take care, darling' I had to double-check that I was the intended recipient of the good wishes. I kissed her, promised not to sleep with the pig, and then crossed the road to the station.

The bike was all fixed up now. Peter had revealed that there'd actually been no problem with the battery. I simply hadn't put it back onto the bike properly. I now realised there was a little button at the top that needed to fit through a little hole. A little bit of jiggling was required to ensure that this happened, but now that was all done, I could leave, safe in the knowledge that my bike would 'help' me as I pedalled my way up hills.

Getting myself and Titch onto the train was the next challenge. I wheeled the bike with my entire 'world' for the next three days fixed either in the basket on the front, or to the panniers and rack on the back. I kept Titch secreted in the sling beneath my coat, as I didn't know whether First Great Western trains operated a 'no pigs' policy or not. I'd had enough last-minute hitches without the station master reaching for a thick rule book and thumbing through the index under 'pigs'.

Thankfully, the guard opened the barrier with no questions and without noticing the lump under my coat. I wheeled the bike through onto Platform 1 with a full five minutes to go. Plenty of time to get to Platform 4 for the Barnstaple train.

It soon became apparent that I'd not followed Kate's instructions to the letter when I'd tied the sling earlier. It was now drooping very low under my coat, and Titch was attempting to wriggle free. Titch, it seemed, had ideas not consistent with the smooth catching of a train. Perhaps she was hungry. Perhaps she wanted to go to the toilet again. Maybe she wanted to get a clear view of what was going on all around her. Whatever it was, sitting still and going to sleep didn't appear to be in her plans.

I struggled to the lift that would take us up to the bridge across the platforms. A middle-aged, swarthy, Spanish-looking couple were waiting, surrounded by suitcases, and they looked at my heavily laden bike and then at me, clearly puzzled that I should be considering this form of transport at such a time of year. Titch wriggled. I held her tight with my one free arm. The couple now knew that there was either something alive inside my coat, or that I was wearing a motorised jumper that gave me a body massage as I moved about. Their eyes fixed on my blue anorak as we arrived at the bridge level. As I moved off, Titch let out a mighty wriggle.

'Titch!' I said, unable to contain myself.

The couple looked on, more confused than ever. I smiled, and hoped that they weren't getting a train from Platform 4. Should that be the case, I'd have to share another short, but uncomfortable, lift journey with them. Their presence meant that opening up my coat and attending to whatever was troubling Titch wasn't really an option, without running the possibility of allowing my secret cargo to become public knowledge on this station.

I couldn't really say what I wanted to tell them: 'Look, relax my Spanish friends – it's a pig. Get on with your journey and stop eyeballing me like you've never seen a pig in a coat before.'

Or better still: *Es un cerdo. Relájese mis amigos espanoles. Continuar con su viaje y dejar de mirarme a la manera de alguien que nunca ha visto un cerdo dentro de un abrigo antes.*

Surprising people by guessing their nationality, and bursting into their native tongue, is something I like to do wherever possible. It mostly backfires, as people have a habit of not resembling their stereotypes. Had I been able to offer up the valid Spanish – the above is offered courtesy of Google Translate – quite possibly this couple would have turned out to be Norwegian. And even Google doesn't know the Norwegian word for 'eyeballing'.

I allowed them to walk ahead of me, whilst I had another surreptitious attempt at reorganising Titch in the sling. I had only one hand available for the task – a task that clearly needed three pairs of hands for it to be done properly. I was deeply disappointed when the couple ahead now stopped at the lift that descended to Platform 4. Oh dear. We were going to share another lift together.

I smiled nervously when I caught up with them. They looked at me with suspicion. Perhaps their few private moments on the short walk across the footbridge had afforded them some time to formulate some theories.

He's a white snake charmer and he has a snake in there. It may kill us if we share another lift with him. Please don't let him be travelling from Platform 4.

His motorised jumper massage equipment has a computer fault. It will probably break through his clothes soon and harm innocent bystanders, should they be contained in a small space with him. Please don't let him be travelling from Platform 4.

The lift doors opened and the three of us got in. Or rather the four of us got in. Titch was now making little grunting noises, so no point in trying to pretend that she wasn't there. I simply couldn't think of what to say, so I smiled again.

I guess the smile is nature's way of trying to set people's minds at ease. I suppose that's why we use it in these situations. We're trying to say to people: 'OK, I know you're nervous of me but I can smile, so I must be all right. Look.'

And then we display our smile. The most sickly, disingenuous smile we've ever managed. It produces the exact opposite reaction to the one intended, giving the impression that we kill for pleasure and are eager subscribers to the magazine *Cannibalism Today*.

We entered the lift and my Argentinian couple (I was attempting to close in geographically) looked away. They were now more comfortable with their noses pressed against the grubby side of a lift than making eye contact with their strange, and possibly dangerous, travelling companion.

When we reached the platform, they fled the lift, almost breaking into a trot. Certainly as much of a trot as their accompanying bags permitted them. By rights, I should have let them 'escape'. However, waiting for the two lifts had meant that I was now running late and the train, exasperatingly up the other end of the platform from the lift, was about to close its doors and pull away. So I began to run, too. This clearly alarmed the couple, who became flustered and attempted to increase their speed, whilst babbling to each other in a foreign tongue.

I was attempting to stay focused on my task, which was

to support a wriggling pig inside my coat with one hand, whilst steering a heavy and overladen bike with the other. Oddly, I still retained the capacity to be mildly irritated by the fact that the language I was hearing a few feet ahead of me was not Spanish. I'd been wrong with my instant racial diagnosis and, in spite of the urgency of my situation, this left me feeling disappointed. And curious still. Was it Bulgarian they were speaking? Turkish perhaps?

'Focus, Tony,' I said to myself.

I was making very slow progress up the platform, because inside my coat, Titch was slipping ever lower down my body. There wasn't time to check, but it really felt as if she'd freed herself completely from the sling now, and the only thing that was preventing her from falling onto the platform beneath us was the arm that I had placed beneath her body to support her. Up ahead the train driver revved the engines, nudging my anxiety towards panic. I could see my Balkan couple boarding the train, not even permitting a glance back in my direction to see where I was. Still a few more yards to go.

'Come on, Tony, you can do it,' I mumbled.

I made it to the first open door of the train, just as the guard blew his whistle. I squared the bike up to the entrance and attempted to lift it onto the train with my one free hand. But the bike didn't shift an inch. I tried again. Nothing. Were the wheels caught somewhere? I looked. No visible problem. The guard blew his whistle again. I heaved at the bike again and almost managed to get the front wheel onto the train, but I lost my balance and nearly fell.

I realised that I simply wasn't strong enough to lift this bike with one hand, and I couldn't spare the other, because

Titch would have surely dropped out of the bottom of my coat. And it wouldn't be a platform she would fall onto now, but onto the railway tracks below, to be crushed by a departing train. It occurred to me that killing Titch in such a manner this early on would not only be disappointing, but probably wouldn't greatly assist the fundraising process either.

So this was it. I had made it to the train on time, but I couldn't get onto it. I watched in horror as the doors closed before me.

'Shit!' I cried. 'I don't believe it!'

Then, as if a prayer had been answered, I saw a boot appear at the bottom of the doors, preserving a chink of light onto the train. I could make out a long-haired young guy the other side of the doors.

'Hang on!' he said. 'Let me help.'

He proceeded to force the doors open using a Samson-like strength, and he leapt onto the platform and lifted the bike onto the train. Titch and I jumped on behind him, just as the doors forced themselves closed behind us.

I was now face to face with a twenty-year-old guy, who smiled a far less creepy smile than I'd managed in the lift moments before.

'It would have been a shame to have missed a train when you were so close,' he said, as we pulled out of the station.

'Exactly,' I said. 'Thank you so, so much. You've really saved us!'

The young guy, presumably a little puzzled as to why I'd used 'us' instead of 'me', proceeded to help me secure the bike next to his surfboard. Happily, I'd arrived at the carriage in the train where there was provision for bulky items.

'Are you going to surf?' I asked.

'I am. North Devon is magic for surfing.'

Suddenly I felt less crazy to be taking on my coast-to-coast cycle at this time of year. Surely it wasn't as crazy as wading into the sea in mid-December in pursuit of large waves.

'Thanks again,' I said.

'No problem. Are you going to Barnstaple?'

'Yes.'

'OK, in that case, I'll help you off at the other end.'

Wow, I thought, what a nice bloke.

Now I was faced with a new dilemma. Where to sit? Fortunately, the train wasn't too crowded, but it was more than half-full, meaning there was nowhere to sit where I wouldn't be adjacent to somebody.

A quick glance around me suggested that the train appeared to be full of those people who put their bags down on the seats next to them, as if to say: 'If you sit here, you bastard, you ruin my life.'

Given that I needed to open my coat and attend to Titch, I realised that sitting directly next to somebody might cause alarm. Had I been in a more playful and mischievous mood, I could have marched my way up the train and sat myself next to the Macedonian couple (another theory had formed), but I was far too sweaty, stressed and exhausted to consider such a thing. The obvious place to sit was next to my surfing saviour, but his seat was quite a long way down the carriage, and placing myself next to him would have seemed creepy and overfamiliar. Besides, I didn't want to chat on this journey. I wanted to get Titch settled and then rest. I still had a long cycle ahead of me tonight.

Then I noticed a little hinged, drop-down seat close to the bike and surfboard that was ideal. It would enable me to stay close to the precariously balanced bike and attend to my mini companion. I pulled the seat down and sat on it. Comfortable it was not, but boy, was I grateful to be on it.

Finally, I was able to open my coat and see what had happened with Titch. Just as I had suspected, she had crawled completely out of her sling, and was nestled at the bottom of the coat, having only been held in place by my supporting arm and the cord ties on the anorak bottom. Strangely, she seemed a lot calmer now. Perhaps because she was able to see what was going on, and I was able to cuddle and stroke her with both hands, and support her fully.

Titch was happy now, and our ninety-minute train journey looked set to be a peaceful one. Fortunately my seating position afforded me a reasonable amount of privacy, meaning that only an elderly couple could really see me, and they were showing no interest. That changed when I attempted to lift Titch back into the sling. Although she seemed quite sleepy now, she still made a gentle, grunting noise as I lifted her and started to manoeuvre her back into her sling. The couple looked up, and saw that I was holding a baby pig. I looked at them, and they immediately looked away. It was as if they had admonished themselves for being so interested in someone else. How rude, they must have thought. I'd half-expected them to smile, and come over to have a look, but no, they looked away, and as far as I can recall, they never looked my way again for the whole journey. Well, why would they? Nothing unusual about a man and a pig on a train.

With Titch comfortably back in place, and more tightly

secured this time, I leant my head back against the glass behind me and closed my eyes. I hadn't intended to sleep, but the shenanigans on the station platform and the general stress of pig travel must have taken it out of me, because I fell fast asleep.

I awoke to the sound of the guard announcing our imminent arrival at Barnstaple. Ah, the magic of sleep. It can give you the impression that you've mastered time travel. Simply go to sleep in one place and then wake in another. No such luxury for the rest of my trip, however. Falling asleep whilst cycling is most certainly a health risk, and I owed it to Titch not to indulge.

My surfing hero helped me off the train, and I thanked him profusely again.

'Have a great time surfing!' I added.

'I will.'

I bet he did, too.

***

It was 15.30. It was not raining. There was some wind, but it was not excessive, and I figured that conditions were pretty good for the first leg of my journey. Technically, of course, this next cycle was not part of the coast-to-coast adventure – this was me getting to the starting point. In years gone by, there would have been a train to Ilfracombe. In fact, as late as the summer of '69,[1] you could take a train from Exeter to Ilfracombe. Alas, the station closed in 1970, mainly because everyone was now driving around in cars.

1   Could that be what Bryan Adams's song was about?

That was what you *did*. No one really knew how much it was polluting the atmosphere, and adverts on TV and billboards persuaded us that the car we drove signalled to the rest of the world how much of a success we were. We pretty much all bought into it, me included, and hundreds of wonderful railway stations became shops, cafes, pubs or private homes. Ah, progress.

A single-track railway link between Barnstaple and Ilfracombe had opened in 1874 and it had been so popular that they'd enlarged it to a double track between 1889–91, even though this had meant demolishing and rebuilding most of the stations along the way, and widening tunnels. Nothing was too much for those pioneering Victorians. Much of the old line had now been converted to cycle tracks and I was going to be using it for a lot of my journey. Not tonight, though. Circumstances having forced me onto the later train from Exeter, I was now running out of daylight for the fifteen-mile cycle ahead. The cycle tracks would not be lit and I wanted to avoid any fate that could be reported thus by local newspapers:

COMEDIAN PLUNGES TO DEATH
BUT IS SURVIVED BY PIG

The hastiest of glances at the map (the morning had been such a rush) had suggested to me that I should take the A361, and I was simply hoping that it was a reasonably 'bike-friendly' route.

I gathered myself outside the station. Titch was nice and secure and was sleeping, having been rocked by the gentle motion of the train. The station appeared to be on the outskirts of the town, and I found myself looking ahead to a big, ugly supermarket car park, brimming with the vehicles that had done so much damage to the railway network. The vehicles with which I was reluctantly now going to share the roads.

'Well, here we go, Titch,' I said, to a sleeping pig, 'let's see how we get on with this.'

I pushed the bike forward and swung my leg over the saddle. A move I can remember doing so much in my youth. I was struck by just how little clearance I was now achieving with my swinging leg. The leg was clearing the bar, like a high jumper's, but with little to spare. I would have to watch that when I became tired. We were now cycling. After just a few revolutions of the wheel, the electric motor kicked in, and I was receiving some much welcome assistance.

All went smoothly as I followed the signposts, and soon I was on a nice, wide cycle track heading over the bridge on the River Taw,[2] a vast modern construction built in 2007 to reduce congestion in Barnstaple town centre. It now afforded me the twin benefits of a speedy exit from the town and splendid views across the Taw estuary.

It was the other side of the bridge that the problems began. The road opened out into a rather cycle-unfriendly dual carriageway, and just as I entered this stretch, Titch began wriggling and squeaking. This time she meant business. I sensed I should stop immediately, such were the

---

2   No films have been made about this, even though the views are prettier than those from the bridge on the River Kwai. However, its failure to have played any meaningful role in the story of Japanese prisoners of war in Burma has biased film-makers against it.

vigorous contortions she was now achieving within my coat. I pulled over at what appeared to be the entrance to an industrial estate, and I lifted Titch out – just before she would have simply fallen out – and set her on a convenient grass verge. Within seconds, the reason for her noisy protestations was apparent, and she launched into a long, and presumably deeply satisfying, wee. I opened my pannier at the rear and foraged around for the Defra approved disinfectant.

It was probably a quite needless precaution and I couldn't imagine how anyone was going to check up on me, but I wanted to do things by the rule book. The foot-and-mouth disease outbreak of May 2001 had paralysed Devon's farming industry. More than three million animals had been slaughtered and burning pyres had become a symbol of the disease. The cost was about £8 billion to the UK livestock industry. So there was another headline I was eager to avoid, one that would be more likely to reach the nationals:

COMEDIAN TORN TO SHREDS
BY ANGRY FARMERS
AS HE AND PIG CAUSE NEW
FOOT-AND-MOUTH OUTBREAK

I diligently sprayed the land on which Titch trod, as she contentedly had a brief investigation of her immediate surroundings, happily snorting and foraging with her nose. I gave her a piece of carrot that she seemed to enjoy thoroughly. Had we been doing the sensible thing, and making this trip in July rather than December, then we could have stopped for an hour at this point, basking in the sun and allowing Titch some valuable R and R. But the clock was ticking, and I was eager to avoid as much cycling in the dark as possible.

'Come on, Titch,' I said, after just a five-minute break. 'On we go.'

To my surprise, Titch allowed me to pick her up and pop her back in her sling with no protest at all. Her owner had been spot-on when he'd called her the most good-natured of creatures.

'You're a good girl,' I said, as I remounted my bike.

I really did need Titch on her best behaviour for this next section – for the safety of both of us. This was an extremely busy stretch of road, and drivers seemed to enjoy flooring the accelerator and testing their cars' capacity for speed.

In retrospect, I never should have taken the A361[3] from Barnstaple to Ilfracombe, and I would advise any cyclist against it.

This road contained some sections that were busy dual carriageway, and others that were narrow enough to make passing a cyclist a difficult manoeuvre, and likely to make impatient drivers take risks. It had its fair share of long and tiring hills, too, ending with a prolonged and steep descent into Ilfracombe that would severely test the brake pads of any two-wheeled device.

Titch had behaved angelically for about ninety minutes, but it turned out that she was just waiting. She was waiting

---

3 In this book, I promise to keep you sporadically informed of trivia that will astonish your friends and make you a major hit at dinner parties. Try this for size. The A361 is the longest three-digit A road in the UK (195 miles). A stunner, I think you'll agree.

for the most inappropriate moment to become restless and make life difficult for me. Night had fallen. Rain had started to fall. The wind had certainly increased in strength. Just outside Ilfracombe, I stopped to phone and ask directions from the owner of the hotel where we were staying tonight. This was a mistake. The gentle motion of my body whilst cycling had eased Titch into her gentle slumber, and now this break in that methodical routine had caused her to wake up. This new state of consciousness clearly reminded her where she was, and that she currently didn't want to be there at all.

All this wouldn't have mattered, had we been in a place where we could stop. We weren't. Titch, with disastrous timing, had chosen to express a strong desire for freedom just as I was freewheeling down the long, steep hill into Ilfracombe, on a stretch of road where cars sped by extremely close to us, and where, ideally, both hands should remain firmly on the brakes. However, I needed one hand free to prevent Titch from escaping and dropping down onto the road. With each wriggle from Titch, the bike wobbled precariously. I became seriously concerned. This was dangerous. If we lost control here, the consequences could be very serious. However, I couldn't stop. The hill was just too steep for only one set of brakes to bring the bike to a halt. If only I had both hands free, but I just couldn't risk dropping Titch. The new headline didn't bear thinking about:

ANIMAL RIGHTS ACTIVISTS SET FIRE
TO HOME OF COMEDIAN
FOR KILLING A PIG BY DROPPING IT
ONTO ROAD OUTSIDE ILFRACOMBE

'Please, Titch!' I pleaded. 'Please! Stay still for two more minutes. Then we'll stop.'

And so it was, with my left hand supporting a small pig beneath my coat, and my right squeezing the brake with all its strength whilst doing its best to keep the bike balanced, that we whizzed down the perilously steep hill into Ilfracombe.

It was an experience I *never ever* want to repeat. It was a close thing, but we made it to the bottom of the hill in one piece, possibly because Titch seemed to respond to the desperate pleading tone in my voice. At the first set of traffic lights we came to, I dismounted and lifted the bike onto the pavement, propping it against the wall. I let out an audible sigh of relief. I had known that this journey could be uncomfortable. I had known that this journey could involve some suffering, but I never imagined that it could be dangerous. And I certainly never imagined that it could be life-threatening.

'Thank you, Titch,' I said, as I gave her an almighty hug, having removed her from the bottom of my coat, where she'd been hanging precariously during our hazardous descent. 'We made it. Thank you. Thank you for not getting us both killed.'

After all, she was too young to die, and I was too handsome.

10

Countdown

Rod – roughly my age, jovial, warm and welcoming in his sleeveless jumper – stood on the porch of Varley House, a well-ordered Victorian guest house with sea views (from the upper rooms). Rod was exactly the kind of host you wanted to meet after you'd had a long, wet, windy, and ultimately unnerving cycle. He was also pleasingly nonchalant about the arrival of a pig. He waited happily whilst I hovered over Titch in his hotel's front garden, hoping that she'd relieve herself. When she did, I repressed my urge for a triumphant punch to the air, choosing instead to attempt to give the impression that I was completely in control of this pig. Little did Rod know how close Titch had been to hospitalising the pair of us just half an hour earlier.

'I'll show you both to your room,' said Rod, with an unexpected deference to livestock.

'Brilliant, Rod,' I said, 'this is so kind of you.'

'Happy to help the charity.'

Several days earlier, Rod had offered a complimentary room and breakfast, within only five minutes of my having sent out an email appeal to the many hoteliers of Ilfracombe.

I had been honest enough to reveal in my mail that I had a pig in tow. It hadn't put Rod off.

'You should both be happy in there,' he said, pointing into the spacious Room 6.

I set Titch down on the floor and we watched as she proceeded to sniff around the room, like she was a seasoned traveller. She seemed to be doing the pig equivalent of what we humans do when we check out where the tea- and coffee-making facilities are, identify the whereabouts of the hairdryer, or snoop around the bathroom checking the complimentary miniature toiletries, assessing how many we should take with us when we leave.

'What are you doing for dinner?' asked a smiling Rod, as he viewed my little friend with interest.

'I was going to wander into Ilfracombe and find a restaurant, I guess.'

'Would you like to join us? My family have arrived and we're going to have a Christmas dinner. We're eating early, so you'll have time to explore Ilfracombe afterwards.'

'That would be lovely, thanks.'

How extraordinarily hospitable, I thought. Pigs clearly bring out the best in people. I did have some reservations about joining them, though, feeling a little like a gate-crasher, but there was something so soothing and warming about a Christmas dinner, and I needed comfort after the journey I'd just had.

An hour later, I was sitting round an extremely large table with seven people I'd never met before, wearing one of those ridiculous paper party hats that are generously provided within eternally overpriced and disappointing crackers. I wonder if this is what I enjoy most about this kind of travel – the fact that you simply have no idea what you will be doing next, or whom you will be meeting.

I've never been fond of the expression 'expect the unexpected', mainly because I have a pedantic problem of logic with it. (Once you're expecting it, doesn't it cease to be unexpected?) However, there's certainly some truth in the way you can cherish the unpredictability that a journey like this can bring. One is forced to 'go with the flow'. In order to make your journey joyous, you accept invitations, you follow advice, you call people up that others have suggested you contact. In short, you allow yourself to become the vehicle that takes you on your journey, and your fuel is the people you meet along the way.

That's why I had a silly paper hat on.

Christmas wouldn't be Christmas without silly paper hats. Not that it was Christmas anyway – it was 17 December. Yes, it's normal to have a work Christmas party long before Christmas (some even begin in November – *quelle horreur*), but family gatherings normally have to wait until Jesus's birthday.[1] Rod, however, had been forced to improvise, since his daughter and family were visiting early as they had to be in Surrey over Christmas, because hubby had to work.

I was impressed by the fact that there were four generations at the table. Rod's wife's mum, Rod and his wife's daughter, and Rod and his wife's daughter's son. Impressive work, especially as the great grandmum didn't look that old to me.

---

1   Just a thought, but do you think Jesus lost out on presents, what with his birthday falling on Christmas Day? Always bothered me, that.

At first, I felt a little out of place in this setting. The conversation didn't seem to flow too well, and I wondered if I was preventing everyone from doing what families do so well when they get together over a few drinks.

Arguing.

It was all very polite. I asked a lot of questions. Rod, it turned out, had just completed a brush with showbusiness, having been a winner on *Countdown* for the previous five days, and holding the honour of being the current champion going into the New Year. I asked if he was confident of winning again, at which point he revealed a state secret: he'd already lost his next show, but it hadn't yet been broadcast. I promised not to tell anyone – a secret that I would find surprisingly easy to keep.

For those of you who are not British and don't know *Countdown* as being the stalwart quiz game of British television (it was the first show broadcast on Channel 4 in 1982),[2] here's the gist of it: the contestants are given a load of numbers and a pile of letters and are encouraged to arse about with them until a studio audience applaud knowingly and the presenter and guests comment smugly.

It's a winning formula and a show not to be missed, if you like staring at a screen and experiencing bemusement and a sense of your own inferiority.

Self-consciously, and without anything approaching gay abandon, we pulled our adjacent crackers, adjusted our

2   The host, Richard Whiteley, began the show with the words: 'As the countdown to a brand new channel ends, a brand new countdown begins.' (I am keeping my promise about providing you with trivia that will astound and impress your friends.)

paper hats, read out the feeble jokes, and wondered at the small plastic toys that were immediately ready for recycling the moment they were in our hands. We had all the seasonal, pointless paraphernalia, but it still didn't feel very Christmassy.

Only after the main course did the subject of Titch and the coast-to-coast cycle come up, and I was urged to fetch Titch from the room and let her join us. This made a world of difference. It turns out that a small piglet snorting and foraging around the room can create informality just as well as a round of gin and tonics. Her introduction was greeted with a chorus of 'Isn't she cute!' and intense fascination from the toddler, Callum, who followed her around, but couldn't quite muster the courage to bend down and pick her up. (Great news for Titch. Toddlers no doubt mean well, but are probably responsible for more abuses of animal welfare than the Japanese whaling industry and Spanish toreadors put together.)

Amidst this fresh conviviality, new and more diverse conversations were struck up, and soon I revealed that Fran was six months pregnant.

'Have you found out what sex it is?' asked Rod's daughter. 'Not that it necessarily makes any difference.'

It turned out that they were one of the 4 per cent that got duff info from the hospital. They'd been told to expect a girl, so imagine their surprise when she gave birth to a boy. I imagined the double take when they saw the penis. Perhaps the only double take that penis would ever get. Who knows?

'We had a whole room done out in pink, and loads of clothes that were no use.'

This made me feel that Fran and I had been right to allow

the sex of our future child to remain a mystery. Not that we were about to paint any room pink, blue, or any other colour. So far – and this could change – it seemed that we were going to do what needed doing when it needed doing, and not before. Currently, my only preparation for father-hood had been to clear the diary for the first three months after the baby was born. During that period, I was no longer available for weddings, parties and bar mitzvahs.

Rod's son-in-law, who had become a father before me, despite looking young enough to be my son, began chat-ting, and told me that he worked for McLaren in Woking. Apparently they sold luxury cars to film stars, footballers, celebrities and anyone else who had more money than social conscience.

'Jay Leno just bought one. I think he paid about £800,000 for it.'

I nearly spat out my mince pie.

The amazing thing is that Jay Leno got a bargain com-pared to the most expensive new car of 2013 – the Lamborghini Veneno, which could be purchased for a mere £2.5 million. Even more amazing is that new cars are cheaper than the vintage ones. Just two months before I set off on this trip (on a mode of transport that costs less than the Lamborghini's ashtray) the car collector Paul Pappalardo sold his Ferrari 250 GTO for £32 million.

When I learn this kind of stuff, it makes me feel a little nauseous. For all the amazing advances we've made in society – in healthcare, social reform, technology and human rights – I still find it staggering that we live in a world where it's socially acceptable for one man to spend this amount of money on a car, while others starve. Plainly we've got a bit more advancing to do before it's job done and Jesus can pop back down and say, 'Well done, chaps.'

* * *

After dinner I was faced with the task of getting Titch tucked up in her little pet carrier, so that I could wander into Ilfracombe and take a look around. Titch, however, was alarmingly like a small child who'd become excited by the recent presence of visiting guests. She seemed stimulated, and was unwilling to bed down in her carrier for the night. She kept getting straight out again and foraging round the room, making grunting noises. I wasn't sure whether Rod had told the other guests in the hotel that he had a pig staying over in Room 6, so leaving a grunting pig unattended while I went out didn't seem the best way to repay his hospitality.

Then I remembered something that Chris had told me at one point, when I'd collected Titch.

'If you ever want to calm her down, then massage her just behind the ears. You can use hand cream, or moisturiser. She loves it.'

So it was that I reached for the moisturising lotion that I had packed specifically for Titch, read the label and checked that it didn't say anything about not using it on pigs, and squirted some behind Titch's ears. The massage that followed was not a pleasurable experience for me, since Titch's skin was far more lumpy and barnacled than I might have expected. However, the effect on her was quite magical. After a couple of minutes, this oddest of rituals reached a climax when her eyes began to close, and soon she was out for the count. I covered her with blankets and tiptoed out for the night with a stirring feeling in my heart. Clearly I was demonstrating excellent aptitude for fatherhood.

It was about a twenty-minute walk into the centre of Ilfracombe from Varley House, and thankfully, the wintry rain had eased off. It was dark and I couldn't see a great deal, but I could hear the distant crashing of the waves on the cliffs of nearby Hillsborough. Known locally as the 'sleeping elephant', this promontory (funnily enough, not that different in profile to the shape of a sleeping elephant) is also a nature reserve and the site of an Iron Age fort. I made a promise to myself to return one day and visit it at a more suitable time. Like, in the daylight.

On the way into town, I did what many people do now when they are out walking, I took out my mobile phone and made a call. I am fully aware of how these ingenious miniature communication portals have begun to be the objects we reach for when nothing particularly stimulating is happening in our lives. Recently, on a train, I had noted that every other passenger around me was either talking, texting or playing a game on their phone. On another occasion, a while back, I'd been in a restaurant in Pittsburgh adjacent to a table where four girls had gone out for a meal together. *All* of them were busy looking at their mobile phones, and were tapping away at them. I wondered if this had now become preferable to talking, and that they were sending messages to each other instead.

The soup looks gr8. Are we having starters? :)

In the days of my youth, I would have had to queue outside a phone box for twenty minutes, listening to someone have a row with their boyfriend, before I could have told

Fran that I was OK, and that Titch was safely sound asleep in a lovely, cosy room. No such inconvenience now. Like most of the rest of us, I could now combine travel with communication, meaning that time wasn't wasted.

Wasted time.

As I walked down to Ilfracombe's picture-book pretty harbour, I gave a moment's thought to this notion. In our culture, we have created language that illustrates how we view time, like nearly everything else, as a *commodity*. Time is just something else that we consume. We *judge* it too. Some time we see as 'well-used', other time we view as 'wasted'. Time can also be bought and sold. We have created hourly rates for our time. Cheeky lawyers may even bill you for chatting to you about the weather or how your holiday was. Time is money.

I cut down a path, aiming to get to the harbour that I could see glistening in the distance, and I ended up by a little cove where the water gently lapped onto the shore, reflecting the moonlight. To my right, I could faintly make out the silhouette of a sleeping elephant jutting into the sea. To my left, a tourist notice informed me of Ilfracombe's less reputable past. Smuggling.

Even though the north coast of Devon was not favourable for landings, with its heavy surf and exposed coves, these shores had the advantage of rarely being patrolled by the revenue vessels, who were busy keeping an eagle eye on the south coast. Place names in the Ilfracombe area bear witness to the town's connections with the smuggling trade. On the east side of the town there's an inlet called Brandy Cove, and to the west, Samson's Cove, named after an infamous local smuggler. As I walked the coastal path towards the bright lights of the quayside, I imagined the tough lives that these smugglers must have had, and I wondered how long I would have lasted if I'd been born into those cruel and harsh times.

'Aha, Master Hawks, and what can ye offer our crew of smugglers?' chief smuggler Samson might have asked of me.

'Well, I don't have a huge amount of smuggling experience, but I do have a nice, gentle wit, and as we near shore with our cargo of illegal contraband, I could keep morale up with a host of wry observations.'

'I see. Wicked John, run the cutlass up 'is arse. Let's see how wry 'e is about that.'

Happily, I was able to enjoy the delightful old fishing port completely free of what sustains it these days – tourists. In fact, had every night been like this one, then everyone would have had to shut up shop and leave. I peered in the windows of the pubs and restaurants by the quay – no doubt heaving in the summer – to see waiters sitting dolefully on chairs reading magazines, and barmen listening to solitary drinkers perched on stools, as they passed ever more incoherent opinions on politicians and football managers with each melancholic pint.

I walked to the end of the pier, where a huge statue was silhouetted against the moonlit sky. Upon closer inspection, it appeared to be a pregnant woman holding a sword aloft, standing on a pile of law books and carrying some scales. You know, as pregnant women do. As I walked around her, I noticed that one half of her belly was open to the elements, so that we could see her unborn baby. I began to worry for her. In spite of two visits to the midwife with

Fran, I was still no expert on pregnancy, but I did know that this would be something that would cause Maureen, our bright and breezy midwife, to tut and offer a little shake of the head:

'Now that's something that we'll need to take a little look at. Not ideal, tum-tum being open to the elements, but ho-hum.'

Only the following morning, at the same time as I learned that this was a Damien Hirst sculpture, did I discover why the pregnant lady's foetus was visible for all to see. Obviously, as Damien himself makes clear, it is an allegory of truth and justice (I was a fool not to see this myself).

You'll have to excuse my cynical tone, but I'm afraid that with most art, I'm completely unable to 'get' what I'm supposed to 'get', and as each artwork is 'explained' to me, I become further distanced from it. I simply don't understand the language of art criticism. Once, walking round the Guggenheim Museum in Bilbao and listening to the audio commentary on some of the experimental modern art, I wanted to tear off the headphones and stamp on them. All that stopped me was the fact that in so doing I might have created a more impressive piece of art than most of what I was observing, and I didn't want to upset the museum's curator.

Verity, as this sculpture is called, is very striking. There. Let me leave it at that, before I embarrass myself. What is impressive about it is that Mr Hirst, a resident of Ilfracombe and the world's richest living artist, has magnanimously *lent* the statue to the town for twenty years. An allegory of precaution and parsimony.

When I got back to Varley House, I could hear Titch

snorting and grunting as I approached the door of Room 6. Clearly my massage had been merely a temporary anaesthetic. I could only guess at quite what the other hotel guests had made of these noises, but I imagined that a few of them would try to avert eye contact with me in the morning.

Titch was wide awake and patrolling the room confidently, as if she'd always lived here. With great respect to Rod's carpets, like a good girl, she'd had a poo and wee on the tiled floor of the bathroom.

'Hello, Titch,' I said, 'did you have a nice evening?'

All pet owners talk to their pets. It's comforting for them, if pointless. The worst pet owners, though, are the ones who think they can understand what their pet is saying to *them*. For example, their dog comes bounding up to them barking, and they declare, 'Oh look, he wants to go for a walk.' Well, I'm sorry, but he might not be saying that at all. He might be saying, 'I preferred it when the sofa was up against the window.' It seems to me a great shame that all over the country dogs are being dragged on walks against their will, when all they really want is the furniture rearranged.

'Goodnight, Titch,' I said twenty minutes later, after another massage behind the ears had rendered us both ready for slumber.

'Tomorrow's a big day,' I continued, even though it appeared that Titch was ignoring me. 'We need to be on good form. First day of the challenge.'

* * *

Being three months old, in pig terms this probably made Titch the equivalent of a human teenager, which is why she slept on soundly as I went to breakfast.

I was the first into the dining room, eager to make a start before the forecasted driving rain and heavy winds kicked in. However, a glance out at the weather suggested that I might have missed my window of opportunity. That had probably been the day before. Or August.

It was the kind of rain that is noisy as well as damp. It positively rattled against the windows, each cascading drop bringing with it a clear message.

Stay inside and read a book today. I don't want to see you. At all.

Rod took my order – a cooked breakfast without bacon (come on, I have a heart) – and I was left to sit and suffer. The torment was only in small part down to the sounds of the weather, most of it was actually being caused by those emanating from the radio. Seemingly, a gathering of overly jovial adults had gathered around a studio microphone to discuss banalities and laugh thunderously at each other's facile quips. These excruciating exchanges were relieved by music – tolerable at most times of the year, but not right now, as I was forced to suffer Christmas song after sodding Christmas song.

Paul McCartney delivered his anthem to the inexorable decline in the quality of his oeuvre, assuring me that he was 'simply having a wonderful Christmas time'. Jona Lewie had apparently left the kitchen (presumably the party had finished) and was doing his best to 'stop the cavalry'. Boney M assured me that 'man would live for evermore because of Christmas Day'. Given the rapidly growing world population and its insatiable appetite for plundering the earth's finite resources, this seemed to be an over-simplification. I made a note to myself not to seek guidance from the words of Boney M.

After a hearty breakfast, I was ready to begin my quest. Whilst teenage Titch slept on, I got the bike ready for departure, successfully fitting the recharged battery. Despite consulting the short video that I'd shot on my smartphone, with Ken showing me how to tighten and loosen the ratchet on the back of the bike, I tried and failed repeatedly. With each attempt, I felt a deep sense of failure. This kind of practical inadequacy on my part was excusable when I was engaged in my normal career (actually, it's not so normal, I suppose), but I was now an adventurer, and as such I ought to be able to look after myself. An adventurer needs to be able to solve problems. When you're at sea, up mountains, in deserts, or even cycling in the wilds of Devon in god-awful weather, there's no Ken the neighbour on hand to sort you out.

I secretly felt a little better when Rod couldn't do it either. It took the help of another guest, who volunteered when he saw the two of us struggling.

'Have you got a pig in that room?' he asked, upon concluding some annoyingly logical ratchet strap work; the question like a payoff for the completed labour.

'Yes, I'm cycling from coast to coast with a small pig, raising money for charity.'

'In *this*?' said the man, pointing outside.

'I'm afraid so.'

The eponymous host of the *Judi Spiers Show* was equally sympathetic.

'This is probably the worst day for starting such an expedition,' she said, not just to me, but to anyone who happened to be listening to Radio Devon.

Judi wasn't wrong, but the odds had always made this likely. I had figured that probably 30 per cent of December days are quite unpleasant, so it wasn't as if this was unexpected.

'I have my waterproofs, Judi,' I said, from the phone in the hotel's hallway, 'and Titch will be snuggled up nice and warm within my coat.'

'I know you were struggling to find accommodation in Great Torrington, but stay on the line after we go off air, and we'll give you the details of a nice lady who has offered to put you up. And folks, don't forget to give generously to Tony if you see him along the way.'

Hmm. I glanced out of the hotel window one final time. As if anyone would be out walking their dogs in this weather.

'That's right, Judi. All donations welcome. I have my very own piggy-bank with me, although probably best not to insert the money directly, as animal welfare may be after us.'

Five minutes later, myself, Titch, the bike, and Rod's family were posing for photos on the hotel's front steps. We winced, rather than smiled, as the wind and rain lashed us. Hands were shaken, thanks duly given, pleasantries exchanged, and then Rod and his clan were lucky enough to dash back inside, leaving me and Titch to begin our quest in earnest.

'OK, Titch, here we go!' I said, with more than a hint of trepidation, and I began cycling.

Almost on cue, as if blessed with a divine intervention,

the rain eased when we began to move. It took only a few minutes to be back at the harbour, where I dismounted the bike, eased it down the slipway, and dipped the rear wheel in the sea.[3] This, Rod had explained, is the tradition for coast-to-coast cyclists.

A car pulled up, and a young woman rushed over to me and thrust a fiver into my hand.

'Heard you on the radio. Love what you're doing. Go for it!' she said, before dashing back to the car and driving off.

'Thanks!' I called after her, and I slid the money into Titch's carrier.

'There, Titch. Aren't people nice?' I said.

I remounted the bike, thinking that I should now cycle for at least two hours, exploiting what was probably only a temporary lull in the foul weather. So it was disappointing when I had to stop only ten minutes later to question one of the few pedestrians braving the conditions.

'Excuse me, but am I going the right way for the Tarka Trail?'

Rod had given me clear directions to this cycle route and I'd made damn sure that I'd paid good attention. It had all made good sense, and I'd been confident of finding it without any problem at all.

'You've come too far,' said the shopping-bag-laden lady. 'You need to turn yourself around, then turn left at the end of this row of houses, go up some steps and you'll see the trail. It's on the old railway line.'

---

3   OK, I've got to be honest here. The rotten tide had gone out, so I ended up dipping the rear wheel in sodden sand. I won't tell *Guinness World Records*, if you don't.

'Thanks,' I said, repressing the need for a loud curse.

Fifteen minutes later, I was no longer repressing the curses.

'Shit, shit, shit, shit, shit, shit!' I shouted.

As soon as I'd got to the foot of the steps that would lead me onto the Tarka Trail, it had started raining again. Hard. Very hard. Torrentially, even. I'd struggled up the steps carrying a ridiculously heavy bike, whilst Titch had decided that it was time for her to have one of her little breaks. After a struggle to keep her in my coat, I'd set her down at the top of the steps and she wandered around aimlessly, contemplating whatever piglets contemplate when they're freed from their baby slings. A gust of wind then blew the bike over and the animal carrier fell off the back.

After righting the bike, I was now struggling with the ratchet strap.

'Bugger, bugger, bugger, bugger!' I now exclaimed. 'How does this sodding thing work?'

Then I began to laugh. It seemed a better alternative to crying. The rain was now so heavy that it was like standing in a shower. Titch seemed to indicate, by standing still and staring at me, that she was ready to return to the warmth of sling and coat, her little eyes almost appearing apologetic. *OK. Stopping was a bad idea. Sorry. You carry on as you were.*

I then got on my hands and knees and sprayed the area where she'd walked with the Defra approved disinfectant (as pointless an exercise as shouting shit and bugger at volume in the rain). The torrential rain washed the pink liquid away, the moment it hit the ground. But Devon had once again been saved from another foot-and-mouth outbreak.

As I stood up, Titch fell out of the sling.

'Shit! Bugger!'

Then the bike blew over again.

'Arse! Shitting bugger shit!'

At this moment I felt a tap on my shoulder, and there stood behind me was a sweet-faced old man under an umbrella. He shoved a tenner towards me.

'Heard you on Radio Devon. Have this for your cause.'

He then turned and headed off, before I could success-fully switch from obscene to obsequious.

'Sounds like it could be going better,' he added, with a hint of a chuckle as he walked away from me, silhouetted against the grey, threatening sky.

Now I really didn't know whether to laugh or cry. I felt numb, my emotions either drowned or drowning. However, the man's generous and kind gesture rekindled my spirits enough to give me the energy to sort the bike out, repack my pig, and set off on the Tarka Trail.

11

A Cavalier Town

It's named after a book I haven't read, *Tarka the Otter* by Henry Williamson. It must be a good book, because it was first published in 1927 and has not been out of print since. It's the story of an otter's life as he splashes about in the water in and around Torrington. A bit like I was going to do today.

The Tarka Trail, in this part anyway, is excellent for cycling. I was grateful to the hardworking, practical men who'd originally laid the former railway track (I'm sure all of them could have easily operated a ratchet strap), as they'd carved out a route that was relatively flat, with minimal gradients.

Appreciating the views and surrounding countryside is not easy when your eyes are squinting, as mine were doing. Horizontal heavy rain is never easy to tolerate when stationary, but forward momentum provides a kind of effect not dissimilar to someone directing the jet from a powerful shower head directly into your face. However, I could just about nod in approval as I made out two picturesque lakes to my right, before we entered one of the many short, former railway tunnels that would be dotted along this route. They would come as a relief, offering momentary respite from the prevailing precipitation.

A couple of miles further on, I was presented with a choice. I'd come to the point where I could take the trail on a more direct route to Barnstaple, or take a seven-mile diversion looping me around the beautiful scenic coastline. On a summer's day, the choice would have been an obvious one. Come to think of it, it was an obvious one today, too. Were I to take the coastal route, I wouldn't see anything, and there'd be a good chance of being blown off my bike.

Thinking only of Titch's welfare, and not my own need to survive, I took the more direct route. I was quite possibly missing out on the most beautiful part of this cycle, so this was disappointing. I would have to return another time to enjoy it. Just like I would with Hillsborough. I hoped this wasn't going to be the trend for the entire journey – identify pleasurable experiences, but completely fail to enjoy any of them first-hand.

Braunton was my first small town. Or should I say large village? That's a poser that needn't concern us, unless this particular copy of the book is now resting in the hands of the North Devon representative of the Organisation That Decides Whether A Place Is A Town Or A Village Or Not.[1]

What matters is that I cycled through Braunton without noticing anything of great note, other than its surf shops. Being the gateway to three of the South West's most renowned surf beaches – Saunton, Croyde and Woolacombe – Braunton has become a surfing hub. It made me think of

---

1 Or O.T.D.W.A.P.I.A.T.O.A.V.O.N. as it's more catchily known.

my heroic saviour from the Exeter to Barnstaple train. I imagined him battling past waves to rescue a poor surfer (perhaps without pig?), who had underestimated the power of the wind and waves and got into trouble.

The trail led us in and out of Braunton quicker than one can say O.T.D.W.A.P.I.A.T.O.A.V.O.N. The rain had eased but the wind seemed to be getting up. Titch warmed my chest as she slept soundly, happily oblivious to the onslaught of the elements. To my right, I admired the sandy estuary of the River Taw. I knew very little about estuaries, and if no one other than me had bothered to contribute to Wikipedia on this subject, then the entry would read:

Estuary: Wide bit of water where a river reaches the sea that birdwatchers are awfully keen on.

There weren't many birds around today. They'd obviously gone to wherever birds go when the weather is lousy. Actually, where *is* that? Most of them build their nests al fresco up in trees, which is excellent for views, but shit for shelter. I suppose, like me, they just ignored the weather and got on with things, although quite where they were today was anybody's guess.

Barbed-wire fencing interrupted the view of the sand and dunes for a while. A sign revealed that this was a military base, RAF Chivenor, a training camp for marines. No one out and about there either. Bunch of wimps.

I hadn't planned on stopping for lunch before Barnstaple, but I was only a few miles away when I passed a delightful-looking cafe on my left. After I'd gone several yards past it, I applied the brakes and had a think. It wasn't a great time to stop, as the rain had eased off and it was a good opportunity to take advantage of this respite. Furthermore, the fact that Titch was sound asleep ought also to be exploited. First rule in the as-yet-unpublished book, *Cycling with Pigs*, would say – *cover as much ground as possible while the pig sleeps*. So in spite of the alluring cafe, everything said 'press on'.

Except me. I was hungry and the cafe looked nice.

The world's great explorers had it easy. They were out battling in the wilds of Antarctica or the depths of the Amazonian rainforests. They never had to cycle past nice cafes. They didn't have to undertake the agonising battles of will like the one I had just briefly fought and lost. Lucky bastards.

I parked up my bike in front of the cafe – a converted railway station called Fremington Quay – and decided to indulge in some creative interpretation of the rules.

I'd been told by the government's farming and animal welfare authorities that I was not to take Titch anywhere where food was being prepared. However, I figured that if I sat at the back of the cafe and kept her zipped up in my coat, then I couldn't possibly be the cause of a major out-break of foot-and-mouth. And anyway, they weren't preparing food in that part of the cafe, only serving it.

I ordered a soup and roll and took up an inconspicuous position on a comfy sofa at the rear of the cafe. From here I could view the ten or so customers happily chatting and dining. The cafe had been tastefully converted, and to my left there was a museum that charted the history of the place. Pictures on the walls explained what had happened here, before it had become a dispensary for cappuccinos and soups.

The area outside this cafe had once been a bustling port.

Coal, limestone, gravel, granite, lead and seed potatoes were all imported, and ball clay was exported. Like so many places in the UK, a once-thriving hub of manual labour was now a place for people to sit on their arses, drink coffee, nibble on cake, and look at pictures reminding them of how this used to be a thriving hub of manual labour.

It took only a matter of minutes for my cover to be blown.

'Is that your bike outside?' asked a lady, clutching a tray supporting an appetising lunch.

'It is.'

'You must have a pig then.'

I can only imagine that this had been the first time she'd followed a line of enquiry that had enabled her to utter those two sentences consecutively.

'How did you know that?' I asked.

'We saw the bike with the pet carrier on it. Then we saw that the pet carrier has Pennywell Farm written on it, and we know that they breed miniature pigs. Plus we heard you on the radio a few hours ago. Here, have this – you deserve it.'

The lady thrust a twenty pound note into my hand, and then asked if she could see the pig. I could hardly refuse her, even though this meant my attempt at remaining incognito might be sabotaged. It was. The lady made such a fuss of Titch that in a matter of minutes every diner in the cafe was paying homage. Some made generous donations, too, once they knew what it was all about.

The disappointment at having been a spectacular failure in 'keeping a low profile' was easily offset by the joy in the faces of the Titch-loving congregation who were now gathered before us. Offers of help and accommodation were forthcoming, and the cafe's owners, Paul and Charlotte, made up a packed lunch of grapes and carrots for Titch, and wrapped up a huge wedge of delicious coffee cake for me.

Paul's accent was far from Devonian.

'I'm Scottish,' he explained, 'I came down here to surf quite a few years back, and I never left.'

Devon appeared to be a great receiver of people. Naturally enough, people move about in their lives, but as far as I could fathom from the people I'd met so far, Devonians seem to stay put and others, like Fran and myself, tend to move in. Locals call us 'incomers', but they don't seem to display any hostility towards us. Paul certainly seemed happy enough. I guess he just needed to look out of the window to know that he'd made the right decision, even in spite of the drawbacks on this particularly wet day.

As we left the cafe, Titch and I were waved off like heroes. Exactly as it should be.

* * *

The warm glow in my heart sustained me as the cycling became more difficult. One of the diners in the cafe had informed me that severe weather warnings had been issued on the radio, and that a gale-force wind would soon be gusting up to 70 mph from the south. The worst was clearly still to come, and yet I was already in great need of the extra power from the bike's battery to sustain a moderate speed. I switched it onto the high setting, gaining a vital bit of extra power and preserving some strength in my legs.

The trail skirted us around Barnstaple and then on to Bideford, which sits on the estuary of the River Torridge – a river that briefly joins up with the River Taw to create a two-river estuary before spilling into the sea.[2]

Bideford has had a colourful history. Although it's now only a small town with a population of about 17,000, in the sixteenth century it was Britain's third-largest port. Sir Walter Raleigh landed his first shipment of tobacco here, affording people the opportunity to take up smoking and pay extra tax to the government, whilst at the same time damaging their own health. It was a terrific deal and many took advantage.

One of Bideford's other claims to fame is that it hosted Britain's last hangings for witchcraft. Following a trial in 1682, three women were found guilty and were then ceremoniously strung up by the neck until they were dead, so that people could stand around and cheer. (There was no Sky coverage of the Premiership back then, so you had to get your entertainment somehow.) These Bideford witches had it easy. Previous witches had been burnt, or tried by the system of 'swimming a witch', which involved binding them and throwing them into water, to see if they floated. Their accusers had come up with the cunning ploy of declaring them innocent if they sank. Dead innocent. Even if there had been legal aid back then, all your lawyer could have suggested by way of a defence was running away

2   It will be down to me when you cover yourself in glory at the next pub quiz you attend, where one of the questions is: *The estuaries of which two Devon rivers join to the north of Bideford and west of Barnstaple to empty into the Bristol Channel?*

– very, very fast. Things have improved now, and we let witches into the government and become judges on TV talent shows.

Shortly after pressing on from Bideford, the southerly wind became so strong, and the rain so constant, that two songs from my past kept buzzing around my head – 'Things Can Only Get Better' and 'The Only Way Is Up'. By singing them, I assumed that they would become self-fulfilling prophecies. However, reality had other ideas and ten minutes later, disaster struck when the battery on my bike ran out of juice. Suddenly the full weight of this bike and its cargo had to be propelled by the dwindling power that remained in my legs. The songs had given me false succour, and had turned out to be flawed. The writer of 'Things Can Only Get Better' had omitted to reveal something else that things could actually get – which was *a bit worse*. The writer of 'The Only Way Is Up' chose to turn a blind eye to one of the other 'ways' that was also a possibility – *a bit further down*.

After the statutory whinge and curse, I did what I always do in these situations, and I tried to look for the positive. This extra-hard cycling, I told myself, would be good for my fitness. I estimated that Great Torrington was about five miles away. A trifling distance for the cyclist with a light bike and no baggage, but for a cyclist with an already heavy bike, laden still further with a dead battery and baggage for both man and pig, five miles represented an hour's hard cycle. Make that more, if you're cycling into a wind that has warranted a 'severe weather warning'.

After ten minutes of this new and far more 'honest' approach to cycling (let's face it, there was an element of cheating in having the electric bike), my thighs were burning. Another cyclist came flying past me – the first I'd seen today (well, this was hardly cycling weather) – as if to mock me and to emphasise the gradual nature of my progress. At the entrance to one of the many old railway tunnels that peppered the trail, a sign for the train drivers still remained in place.

SLOW.

Hmm. Like I had any choice.

And still the wind began to blow harder and harder.

'Why does it have to be against us, Titch?' I called out.

A wind of this strength behind us would have simply whisked us along. A perfect use of a renewable energy. Wind power without the unsightly turbines.

Doing earnest 'let's look for the positives in this' work, I identified that the rain had eased slightly, and that this new speed – snail's pace – was giving me the opportunity to take in the beautiful countryside that now surrounded me. I was cycling along the riverbank close to the spot that Henry Williamson described as Tarka the Otter's birthplace. Rolling green hills, with sparkling streams dashing down into the waiting river below, were dotted with pretty hamlets where stone, thatch, and church spires combined to create a feeling of timelessness. Devon at its best. One day I would come back here, so that I could enjoy the feeling of beauty and peace. Currently the gale-force wind in the face was just taking the edge off it.

The scarce December light was fading by the time my tired body hauled the bike alongside the remnants of Torrington's former railway station. It was now a pub, called the Puffing Billy, but it appeared to be out of puff today and was distinctly closed. So, too, was Torrington Cycle Hire, the only adjacent building. If this was Torrington, it was far from Great.

A hardy man, walking his dog, approached me. I decided to engage in my first human contact since lunch.

'Excuse me,' I asked him, as he drew within range, 'but where is Great Torrington?'

He turned and pointed behind us.

'At the top of that bloody great hill,' he said, unceremoniously.

He looked at me, then down at the bike.

'Rather you than me.'

And with those rather unhelpful words, he continued on his way. His dog glanced back at me with an apologetic look in its eye, almost as if it was wanting to say:

'He *does* this. He's lovely really, but he has this unfortunate direct manner that comes across as unsympathetic. I'm sorry.'

Nice dog.

Unfortunately for me, Great Torrington had originally been built by the Saxons on a steep ridge overlooking the valley of the River Torridge, so that potential conquerors would be knackered by the time they arrived. Years on, regardless of whether conquering was on the mind or not, the same applied for a traveller with a heavy bike and a pig.

Pushing a bike up a hill is not good for the dignity. It says to those around you that you lack both fitness and determination. Admittedly, on a day like this, the only people who were around me were speeding past in cars. I was saved the humiliation of being overtaken by pedestrians. Five minutes into the gruelling climb, I passed a sign welcoming motorists.

GREAT TORRINGTON – A Cavalier Town.

This, I assumed, was a reference to the town's civil war connections, rather than to its general attitude. Town and city administrators are keen to find adjectives that they believe will set them apart from the others. They are always too complimentary. Names have varied from the modest, 'THE FRIENDLY CITY', right the way through to the downright arrogant, 'THE GREATEST CITY IN THE WORLD'. For my own part, I don't want to visit somewhere that is bigheaded enough to describe itself thus. I'd have more respect for somewhere that had the honesty to admit that it's overpopulated, heavily polluted, and generally lacking in any attractive qualities. Here's a suggestion that simply rolls off the tongue.

SHANGHAI – The Shitty City.[3]

Great Torrington likes to boast about its connection to the English Civil War and in 1646 the parliamentarians defeated the royalists in the aptly titled Battle of Torrington. This marked the end of royalist resistance in the West Country, and was a significant milestone on the road to the British being bold enough to get rid of the iniquitous and undemocratic system of monarchy, for a full *eleven* years. You've got to hand it to us Brits – when we do something, we do it half-heartedly.

Finally, tired and sodden, I made it into the town's long

---

3   I've not been to Shanghai, but regardless of whether it's true or not, this is too good a strapline not to use. (A note to Shanghai's city planners – feel free to use this. No need to ask my permission – it's yours.)

main street, and went straight into the first pub I reached, The Torrington Arms. I was hugely relieved to have made it to somewhere warm, dry, and un-blustery. The pub was simple and unpretentious and reminded me of many of the Irish pubs that I'd come to know on previous travels. A scattering of mature gentlemen were slowly wiling away their afternoon, supping on pints and putting the world to rights. In a dimly lit adjoining room, another bunch of mature gentlemen were in the last throes of a Christmas lunch. They were engaged in what appeared to be measured and even-tempered discourse, even though all views set forth were being completely undermined by the fact that they were all wearing silly Christmas party hats.

Keeping Titch concealed, I wandered to the bar and ordered a soft drink, knowing that I would still have to find my digs for the night and that more cycling would be required. I asked nicely if I could put my bike battery on charge. The lady behind the bar said that she would love to help, but that the pub didn't belong to her, and that the owner wasn't around for her to ask. This wouldn't have been too much of a problem, had my overnight accommodation been as close to this pub as I'd been expecting. After showing the address to the barmaid and the solo drinker next to me, we established the rather alarming fact that the accommodation on offer was six miles out of Great Torrington. At the top of a hill.

My heart sank. This was calamitous. Extreme measures were called for. I had to come up with something to get my way. How could I persuade this barmaid to relax her grip on her responsibilities and let me plug a battery in for half an hour? Then I had an idea.

I stood back, cleared my throat volubly, waited till I'd got everybody's attention as if I was going to make an important announcement, and then I began. A slow unzipping of my anorak. I did it in an alluring way, much like a glamour model might unzip clothing in a TV advertisement. The men looked on, but with far less interest than if I had actually been a babe disrobing. The barmaid just looked confused. I continued unzipping. Finally, I reached the point where Titch's head was popping out of the top of the sling.

'Oh my God! It's a pig!' exclaimed the barmaid. 'It's gorgeous!'

Five minutes later, the battery was on charge, and I found myself surrounded by all the pub's drinkers and several of the gentlemen from the Christmas party. All wanted to know the story, and to stroke and fuss Titch. One of the low-key seasonal revellers introduced himself as Derek and immediately thrust a twenty pound note into my hand.

'Take this for your cause,' he said. 'You have a delightful pig.'

Derek told me that his luncheon party was a group of former teachers and headmasters, who got together every year to catch up on each other's lives and to moan about the incumbent education secretary, whoever that happened to be.

'I'm afraid we're currently stuck with Mr Gove,' Derek said, rolling his eyes. 'By the way, where are you staying tonight?'

'A kind Radio Devon listener has offered me a bed for the night. It's about six miles up the road.'

'You can stay with me and my wife, if you like. We live just around the corner.'

Boy, was it tempting. I really couldn't face another session of cycling, even if the battery was sufficiently charged. The passage of time meant that the hostile weather was now unhelpfully supplemented by darkness.

'That's so kind. The trouble is, I've promised this lady, and she's cooking a meal especially.'

Derek then applied his analytical educator's brain to the dilemma and came up with an excellent solution. On my bike, I was to follow him and his wife in their car – she was picking him up shortly – to their house. There we would deposit my bike in their garage and put it on overnight charge. Then his wife would give me a lift up the road to where I was staying. Either my host could give me a lift back to pick the bike up in the morning, or they would come and collect me.

'That would be amazing – but will your wife mind?'

'She'll be fine. Especially when I explain about the pig.'

As it turned out, not for the first time in a pub, a man was being a little overoptimistic about the goodwill of his wife. After I'd unplugged my battery, thanked the barmaid and said my goodbyes to the remaining drinkers, I emerged onto the dark street to find Derek involved in a very uncomfortable conversation with a woman in a car, whom I assumed was his wife.

'A *what*?' the woman said.

'A pig,' replied Derek.

'How much have you drunk?'

'Not very much at all. It's a pig. A small pig.'

'You want me to take a small pig in the car?'

'Not in the car. It'll follow on a bike.'

'You're pissed.'

'I'm not. It's very straightforward—'

At this point, I did the decent thing and walked up to the car, unzipped my anorak and revealed Titch to the distressed driver.

Immediately her countenance was transformed. Irritation to adoration in 0.1 of a second. Words were replaced by the joyful sounds usually heard only around cute babies.

'Aaaaah . . .' she said, reaching out to stroke Titch.

My little friend had done it again. In a moment, Titch had instilled serenity into a tense situation. Perhaps I was onto something here. Maybe after this trip, Titch and I could lend our services to the negotiators in the Middle East peace process. Just as things reached a very heated point, I could produce Titch and restore a sense of equilibrium.[4]

I'll set up the website shortly:

www.porkpeace.com.

* * *

'Enjoy your stay, and see you in the morning.'

People are nice. For a long time I've held the belief that human beings are inherently good. In spite of all the bad

---

4   Even if things went badly wrong, Titch wouldn't make it onto the menu, provided I was on hand to quote from the Old Testament and the Quran. 'And the pig, because it has a split hoof, but does not chew the cud; it is unclean for you. You shall neither eat of their flesh nor touch their carcass.' Deuteronomy 14:8. 'He has made unlawful for you that which dies of itself and blood and the flesh of swine and that on which the name of any other than Allah has been invoked.' Quran, Al-Bagara 2:173. For more details, go to: www.God'snotkeenonbacon.com

things that are done in the world – and these are usually the ones that make the news bulletins – millions of daily acts of kindness go unreported, sometimes even unnoticed.

Take this situation, for example. Derek's wife had disrupted her afternoon and driven me fifteen minutes up the road to deliver me to another lady, who in turn was offering an evening meal and accommodation to a stranger and a pig. What the world needs is for ladies like this to be in charge. I'd like to see them running countries like Syria and Iran. More tea, less war.

As the car pulled up outside at a nice rural, thatched cottage and I was passed from one kind middle-aged lady to another, I couldn't help wonder why they were doing it. There was absolutely nothing in it for these people. They weren't giving for reward, or out of guilt, shame or a sense of duty. It seemed to be natural giving. What a nice thing, and yet such a rare commodity. How did we get off-target from natural giving? It probably started thousands of years ago, when we began to adopt the wild thinking that human beings are innately evil. Penitence was required, and people were taught to hate themselves for what they were doing. Violent thinking ensued and then, naturally enough, violence itself. Domination cultures flourished, resulting in an extraordinary statistic about American TV from just a few years back. Between 7 p.m. and 9 p.m. in the evening, at the times when most families were watching TV together, in 75 per cent of programmes, someone either kills somebody or beats them up – usually at the climax of the programme. To use the vernacular of the Americans who produced this stuff: 'Go figure'.

'Would you like a cup of tea?' said benign Nicky, as she welcomed me at her door.

One can't always go by appearance, but it would be hard to imagine a woman less likely to kill or beat someone up. Certainly the latter. If murder did happen to be her thing, then she had the build of a poisoner, rather than one who favoured bludgeoning.

'Yes, please,' I replied, 'and thank you so much for doing this.'

'It's nothing. I don't normally phone in to radio stations, but I just felt the urge to do it this time.'

'It's very brave of you to take a strange man into your house.'

'Oh, I don't think you're so strange. I've heard you on the radio and you don't sound like a murderer.'

As someone who still enjoys his broadcasting forays on the radio, it was a great comfort to know that I didn't sound like a murderer. Presumably this is why the bookings had flooded in over the years.

Over tea, we established that Nicky lived alone in this cute and homely cottage. Her children had flown the nest and had begun families of their own. Nicky had tried living with her current partner, but things seemed to work out better if they lived apart and spent weekends together.

'Whatever works for you,' I said.

This happened to be exactly what I believed, although I probably would have said it, even if it hadn't been. Nicky and I were still in the social territory where convention has it that we agree with everything the other says. Only after a few hours, and usually a glass of wine or two, can we lock horns with someone and actually dare to challenge their views. Until then, this is the kind of exchange one might indulge in:

'I've put five sugars in your tea, because I think sugar – like corporal punishment for the dropping of litter – should be compulsory.'

'I couldn't agree more. I don't suppose I could have another teaspoon, could I? I love it.'

Nicky liked Titch, although she wasn't as bowled over as many before her had been, and I sensed that she wasn't a natural animal lover. All the more power to her elbow for inviting a pig into her house. I still wasn't entirely sure of her motive. Was she a fan? Had I walked into a Devonian version of the plot of Stephen King's *Misery*? Or did she just want to help me, in my effort to help some people who had a pretty tough time of things in a far-off European country? I hoped it was the latter.

As if to spite Nicky for her generosity of spirit, Titch let me down socially. Whilst Nicky cooked our fish dinner, Titch had a poo in the corner of her kitchen, and a wee on her living-room carpet.

'Don't worry, it'll be fine,' Nicky said, suddenly aware of the less-attractive implications of having a pig round for a sleepover.

Feeling almost as guilty as if I'd been the culprit, I swept up Titch's poo (easy, nice dry pellets) and scrubbed away at the carpet with government endorsed disinfectant.

'It'll be fine,' said Nicky.

'Yes, I think so,' I said, slightly conscious of the fact that the government disinfectant might be about to cause more staining than Titch had done.

'Dinner is served,' said my charming hostess.

A delicious plate of home-cooked food was served up, and a pleasant evening was spent gently probing for information about each other's lives, whilst Titch nibbled on carrots and did mock foraging around the kitchen. The exhausting day was taking its toll and by 9.30 p.m. I was struggling to keep my eyes open. Unfortunately for me, Titch looked wide awake. This left me in a situation that I had never been in before. As a guest in someone's house whom I had never met before, I wanted to go to bed earlier than the host, and the small pig that I had brought with me. There seemed to be no precedent for the social etiquette that was required at such a juncture.

'Titch looks wide awake,' I said, testing the water. 'But that's because she slept all day whilst I cycled. Would you mind if I go to bed early?'

'No problem,' replied Nicky, 'I'll make sure Titch is in her little bed before I turn in. Sleep well.'

'I will. I'm so tired, I'm sure I'll sleep like a baby.'

This had been a ridiculous thing to say. If I were to sleep like a baby, that would mean that I would wake every few hours screaming at the top of my voice, and then shit myself. I didn't want to do that. Not until I knew Nicky better.

I climbed the stairs, relieved that I had escaped more conversation – not because it was tiresome, but because it was tiring, to an already exhausted man. As I crawled into my wonderfully snug bed, I smiled to myself as I heard little snorting and grunting sounds from downstairs. Titch, adaptable as ever, was bonding with her new companion for the night. I felt consciousness easing from me. Restorative sleep, healing sleep, was only moments away.

* * *

'Did you sleep well?' asked Nicky, as she prepared breakfast.

'Slept soundly, thank you. I see Titch is still sleeping. How was she last night?'

'As good as gold. She's a lovely little pig, that one.'

Nicky was right. Of all the pigs in the world, surely I couldn't have chosen a better one to have had as a travelling companion. Once people laid eyes on her, they became transformed. They turned from honest, decent citizens going about their business, into people desperate to do everything they could to help. At least, I assumed that this transformation was caused by the 'Titch effect'. Perhaps I was underestimating my own boyish good looks and cheeky charm.

After breakfast Team Hawks kicked into action. Nicky drove us to Derek's house where the bike was removed from the garage, and where Derek and his wife helped me pack the bike. Pleasingly, they struggled just as much as I did with the ratchet strap. Ken had made its operation look so straightforward, and yet this strap seemed to reveal something about the way our brains are formed. Evidently there are two kinds of people in the world – those who can operate ratchet straps, and those who can't. Derek was in the second category but, unlike me, was unwilling to accept it. He struggled away with a dedication and zeal that only served to make his disappointment more profound.

'I'll just wedge my rucksack underneath,' I suggested, after a full five minutes of uncomfortable struggling had failed to release the strap.

Bungies were added to further secure the bag, and I announced that Titch and I were ready to hit the road.

After a round of last goodbyes, I tucked Titch into her sling, zipped up my coat and set off.

The weather today was considerably drier. The forecast was better too. Good. Today was set to be a tough day, as I was booked into a hotel in Tavistock and getting there would involve over fifty miles of tough cycling.

As I headed up Great Torrington's High Street, I had a good feeling. Everything seemed in place for a smooth day ahead.

How wrong I would turn out to be.

12

Allez Tony! Allez Titch!

'**Y**ou sodding, sodding thing!'

I'd only been back on the Tarka Trail for five minutes when the battery on the bike had completely cut out again. As usual, I was doing my best to solve the problem by shouting at the bike. It was a method that has never, and never will, work. Nonetheless, I continued.

'You're a bastard battery! Bastard, bastard battery! You've been charging up all night, so what possible reason could you have for not working??!!'

No answer was given. Presumably because the battery was out of power.

I resorted to a tactic that I use whenever anything technological fails on me and, given its absurd simplicity, is surprisingly successful. I turned the battery off, and then back on again.

It worked.

Seconds later we were back on the road (or rather trail) again, and I was feeling rather sheepish about the way I'd spoken to the battery. I had overreacted and there had been no need for the shouting. The full power of the electric 'pedal assist' was sweeping us forward at a good pace towards a walker in the distance with two large dogs.

Despite ringing the bell on my bike, the walker made no attempt to move to one side of the trail and to gather in his pets. As a result, I had to slam on the brakes and I lost all momentum. The bearded, long-haired man, who was younger than I would have expected to see out walking at this time, apologised profusely.

'I'm so sorry, I didn't hear you.'

'Don't worry,' I replied, as I wobbled past, nearly all of the valuable speed lost.

Momentum is a precious thing on a bike. No wonder town cyclists hurtle through red lights on pedestrian crossings, carefully steering their way around the walkers, only to be chastised with an admonishing:

'Can't you see that's a red light?!'

In our life on the streets, we humans readily join clubs. On foot, we're pedestrians. On bikes, we're cyclists. In cars, we're drivers. It's important for each group to hate the other and to consider them idiots. This is the way things work, and it's best not to meddle with it. Such is our schizophrenic nature, even when we switch clubs (as we do regularly, the cyclist becoming a pedestrian once dismounted), we instantly align ourselves with the bigoted views of the new club.

I was currently pissed off with pedestrians, especially when I realised that the power in the battery had cut out again. Whatever had happened during the deceleration required to pass the man and his dogs, this had been enough to upset the fragile temperament of my bike battery. It was behaving like it was hung over. Had it been on charge overnight? Or had it been out drinking in Great Torrington with Derek and his educationalist mates?

Feeling the heavy weight of the bike in my already aching legs, I let it drag to a halt, and I dismounted. I began fiddling with different cables in a hopelessly uninformed way. Once again, I opted for the sophisticated 'turning off and on' method, as used by NASA and air-traffic-control technicians. But I didn't leave it at that. I crossed my fingers, too. No point in leaving a job half-done. I was just about to swing my tired leg back over the saddle and test the efficacy of the process, when a voice interrupted me:

'I'm terribly sorry about that, I really caused you to lose momentum there.'

The bearded, long-haired, dog-walking pedestrian had caught me up, and was now displaying a surprising understanding of cyclists. Not that it mattered anyway, as I'd dismounted now and could talk to him pedestrian to pedestrian. We chatted politely and he actually proved to be very helpful, especially when I played my trump card of revealing Titch. When I explained that I was supposed to do an interview with Radio Devon quite soon, and that there appeared to be no phone signal down here in this scenic valley, he introduced himself as Simeon and explained that he had a cafe a few miles further down the track.

'It's normally closed this time of year, but I've finished walking the dogs now, so I'll drive up there and open it up for you. You can make the call there.'

He then left the trail with his dogs, to get on with the job of opening up a cafe especially for me.

I should travel with a pig more often.

The NASA technology worked, and I made it to the

Yarde Orchard cafe and bunkhouse, as it billed itself, without further technical glitches. Simeon was waiting in the doorway of the wooden hut that appeared to be the cafe.

'Come on in, the coffee is brewing,' he said.

I was rather pleased now that he'd not heard my bicycle bell, causing us to meet on the trail. The Yarde Orchard was a cool place. Simeon explained that in spring and summer they host people who are doing the coast-to-coast trail, either putting them up in yurts, the bunkhouse, or in their own tents. I was pleased to learn that they provide freshly cooked breakfasts, using ingredients that are only sourced locally.

This has to be the future of the way we do things on this planet. Quite how we came up with an economic system where it is sometimes cheaper to buy something that has travelled from the other side of the world, than a product that has been produced around the corner, is baffling. We need to re-embrace concepts that have been far from the zeitgeist in the past fifty years. For example, we can celebrate the fact that *simple is good*, and *small is beautiful*. It's taken me long enough to wake up to this, but wake up to it I have. In the past, most of my selections in shops and supermarkets were based on price, without realising that the cheap product wasn't necessarily cheap at all, the cost was just hidden. You simply pay later, when the full cost of the environmental and social damage is totted up.

'Do you want a bacon sandwich?' asked Simeon.

I coughed and pointed to the small creature who was sniffing around beer bottles in the bar area.

'Oops,' said Simeon, with a smile, 'take your point.'

'All this talk of local ingredients might be making Titch nervous.'

'Quite agree. Toast?'

'Toast sounds more like it.'

Just like Paul from the Fremington Quay cafe the day before, Simeon had moved down to Devon to enjoy a life where nature and the outdoor life was prioritised. And just as with Paul, the benefits of this showed clearly in his face. Happy, open, stress-free.

'Where are you hoping to get to by tonight?' Simeon enquired.

'Tavistock, if I can.'

Simeon inhaled sharply, much as mechanics do when they're about to relay unwanted news regarding the state of your carburettor, or similar.

'That's quite ambitious.'

'The Bedford Hotel have offered me and Titch a complimentary room for the night, so we want to make it there.'

Raised eyebrows now.

'The Bedford? Lucky you. That's a very nice hotel.'

Simeon then directed me to the cafe's telephone and I got on with the job of updating my progress with Radio Devon. As I waited for a suitably anodyne piece of mid-morning radio music to finish – it was Simply Red's Mick Hucknall wanting to fall from the stars straight into his lover's arms, a reckless act if ever there was one – Simeon pottered in his kitchen and oversaw Titch's explorations behind the bar. When we went on air, Judi announced that we had already reached half of my fundraising target of £10,000, and she put out another appeal for donations. Simeon listened proudly, as I plugged his fine establishment. Then, interview over, he gave me some helpful hints on the best route to take from here (the trail divided in a couple of places), and by 10.30 a.m. Titch and I were on the road again. Revived, refreshed, rejuvenated.

* * *

Evidence of the storms that had raged during the night came in the form of a tree that had blown down and was blocking the trail. Passing it involved a lot of clambering and bike carrying, all of which disturbed Titch in her sling (she'd not yet settled from the recent excitement of beer-bottle foraging). Never mind, I was in such good spirits that I managed it all without even a hint of a 'tut' crossing my lips.

A return to verbal abuse of the bike came seconds later, though, when it became apparent that this loss in momentum had once again resulted in the battery packing up. This time, turning the battery off and then back on again didn't work its magic. Given this failure, I was keen to avoid what for me is usually the next stage – becoming tearful. Clearly there had to be some fault that was caused by the bike stopping and starting. Blessed with a mobile phone signal, I called Peter from the electric bike store. Unfortunately he wasn't there, but Luke, his young apprentice, talked me through some possible checks I could do, and suggested cleaning a few contact points on the bike where the electrics might have been effected by the extreme weather.

I knelt down beside the bike and got my hands dirty. Literally. One of the points that needed cleaning was behind the bike chain, and soon my hands were blackened with oil. Once peddling again, I learned that whatever I'd just done was effective enough to make the battery work on a kind of 'part-time' basis. It kicked in at times, and at others it flatly refused. There seemed to be no logical reason for its irrational behaviour. It just seemed to be *in a mood*.

With Titch now happily asleep in her sling, my legs laboured and edged us ever onwards. We passed through a small, sleepy village called Sheepwash. I assumed it had got its name from being the place where they used to wash the sheep. No doubt I would be cycling through Sheepshear next, and then Sheepshag – where I wouldn't be stopping for lunch and getting to know the locals. For about the fifth time on my travels, I cycled past an impressive-looking property called 'The Old Rectory'. I began to wonder why I'd never seen a building called 'The Young Rectory'. Or even 'The Middle-aged Rectory'. It seemed that for some reason no rectory construction had taken place in recent years. This raises an important question. Where are we housing our young rectors? Clearly some kind of rectory 'new-build' scheme is needed in the English countryside, and fast. But do we hear this debated in the British parliament? Is it any wonder that people are becoming disillusioned with our politicians?

It was right in front of the muddy entrance to a farm, a few miles outside a place called Hatherleigh, when the chain decided to come off the bike. Cyclists will know that this happens from time to time, for no apparent reason, but quite possibly in proportion to the number of red lights one has ignored in the previous fortnight. It's vengeance from the Greek god of sensible cycling, Cyclips.

I had jumped no red lights, and this act of retribution was therefore unjust and simply spiteful. Gods can be like that, though. It's their prerogative. It's what makes them god-like. If they were consistent and bound by the rules, they'd be far more like civil servants, and less likely to strike awe into our hearts.

Putting a bicycle chain back on requires manual dexterity and patience, neither of which has been granted to me in abundance. My first attempt didn't get off to a good start. I lifted the bike onto its built-in bike stand and then looked on as an untimely gust of wind meant that it immediately fell over. I lifted it back up again, noting that the tumble had dented one of the brake levers on the handlebars. For me, this is one of the most disappointing aspects of trying to do practical things myself – the fact that I so often make things worse, rather than better. Good intentions fail to convert into results. I hate having to admit this, but I am a hopeless liability, and there can be few tasks that expose this failing more efficiently than the one of having to put a bicycle chain back on.

On my hands and knees, I did my best. I grappled with the chain. I wrenched it. I gently manoeuvered it. I shoved it, guided it, forced it, eased it, twisted it, bent it, and then, when all else had failed, I shouted at it. My hands were black with oil. With each failed attempt, my spirits nose-dived. It began to rain. Consecutive gusts of wind blew the bike over three more times. A man who had been watching from a distance approached. He was dressed like a farmer, and given his current location, there was every reason to suspect that he was one.

Just as he drew near, Titch seemed to take this as a cue to

try and escape from the sling. Perhaps all my awkward movements had woken her, or maybe she needed a bathroom break. Whichever it was, she wanted out, and she wanted out now. Fearful that bringing Titch into contact with a real-life farmer, at the entrance to a real-life farm, would be in severe breach of the livestock movement orders to which I'd agreed, I supported Titch with my left hand and attempted to calm her.

'Problem?' said the rather stern-looking farmer, combining brevity and shrewdness in equal measure.

'Yes, I can't seem to get my bicycle chain back on,' I said, using the word 'seem' quite needlessly.

'Here,' said the man, falling to his knees and seizing the initiative.

'Thank you,' I said.

The man began grappling with the chain, much as I had done. Simultaneously, Titch redoubled her attempts to escape. I gripped her firmly, but couldn't prevent her from letting out a couple of protest snorts. The farmer immediately stopped and looked at me. I returned his gaze with a kind of apologetic look and patted my stomach, as if to explain away the noises as my own gaseous emissions. The farmer eyed me guardedly. Presumably, as someone who worked with livestock on a daily basis, he knew the difference between a pig and a fart. (It may well be one of the final tests they set you before you're admitted into the National Farmers' Union.) However unlikely, supposing that the noises were caused by a fart was still less of a jump than believing I had a pig stuffed inside my anorak, so the farmer shrugged and returned to the job in hand.

'There,' he said, pointing to a chain successfully back in

place, and completing an interaction with me in which he'd lavished all of three words.

'Thank you so much,' I said, as he idled off.

I felt a mixture of relief and irritation. It was splendid news that the chain was back on, but yet again exasperating that I had been unable to complete the task myself. I remounted the bike, feeling like a failure. The rain strengthened, and the battery decided that spasmodic working was now too much for it. The hill ahead looked daunting.

'Shit,' I said, accurately summing up the kind of day I was currently having.

I decided to try and make it to the next village or town and phone the bike shop. Reaching Tavistock before it got dark now seemed a distant prospect – a great shame, since I had been so looking forward to a night in a luxury hotel. The chance seemed to be gone to show Titch just how different this quality of accommodation can be to a sty.

I was extremely tired after an hour and a half of wheeling the bike up the hill to the small market town of Hatherleigh. I glanced at the map. I was still less than halfway to Plymouth, and yet only that morning, I'd announced on the radio that I would be arriving there at noon the next day. In less than twenty-four hours. I was hopelessly behind schedule.

I chose a small cafe in Hatherleigh's main drag. It was a mark both of the nature of this challenge, and the advancement in my years, that I was choosing cafes ahead of pubs as my points of refreshment. Alcohol and cycling don't mix terribly well. Over the last decade, I'd also become what hardened drinkers refer to as a *lightweight*. One drink and I'm tiddly, two and I'm sloshed, three and I have a hangover in the morning. It was a shame, because by and large I like the atmosphere of pubs, and although they are all geared up handsomely to cater for the non-drinker, ordering a pot of tea and a piece of cake still seems vaguely impolite. After all, they've gone to all that trouble of changing those kegs, choosing those wines, and refilling those upturned whisky and gin bottles.

They looked after me well in the incongruously named Cafe de Ville. The owner had heard about my antics with Titch on the radio, and complimentary soup and a roll were immediately forthcoming. Following this trip, it would take some time to get used to that old-fashioned notion of actually *paying for things*. The adulation of Titch followed from the dozen or so other cafe users shortly afterwards, just as soon as I unzipped my coat. Donations in fivers and tenners flowed thereafter. Well, I thought, the journey may not be going as planned, but the funds were still rolling in.

Peter in the bike shop sounded a little depressed. No doubt he'd lent me the bike so that I could sing its praises whenever I spoke on the radio and boost sales for his business.[1] So it was not the best of news for either of us that the damn thing had broken down.

'Stay where you are,' he said, 'I'm sending Luke out with a new battery and a load of tools. We'll get you back on the road in no time.'

The cafe emptied of diners, all wishing me and Titch well as they departed. Now the wait. Honiton to Hatherleigh was well over an hour's drive for young Luke, and sitting

---

1 AXcess Bikes, Honiton. Good bloke, Peter. Just don't buy the second-hand bike with the bent brake levers.

there alone, I felt like the forgotten ten-year-old I'd been so many times at 4 p.m. on weekdays in the 1970s. My dad, a self-employed builder, was supposed to pick me up after junior school, but so often work held him up. I would stand there, a forlorn figure, watching as each vehicle turned the corner and failed to be my dad's grey pick-up van. All around me, happy children were reunited with their lovely, loving mums, and whisked off for tea and *Blue Peter*. I waited. Yes, he always turned up, but the feeling that perhaps I'd been forgotten was never far away. Well, I was a big boy now, old enough to be Luke's dad, in fact, but I still felt that tinge of insecurity. Medicinal latte and chocolate cake came to the rescue. Complimentary, of course.

* * *

'I think yesterday's heavy rain got into the electrics somehow,' said Luke, once he'd checked the bike over. 'I've put a new battery on there, and you should be fine.'

The trouble was that it was now nearly 2.30 p.m. The brighter weather of the early morning had long gone. Rain clouds loomed overhead and the prospect of darkness engulfing the trail in ninety minutes or so seemed very real. It was still about thirty miles to Tavistock, and three-and-a-half hour's cycling on a normal bike. With a freshly charged battery performing well on its highest speed setting, and with me cycling my heart out, perhaps I could shave an hour off that time. That would leave me cycling the last hour in the dark. I searched both panniers at the rear of the bike for the front light that Peter had given me. It was nowhere to be found and had obviously fallen out, a consequence of my botched job of keeping the panniers secure with bungies.

'Crappy plastic zips!' I blurted.

Without a front light, cycling on an unlit trail would be impossible. Now I was faced with the pressing question of where Titch and I would sleep tonight. We had nothing else booked, and there didn't seem to be an awful lot marked on the map on the approaches to Tavistock. The rather cowardly option would be to play safe and find somewhere to stay in Okehampton, which was now only nine miles away. However, failing to press on further would leave a colossal task for the following morning to make Plymouth by midday. So I chose to continue without a real plan – almost in homage to the way I'd lived my entire life thus far.

The race against time was on.

Titch insisted on a wee break just outside Hatherleigh, which didn't help matters, but I did my disinfecting duty with due diligence.[2]

Both the bike and my legs performed well, as we negotiated the hilly country lanes outside Hatherleigh. An hour later, the trail then painstakingly criss-crossed us through the town of Okehampton, before we found ourselves close by the station and at the beginning of the Granite Way – an eleven-mile cycle path that runs along the north-west edge of the granite massif of Dartmoor.

'Good,' I said to myself, 'now we can nail it.'

Titch had other ideas. Just as I got up to my optimum speed, she began her wriggling escape act, and managed to

---

2 I think I'll use the last bit of that sentence as a vocal warm-up before shows in future.

free herself from the sling and into my coat. She'd recently had a wee. Could she now need a poo? I stopped and allowed her to wander about, but she showed no such inclination. However, when I went to pick her up so that we could continue on our way, she squeaked in protest. What was wrong? This was an extremely untimely moment for Titch to discover a rebellious quality. Then it came to me.

'Ah, you must be hungry!' I said.

Titch looked at me with a look – as close as a pig can get to saying: 'Of course I'm hungry, you idiot. What else do you expect me to be, if you don't feed me?'

Titch fairly demolished the carrot that I produced for her. And then another one after that. Poor thing had been hungry and had sat politely through me devouring a soup, roll and piece of cake, but she hadn't wanted to make a scene in the cafe.

'You really are a nice little pig,' I said, as I looked down on her, munching away.

Serious cycling then began in earnest. I tried to imagine that I was in the Tour de France – sleek, super-fit, and pumped full of performance-enhancing drugs (rather than cake). I imagined an enthusiastic crowd cheering us on.

Allez, Tony! Allez, Titch!

It worked. My thighs and calves combined in perfect harmony, as we crunched away the miles. We now had spectacular views over Dartmoor, up towards its highest point at 2,037 feet. The sun obliged by bursting through the clouds, combining with the rain to create a spectacular rainbow. We crossed the Meldon Viaduct, an impressive wrought-iron and cast-iron structure built by the Victorians, standing 150 feet above the wooded valley below. In other circumstances, I might have stopped to take in the breath-taking view. But not this afternoon. Every second of daylight was invaluable.

At the first opportunity, I left the trail and joined up with the road. It was getting harder to see, and with no front light, the possibility of riding into a bush or ditch was an alarmingly distinct one.

When we made it to Lydford, I was still harbouring some hope of being able to press on to Tavistock. A spotty youth, who was loitering unproductively at the village crossroads, comprehensively dampened those expectations.

'Is there a hotel in the village?' I asked.

'Yeah, I work there. The Castle Inn. Just down there on the right.'

'Thanks. By the way, how far is it to Tavistock?'

The lad dropped his head and shook it, as if I had just posed the hardest question he'd ever been asked.

'I don't know by miles. But it's forty-five minutes by car.'

My head dropped now, as if I'd just received the worst answer I'd ever been given to the hardest question that had ever been asked. I'd been sure that it was closer than I was now being told. From what this lad was saying, there was still a further two hours to cycle – at least.

A plaque in the entrance to the Castle Inn announced that it was built in 1550, which, by the 24-hour clock, was only fifteen minutes earlier than I was making my arrival. It was a cosy and charming bar. The kind that makes brash American tourists say, 'We just luurve your English pubs. They're so cute.'

The landlady was talking to four drinkers who were sitting on bar stools. The rest of the pub was empty, and yet it had the feel of being half-full. I was hoping that 'Titch magic' would work its spell. I would reveal Titch, a huge fuss would be made of us, and accommodation and a lovely evening meal would be immediately forthcoming.

It didn't happen that way. The revelation of Titch brought smiles, one vaguely humorous remark, and a £1 donation. Even when I explained about the fading light and my need for accommodation, there was no proposal of a bed for the night, not even as a guest paying the full rates. Perhaps the hotel part of the pub was closed at this time of the year. Even if it were open, stopping this early in a village of this size would make for a very long evening ahead. Either I could sit in my small hotel room − or drink in the pub. There didn't seem to be any other options. Six hours drinking in a bar would no doubt result in some stories, but would make arrival in Plymouth at noon the next day most improbable.

'How far is it to Tavistock?' I enquired.

'It's about nine miles,' said the landlady.

Nine miles? Surely nine miles wouldn't take forty-five minutes in a car? The boy at the crossroads was clearly an apprentice village idiot, placed there as part of his training. Nine miles was doable.

'I can take the roads all the way? Not cycle tracks?' I checked.

'Roads all the way. Bloody hilly roads, mind.'

'Thanks,' I said, making a hasty exit for the door.

Provided that my back light worked, Tavistock, and the prospect of a quality hotel, now seemed back on the cards.

'Yes!' I shouted. 'At last something is going right!'

The rear light illuminated on demand and I could now

be seen by any cars behind me. Better still, the clouds had lifted and the evening sky was clear – the twilight offering sufficient light for me to see the road ahead. All I had to do was continue doing what I'd been doing for the last two hours. Cycling my bloody heart out.

* * *

There may not have been a crowd to welcome me, but it still felt like a magnificent victory. I may not have been Bradley Wiggins or Chris Froome winning the Tour,[3] but as I locked my bike outside the Bedford Hotel, I felt like a champion. I'd beaten nobody, but I'd won a hell of a prize. A comfortable night in what appeared to be Tavistock's best hotel.

I reckon even without my current feelings of euphoria, I would have had a very high opinion of this hotel. Currently, I ranked it as the best hotel in the world. Built on the site of a Benedictine abbey that had been looted and dissolved by Henry VIII,[4] it was designed by Jeffry Wyatt, the same architect responsible for Windsor Castle. This hotel is

3 French readers look away. Oh no, too late. You've already read about the two consecutive British victories when there hasn't been a French winner for over thirty years. Sorry.

4 Henry VIII was a colourful figure – for some an overweight, misogynistic and bloody tyrant, for others a Renaissance king who was a scholar, played and composed music, and was a first-class hunter. For me, what's most impressive about him is this ability he had to dissolve monasteries and abbeys. Most of us live our lives occasionally dissolving an aspirin, and we leave it at that. Not so, Henry. He dissolved over 150 of these huge edifices. He didn't knock them down. He *dissolved* them. I don't think he gets enough credit for that.

castle-like, too, built with battlements in an austere grey stone.

Right now though, it couldn't have looked more welcoming.

At reception, I was met by a girl who had clearly had a hard day. She looked tired, and her manner was grumpy. She looked at me through dead eyes and made the phonetic sounds, 'Yes, can I help you?' but seemed to mean, 'Oh no, not another, what do *you* want?' Her manner changed when I gave my name.

'Tony Hawks?' she said, looking up at me. 'It says here that someone of your name is arriving with a pig. Is that right?'

'Yes, it is,' I said, with a smile.

Now it was party-trick time. It had worked before, but surely this was going to be its most severe test. Slowly, I unzipped my coat and revealed Titch to this poor exhausted girl. In an instant the look on her face transformed. A huge ear-to-ear grin wiped away the grimace, and she let out a loud 'Aaah' sound that caused her colleague to appear from the adjacent room, to see what the cause could be. She was then instantly struck in the same way and the sound was doubled. They both called out a name, barely able to contain their excitement.

'Simon! Simon! Come see! It's amazing.'

Simon turned out to be the hotel manager who had made the kind gesture of offering me and Titch a complimentary night at this fine establishment. He was far less excited than his junior staff members, but that wasn't difficult. Instead, he managed to explain some practicalities about the hotel, including where breakfast was served and most important of all, where the room was. The room! I simply couldn't wait to get to that room. I had been dreaming of a hot bath in a nice, comfortable room for most of the day, it had been what had driven me on through the exhaustion of the last hour.

I could still hear the receptionist's howls of delight as I headed up the corridor to my bedroom. The route to the room took me through a luxurious area where guests were having early-evening drinks. Titch's head was still visible, and one or two seemed to do a double take.

'Did that bloke have a pig in his jacket?'

'He can't have done. This is the Bedford Hotel.'

I threw open the door to our bedroom. The room was gorgeous.

'Yes!'

We had made it.

13

Mayflower Steps

Titch and I were so happy in this lap of luxury. I set her down, and she began her immediate faux-foraging as I checked out the bathroom. Perfect. A big corner bath. Better than I'd dared hope for.

Whilst the bath was running, I fed Titch, punched the air a few times, and set up my smartphone by the bath to play classical music. There was even some 'tranquillity' bath foam, which I tipped in for good measure. This was going to be pure relaxation.

And it was. As Titch snorted and sniffed around the main bedroom, I slid into the lovely, hot bath whilst the sounds of Beethoven's piano concerto in C minor filled the room, in a manner totally disproportionate to the size of the device that was emitting them. Five minutes later, I was as close to heaven as a man can be on earth. I was currently experiencing a feeling that is rare and special in life. I was getting absolutely everything I wanted. There was nothing I could add to this moment that could have improved it. I allowed my mind to drift off, soothed by the genius of Ludwig van B. Until disaster struck.

I was shaken by a sudden, deafening sound, and the water began convulsing and overwhelming me. The ground shook. It seemed impossible, and yet it was clear enough – we were experiencing an earthquake. In a state of panic, I reached for the side of the bath and attempted to haul myself out, but I slipped and fell, my head hitting the side of the bath. The sound continued, and everything was shaking.

I was still conscious. I opened my eyes and saw, through the steam-filled room, a red light was flashing in front of me. I looked up and noticed that the ceiling was still intact. The floor around the bath had also not collapsed. The sound and shaking carried on, but whatever had happened, I had escaped the worst of it. The epicentre, wherever that was, must have taken the brunt. I looked again at the mysterious red light, and I waved away the steam that was obscuring it. Three letters started to become visible. An S. Then I made out a P. A final letter – yes, A. What did that spell? It spelt SPA.

Ah. I felt a little silly. It hadn't been an earthquake. Of course not. Dartmoor is not known for them, after all. No, I was sitting in a spa bath which, for some inexplicable reason, seemed to be equipped with some kind of timer – meaning that it could erupt and frighten the living daylights out of a bather at any given moment. In this case, me. Perhaps a poorly paid maid exacted a kind of abstract and indiscriminate revenge on wealthy guests, by setting the timer after each clean of the room. Perhaps she was sitting at home now, smiling quietly to herself.

Maybe she also knew that the controls on this spa bath were utterly unfathomable. Whichever sequence of buttons I hit, and in whatever order, I was unable to turn this earthquake off. It raged on, in spite of my desperate button-pushing and howls of frustration.

'WHY DON'T THEY MAKE THINGS WITH SODDING ON-OFF BUTTONS ANYMORE?!!' I screamed.

Titch appeared at the door, displaying a kind of inquisitive look. She didn't have an eyebrow to raise, but had she been blessed with one, that's what she would have done with it.

'It's OK, Titch,' I said. 'It's the spa, not an earthquake.'

It had been a long day and clearly I was losing my grip on it. Not only had I imagined a cataclysmic event, but now I was needlessly reassuring a quite clearly undisturbed pig.

I didn't get out of the bath. No, my heart had been set on a half-hour bath, and a half-hour bath was what I was going to have. Yes, I had to suffer the ignominy of being shaken to my very core by the fierceness of the spa (the maverick maid had clearly put it on its highest setting), but I was not leaving. Yes, it was difficult to relax, such was the force of the aquatic assault that I was now undergoing, but I would not let the evil maid win. Instead, I would sit there, being shaken, pushed, bashed, battered and buffeted by this man-made mayhem. The perfect storm in a tub. Incredible to think that people pay extra for such a thing.

I left the bath a dazed man. If not a jibbering wreck, then not far off it. Instead of feeling tranquil, I felt like I'd been mugged – the only difference being that I still had my mobile phone.[1]

---

1   OK, and that I was naked. Only very zealous muggers steal the clothes off your back, too.

I lay on the bed in shock. To my left, I could see Titch looking up at me, longingly. She had probably never seen such comfort. A big double bed in a quality hotel. Would Titch ever have a chance of experiencing this again? Wouldn't she be returned to her sty as soon as she was back on the farm? How could I deny her this opportunity to experience a measure of luxurious comfort?

I leant down and lifted her onto the bed.

'Here, Titch,' I said, as she let out a little satisfied grunt, 'this is how the other half live.'

She examined the bed, sniffing every square inch, and I laid my weary head down in an effort to recover from a spa that had clearly been on its 'Niagara Falls' setting, and immediately I fell asleep.

An hour later, I woke to find Titch snuggled up by my side. Pigs like to keep warm, and in their natural habitat they would rest alongside each other to maximise bodily warmth. It was definitely a good feeling having this warm little pig at my side. I stroked her, amazed at how well we'd bonded as a team on this trip. A terrible thought then occurred to me. What if a maid had called on her evening round whilst I'd slept? They often do that in posh hotels – freshen up a room at the end of the day. What if she'd knocked on the door, received no reply, and opened the door to discover a man stark naked on the bed with a pig? Yes, publicity for this trip would help the fundraising, but not necessarily the kind that would surround that story. Sleeping naked with a pig is bad enough, but doing so with one that also happened to be under age would put me in a class of my own when it came to deranged perverts.

Titch was sleeping soundly, so I left her on the bed as I

dressed and headed out into town to grab a quick bite to eat. Tavistock appeared to be a nice market town, but I didn't see much of it – just the walk from the hotel to the pizza restaurant where, alas, yet another Christmas party also happened to be taking place. I dined alone, trying to fathom the nature of my adjacent revellers by using a combination of people-watching and eavesdropping. They were a docile young crowd, abstemious and sensible. A far cry from some of the festive rabble who had tormented me from time to time in London. In the mid-1990s, when I'd been making fairly regular appearances on TV, during the party season I used to avoid public transport, for fear of being recognised and then 'bothered'.

On one occasion at around 4 p.m., a full three weeks before Christmas Day, I figured that taking the tube home would be safe. To my great alarm, at Leicester Square, a huge party of inebriated office workers entered the train and shouted, jostled, and gave dreadful renditions of Christmas songs that were already dreadful enough before being submitted to this indiscriminate slaughter. I braced myself, closed my eyes, and hoped that I would be left alone if I gave the impression of being asleep.

No such luck. Soon I heard a rowdy male voice pipe up.

'Here, that bloke over there, isn't he off the telly?'

I'd been rumbled. Never mind, I could ride this out if I kept my eyes firmly closed.

'Where?' asked a screechy female.

'There. Opposite. I'm sure he's off the telly.'

'Which one?'

'The one who's pretending to be asleep.'

My heart sank. I was about to be ridiculed by this riotous

group, whilst being closely examined by the rest of the carriage, inwardly asking the question, *Is* he off the telly? *I* don't recognise him. There weren't many options open to me. I could hardly rise to my feet and declare at the top of my voice:

'LOOK, MATE, I'M NOT PRETENDING TO BE ASLEEP. I *AM* ASLEEP. SO KEEP IT DOWN, BECAUSE I DON'T WANT YOU TO WAKE ME!'

Actually, I could have said that and, in retrospect, I think it's precisely what I should have said. Instead, I just sat there meekly whilst the mouthy young man ridiculed my pretence at slumber and his mates had stabs at why I might look so familiar.

'IS HE A NEWSREADER?'

'NAH, HE'S THE BLOKE DOES THAT PROGRAMME ON ARCHAEOLOGY.'

'NAH, HE DOESN'T LOOK CLEVER ENOUGH.'

Five more stops. That's how much longer I had to endure this humiliation. And that's why I'm happy to earn my living from books and radio.

I allowed myself two large glasses of red wine to help wash down the excellent pizza. Why not? A luxurious room was awaiting me and that was worthy of celebration.

When I made it back to the hotel, Titch was asleep where I'd left her. I lifted the duvet and snuggled in next to her.

My life had come to this.

I was sharing my bed with a pig.

* * *

Nothing happened, honestly.

OK, I'll admit that I enjoyed it. Waking up and having

the cutest little pig lying next to me was not a horrible experience. However, I am greatly relieved to inform you that I didn't find it sexually arousing.[2] Titch was not eager to wake up and begin the day. There was the faintest of grunts where she acknowledged my presence and then she was straight back to sleep again.

At breakfast, a CD blasted more distasteful Christmas songs at me. The worst was 'Santa Claus is Coming to Town'. This song tells the story of a cruel man with a white beard, who knows if children are 'naughty or nice' and doles out presents to the good ones and ignores the rest. It's copied out of the Republican Party manifesto.

When I made it back to the room, the teenager was still asleep on my bed.

'Come on, Titch!' I announced. 'It's time to get up. Triumphal arrival in Plymouth in just a few hours.'

Two snorts by way of riposte. It was almost as if she didn't understand the magnitude of the day ahead. A phone call over breakfast had established that it wasn't going to be as much of a disappointing anticlimax as I'd envisioned. Being both incompetent and a bit lazy, I'd failed to organise – or get anyone else to organise – any kind of party or celebration for me and Titch in Plymouth. The regional TV

---

2   OK, I accept that if I had found it sexually arousing, then I wouldn't have admitted it here (the slim chance of a knighthood would have further dwindled). However, if Titch and I had embarked on any kind of sexual relationship (either with or without her consent), then I would simply have omitted this whole section. And I haven't done. So I'm innocent. See? Besides, I made a promise to myself many years ago that no matter how lonely I got – no livestock.

news people had been on the line, though, and they were going to meet us at the Mayflower Steps at midday, and film a nice interview. After that, I would take Titch on the train to Totnes, where Fran would meet me and we'd return Titch to Pennywell Farm. Yes, this was our last day together.

I tried not to think about it, as I prodded Titch and woke her from her deep and seemingly peaceful slumber. If possible, I wanted to leave the bedroom in the same state I'd found it. They'd been good to me at this hotel, and I didn't want Titch fouling the room and me having to scrub away at the carpet with my Defra disinfectant. Circumstantial evidence had provided me with the information that Titch liked to have a wee just as soon as she got up and, having processed this, I now had a brilliant idea. Why didn't I lift her straight into the bath?

'Come on, Titch,' I said, as I lifted her gently towards the bathroom, 'I promise not to put the spa on.'

Like all good ideas, it needed to be tried, and Titch seemed a little bemused. Her hooves had not been designed with baths in mind. Mud, yes – ceramic, no. Wet ceramic especially. The bath hadn't fully dried out from the previous night's trauma and Titch's little trotters slid and slipped. Momentarily she seemed like a tap dancer on speed. The clatter of her tiny hooves was complemented by some squeaks and snorts, but soon she settled and found her footing. To my amazement, she then placed her delicate derrière over the plughole and emptied her bladder.

'Way to go, Titch!' I said, desperately needing someone to high-five. 'You little beauty.'

Titch was toilet-trained and ready for high society. We just had to await the appropriate invitations.

The local press greeted us as we prepared for departure, and the hotel staff posed for a photo with Titch, myself, and the loaded bike outside the establishment's stately front entrance. I was then introduced to a man called Andy, perched on an impressive-looking mountain bike. He was the owner of Dartmoor Cycles and announced that he was going to escort me out of the town and onto Drake's Trail, the last leg of my epic adventure.

Francis Drake is big in this part of the world, and a large bronze statue of him welcomes visitors arriving to Tavistock from the west. Drake was born at a farm just up the road, and his vast and dubiously obtained fortunes had enabled him to purchase Buckland Abbey, eight miles away. Of course, he spent most of his time at sea, circumnavigating the globe and plundering treasure from Spanish vessels. I remember being taught at school that he was a hero. The word 'pirate' was never used, but I urge you to do a little research on him and you can decide what nomenclature is best suited – 'heroic pirate', perhaps? (Although it would depend how 'heroic' you considered slave trading to be.)

I'm pretty certain he had nothing to do with the 21-mile cycle and walking route that links Tavistock and Plymouth. He's simply lent it his name, posthumously, that's all. I'm not sure who organises this kind of stuff, but I'd like to let it be known that after my demise I'm prepared to lend my name to future projects with which I have had no connection whatsoever. Feel free to name rivers, seas, inventions, life-saving drugs, and new species of wildlife after me. It's a gesture that I'm quite happy to make.

The crisp morning had transformed itself into an unusually bright and sunny one by the time Andy, our personal guide, left me and Titch on the trail by the entrance to the Grenofen Tunnel. This former railway tunnel is 374 yards long and was built in 1859 by Brunel. In spite of having two very silly first names (neither Isambard nor Kingdom were on the list for us, if Fran gave birth to a boy), Brunel had to be the greatest of the Victorian engineers.

At the time of writing, I am the same age as Isambard was when he met an untimely death, after suffering a stroke aged just fifty-three. There are not many similarities between us, and I hope that age of death doesn't become one. I have concentrated less of my time on building railway lines and bridges, with the result that he has really trounced me in this domain. (I have built twenty-five fewer railway lines, and more than a hundred fewer bridges.) He also came quite a bit higher than me in a 2002 public television poll conducted by the BBC to select the '100 Greatest Britons'.[3] Brunel, however, lived his whole life failing to bond with fridges, Moldovan footballers and pigs in the same way that I have, and as a result he may well have considered his life a failure.

Not all of Brunel's work has survived. Not long after exiting the Grenofen Tunnel, we crossed the brand-new and extremely impressive Gem Bridge, a viaduct built to replace Brunel's effort, which had been so crap that they'd had to demolish it in the 1960s. Thereafter, the picturesque trail proceeded to lead us ever onwards through wooded river valleys and open moorland, where sheep and horses wandered freely. On occasions they had ambled

3 Brunel was placed second, behind Winston Churchill. Owing to an administrative error, I didn't feature.

onto the trail itself and required, in homage to Drake, circumnavigation.

Drake's Trail became the Plym Valley Trail and Plymouth drew ever closer. The sun shone, the bike performed well, Titch slept, and mile after mile, decorated by exquisite scenery, was completed. Everything was going well. Too well for me to feel comfortable. I am a positive person and not one who expects setbacks, but something inside me couldn't accept just how wonderfully things were progressing this morning.

The reason for this gentle but persistent anxiety made itself known to me when I stopped to open a gate, shortly after we'd passed through a town called Yelverton. I looked down at the rack on the back of the bike and, to my horror, I saw that my rucksack was not there.

'Oh no, Titch!' I cried out. 'The damn thing has fallen off. Bloody useless, shitty, ratchet strap!'

That morning, like every other morning, I had been unable to loosen the ratchet strap. That morning, like every other morning, I had wedged my rucksack under the intransigent, unreasonable and loathsome strap, and fixed it in place using the stretchy bungee cords. Evidently, this morning I had not made a good enough job of this. Result? Major setback.

What should I do? I could cycle back, retracing my path, and I would probably find the bag lying on the trail somewhere. However, I'd been cycling for over ninety minutes, and the bag could have fallen off quite soon after I'd left Tavistock. There was now less than an hour to go till the midday TV interview. The best option seemed to be to press on and hope that the bag was handed in. Quite where it would be handed in, and who by, remained a mystery. I alerted Radio Devon to my predicament and they kindly agreed to ask relevant Devonians to keep an eye out.

I continued cycling, my mind mainly preoccupied with trying to identify exactly what I'd put in that bag. The good news was that it was mostly clothes, all dispensable, and some of which Fran had been trying to get me to burden a charity shop with anyway. The not-so-good news was that the cash which people had been handing me along the way was in the front pocket. I wondered if there was anything in the bag that would identify me and help any finder to locate me. Sadly, I thought not.

'Shit!' I said, just as we hit the outskirts of Plymouth.

It had been a disgruntled curse, relating to the loss of the bag, but it also served as an apt description of our new surroundings. Flyovers, superstores, and industrial units were replacing the jewels of nature that had been on display for the last two hours. Man – ingenious, resourceful and industrious – had a gift for creating the ugly, something he demonstrates regularly on the fringes of cities and towns. The now somehow weary trail led us alongside the River Plym – no longer pretty, but grubby and functional – and towards the historic part of the city. It was here, I dared to hope, that a small TV crew was waiting expectantly.

I thought that I had allowed plenty of time for this final leg of my journey, but the drawn-out entrails of the city seemed to go on and on, and it was clear that I was up against the clock once more. Eager cycling, coupled with a well-performing bike, meant that I cycled into the area that I took to be my arrival point at 11.57 a.m. Pretty good timing.

Two men – one with a dog – applauded. A photographer waved, and a cameraman and colleague with a microphone gave me a thumbs up. This part of Plymouth looked decidedly different to what I'd seen so far. The old harbour had escaped the destruction of the Blitz and resembled a quaint and authentic fishing port. It could easily have been the film set of a period drama.

No drama today, however. Five men and a dog hailing the triumphant completion of a coast-to-coast cycle by man and pig. I unzipped my coat, revealed my cargo, and further polite and disjointed applause was elicited. Two passers-by, oblivious to the nature of our presence here, stopped and admired Titch.

'Where are the Mayflower Steps?' I asked the photographer, after he had introduced himself as a freelancer hired by the local rag.

'Right behind you.'

These steps are so called because they are believed to be the ones that the original Pilgrim Fathers descended, before setting sail for the body of land that has since become known as the United States of America. Religious dissenters, they were pious, pure and pissed off. I don't know a huge amount about them, but my guess is that they were keen to set up a community where 'going large' with burgers and fries was not an option.

They may have had limited success to start with, but the settlers who followed them engaged on a greed 'free for all' that has created the economic climate for the world's largest number of dollar billionaires,[4] not to mention the highest

4 442.

number of privately owned guns per capita. These Pilgrim Fathers were no doubt an austere bunch, and their daughters would have been incredibly difficult to 'get off with', but the simple values by which they had chosen to live would not have got their country to Number 2 in the shameful chart of the world's worst polluters, and then stubbornly refuse to do much about it.

Titch and I did our photos and chat for the media, whilst I simultaneously chomped on some fish and chips, kindly donated by a nearby establishment.

'Here, you must be hungry,' a girl in a Rockfish T-shirt had said, proffering a healthy portion of England's most famous seaside fare. 'Here's our donation to the cause.'

One of those wooden forks would have been good, but it wasn't part of the package. As a result I ate the fish and chips with my unwashed hands; the same hands that had been handling a pig all morning. Fran would have been appalled, being someone who sticks rigidly to conventional advice when it comes to food hygiene. I always defended my rather *laissez-faire* approach – currently peaking with this latest effort – by claiming that a certain exposure to germs helps build up our immune systems. I'd never really looked into the science, or indeed the validity of the claim, but the information was extremely useful in enabling me to defend a need to be something of a slob from time to time.

Needless to say, doctors and nurses don't handle pigs before treating patients, and this fact certainly adds strength to Fran's argument. On the other hand, I am still here – typing this – so I have survived. There. It's not always a bad thing to rebel against the conventional wisdom of the day. Next time you see a rather bossy 'Now wash your hands' sign in a bathroom, walk straight past it. Leave it five minutes and then wash them. Show them who's boss.

I was deeply grateful for the media presence. Not only did these interviews prevent a damp squib of a finale, but they ensured that Titch and I would be on TV in the front rooms of many a West Country home this evening, and in the papers on their breakfast tables in the morning. I just hoped that a few viewers and readers would dig deep and make a small donation. Moldova awaited.

The regional news crew finished their filming by getting me to cycle around Plymouth Hoe, with Titch hanging cheekily out of the sling, turning on her charm for the camera. This was the spot where, more than four hundred years before, Drake had nonchalantly finished his game of bowls before preparing to do battle with the Spanish Armada. This story is most probably apochryphal,[5] since there were no eyewitnesses, and the first written account of it was given thirty-seven years after the event.

I mean, why would you wait that long before jotting down a momentous event? For me, the worst offenders in this department have to be the writers of the gospels. Most scholars accept that they were written a good twenty or thirty years after the death of Jesus. Well, what were the great scribes of the day up to?

'Hey, Matthew, that was a cracking story, wasn't it?'

'What was?'

'Jesus's life. Overturning the tables of the money lenders, turning the water into wine and feeding the five thousand. Talk about drama. I bet you can't wait to write about that!'

---

5 Apocryphal is a word academics use instead of saying 'bollocks'.

'It's on my list. I'll get to it when I've finished "The History of the Pebble" and "Sandals – Leather's Great Prize."'

'I see. You're confident of getting all the facts right?'

'Facts, schmachts.' Pointing to his friend's feet. 'They're cracking sandals, where did you get them from?'

Suddenly, Titch and I were alone again. The camera kit had been packed away, warm goodbyes and wishes had been offered, and cars had been driven off. An ordinary weekday in Plymouth. I may have been on the hallowed turf of Drake's nonchalant bowls' game, but there was no sense of history now. No celebration lunch awaited us. Nosh had already been unceremoniously dispatched out of sheets of newspaper by my grubby, multitasking hands. The party was over and Plymouth City Council could stand down any staff that they had earmarked for clearing up the debris.

I successfully followed directions to the railway station, thus completing my last obligation on the pedalling front. I bought a ticket to Totnes, and made it to the platform with considerably more ease than when I'd set off earlier in the week. I was a veteran of pig travel now. I understood Titch, and she knew how to communicate to me. Quite what she thought I'd been up to every day was anybody's guess, but she'd grown to accept my need to pick her up, shove her in a sling, and cycle her about the country. Pigs, bright beasts though they are, probably don't grasp the concept of fundraising. Titch didn't need to know. She just went with the moment. She was Zen. She was mindfulness embodied. A cool little pig.

The train journey, unlike the two-wheeled extravaganza

that I had just completed, was swift and uneventful, and it was not a happy one. I knew that I would soon be saying goodbye to Titch. Buying her off Chris was not an option. He'd made it very clear from the outset that she was not for sale.

'She's too precious,' he'd explained. 'A pig with a lovely temperament like hers is very rare. We'll need to keep her for breeding.'

So it was definitely goodbye Titch. Lovely Titch. Sweet Titch. No longer would I be able to transform the mood in a room with the unzipping of my coat. Oh, I could try. But I'd need to be wearing one hell of a jumper.

Thinking about the missing bag was hurting, too, especially the loss of a fairly decent wedge of money that was meant for a far-off children's care centre.

'Bollocks,'[6] I mumbled under my breath, causing a nearby elderly lady to raise an eyebrow, and banish me from her list of passengers in the carriage with whom she was prepared to engage in eye contact.

The train pulled into Totnes station, and Titch and I made our way out to the car park.

'Tiiiiitch!' said Fran, as she rushed towards us.

Right at the very last minute, she remembered the conventional running order for greetings following time away from your partner and, quite properly, she kissed and hugged me first, before turning her attention to the piglet.

'How is she?'

---

6   This is something non-academics say, following three days of failing to understand how a ratchet strap works.

A look from me.

'I mean, how are you both?'

That's better.

'We're good, thanks.'

'Where's your bag?'

'I'll explain on the way to Pennywell Farm.'

The warm and comforting familiarity of Fran, the smells and touch of the van and the feel of 'normal' transport, all set to work on dissolving the memories of the week's events. Did I *really* do that? The flimsy nature of memory was under assault from the solid, unflinching, towering stature of the present. Had all that stuff *really* happened? My sense of time was skew-whiff. Posing for the photo with the staff from the Bedford Hotel seemed like something that had happened at the beginning of the week, not just a few hours ago. Collecting Titch and introducing her to our home, standing in Ilfracombe harbour and staring up at a statue of a pregnant woman with half of her belly exposed, getting down on my hands and knees and disinfecting the ground on which Titch had walked – these all seemed like things done months before.

As we arrived at the farm, my mobile phone rang. It was Radio Devon telling me that my bag had been located. A dog walker had found it by a gate and had carried it to a local shop. The kind owner of said shop – Richard, at the Corner Shop, Yelverton – had found in my bag a business card that I'd been given at the cafe in Fremington Quay. He'd called the number on the card and spoken to its owner, who must have guessed that the bag had been mine, and directed him to Radio Devon.

'Sorry, Fran, but we'll have to drive all the way back from

where I've just come. But it's worth it. There's a lot of money in that bag.'

* * *

Titch sat on my lap as Fran drove us back across Devon. Richard, kind Richard from the Corner Shop, had returned my bag and the fundraising money was all present and correct. As we left Yelverton and headed back across Devon once more, I began to see sections of route that I had cycled only that morning. Distant memories from a few hours ago. I stroked Titch and realised that this lovely, warm, little creature would be out of my life soon.

I've never liked goodbyes much. They rarely happen at a time that is ideal for all parties involved. Either the other party would prefer you to stay longer, or you would like to hang around but they're anxious to see the back of you. Finding the right words is hard. We may have to dance around the truth. 'Thanks so much for having me, I'll definitely be in touch if I'm passing this way again' could easily mean 'I'm glad I'm out of here. In any other circumstances I would have stayed elsewhere. Take a good look at me, because you'll never see me this close up again.' Equally, being on the receiving end of 'It's been an interesting visit, stay in touch' may mean 'You're hard work. Go. And please, limit any future communication to email. OK?'

There'd be no need to find the right words for Titch. She heard only sounds with no meaning, much like it is for us when we listen to a politician. The van pulled in to Pennywell Farm and I felt a tug in my heart. Titch. Little Titch. She'd be gone soon.

My little Titch.

We were welcomed warmly by a hearty Chris, who led us to Titch's pen, firing pig anecdotes at us, and keeping my mind from the sad moment that awaited us. Moments later, I was standing and holding Titch, ready to lower her into her sty and to reunite her with her two cousins. I cleared my throat, which for some reason had a little lump in it.

'So this is goodbye, Titch. You have to restart your life with pigs instead of humans. Let's see if you can stand it.'

And in she went. Her two considerably larger cousins immediately began jostling her, in a manner that looked less than welcoming.

'They'll bully her for a bit,' said Titch's lucky owner, Chris. 'They'll want to establish who is boss for a while.'

'Can I come visit her?'

'Yes, you can come visit. She's your special friend now.'

She was indeed. Just how special I didn't bother to say. It was none of Chris's business who I slept with.

14

What's In a Name?

My uncomfortable feelings about the Dartmoor National Park Planning Authority had been entirely justified. When we got back to the house, having returned Titch to the family fold, a letter awaited us giving notification that our planning application had been refused. This wasn't great news. We'd rather set our hearts on the new kitchen extension. Never mind. We consoled ourselves with two facts.

(1) We were only weeks away from an event that would put it all into perspective.

(2) We could appeal against the decision. This was what our architect advised, on the grounds that their objections were without foundation and they had failed to follow their own planning guidelines.

As it turned out, we had support amongst our community.

Every member of the local parish council wrote letters to the National Park in support of us, and many people in the village stopped to encourage us and tell tales of woe regarding their own failed planning applications. We may have been refused, but there was no point in getting angry or fed up about it. Life, like President Putin, is too short.

Unappealing a prospect though it was, we would appeal.

* * *

The rain continued to beat down throughout a brutally wet winter. Sod, the malevolent and spiteful God whom I first described in Chapter 3, had decided to make us suffer in return for the blissful hours of sunshine He had provided over the summer. High winds and driving rain did the job exceptionally. Inundation was what He chose for many. We were lucky enough to live at the top of a hill and our only discomfort, beyond many an unpleasant dash to the car, was the sound of brooks and streams running high as they gushed down to swell the rivers in the valley below. Surprisingly, the kale that we had attempted to grow in the summer and which had been decimated by the caterpillars, started to make a comeback. So there you have it – endless winter rain is better for kale than it is for those living on flood plains in Somerset.

As I re-emerged into village life, post-Titch, there was some excitement amongst the villagers who had followed my progress in the local media. 'Where's Titch?' was the most common question, just as 'Where's your fridge?' had been the most prevalent after I'd completed *Round Ireland With a Fridge*. It seems that people, deep philosophical beings that we are, need to know the whereabouts of things.

'I READ ABOUT YOU IN THE PAPER!' called Reg, at his customary volume that was, let us say, enthusiastic.

Reg lived with village hall committee member Ann, but

they were not a *couple*. As far as I understood it, 86-year-old Reg had formerly worked for Ann and her husband. When the husband had become terminally ill, he'd asked Reg to look after Ann once he had passed away, and that was what Reg had done. Ann and Reg lived like incredibly old student flatmates. I'd been popping round to their little farm (nobody seemed to be sure which one of them owned it) to buy eggs for quite a few months now and I'd always enjoyed our little exchanges, which often became extended over a cup of tea and biscuits. I'd grown to like the way Reg bellowed at you, as if you were the other side of the room.

'YOU GONNA TAKE MY TRACTOR OUT ON A FUNDRAISING TRIP?' he demanded.

Reg, like Ken, was a great lover of tractors. Men in the countryside seem to develop this trait, just as men in cities grow to like Porsches, or develop irrational loyalties to football clubs. Reg had renovated a 1960s' Zetor, a Czechoslovakian tractor, and he was inordinately proud of it. Having read about my antics with the pig, he now saw me as a man who would take on any challenge that was laid before him, and he wanted to see his tractor in the headlines after I'd driven it from Lands End to John O'Groats.

'I'm not sure that I'll have the time once the baby's born,' I pointed out.

Reg shot me a look that came straight out of the *Confirmed Bachelor's Handbook*. As a man who had never married, nor sired any offspring, I suspect that he couldn't comprehend why anyone would willingly subject themselves to such a fate. I hoped that in the years to come, I would be able to make a strong case in its favour. For the moment, I just felt like a man on parole awaiting a lengthy trial, the verdict of which was far from certain.

'WHAT WAS THAT PIG OF YOURS CALLED?' demanded Reg, changing the subject completely and, pleasingly, failing to make the more common enquiry as to its geographical location.

'Titch,' I replied.

'GOOD NAME!' he said, in a tone that suggested I needed his approval. 'GOOD NAME!'

Reg was right. Titch, of course, was an excellent name for the pig that I had just spent so much time with. It was a name that meant something, and most names don't. Not that Fran and I had any names lined up for our future progeny, and one of the problems with having chosen not to identify the sex of our baby was that we had to refer to the bump as 'it'.

'*It*'s due on the twenty-fourth of March.'

'*It*'s getting bigger.'

'*It*'s kicking.'

Given what we'd been told in one of the many books we were beginning to plough our way through, calling the baby 'it' could be detrimental. According to some American doctor with a lot of letters after his or her (or its) name, the baby can hear our voices long before it is born. Apparently we ought to be talking to, encouraging, and singing lullabies to our baby. So identifying our baby as 'it' might mean that 'it' would arrive in a grumpy sulk.

'Oh, you've given me a name *now*, have you? Why bother? Why not just carry on with the "it" business that I've had to endure for the last nine months? Don't mind me while I cry for four hours. It's called revenge.'

Not that we'd have been able to come up with a name, even if we'd known the sex. Naming a child, we were now discovering, was fraught with complications. There are all sorts of factors that we hadn't considered. For a start, when we parents name our child we make a statement about *us*. Calling a boy John, or a girl Sarah (perfectly nice names), might indicate that we're unimaginative or boring. Why? Because these are really common names, and there are hundreds of Johns and Sarahs already. However, going too far the other way and naming one's child after a fruit (Apple) or a country (India), then we might be declaring ourselves to be so unimaginative and boring that we need to give a clear signal to the world that this is exactly what we're not.

Of course, we don't have to pick the name from those available from our own cultural name pool. There's a boy's name that is quite popular in Spain and South America.

Jesus.

Was that an option if we had a boy, I wondered? Or would that be placing too much expectation on the lad? Seemingly not a problem for the Latinos to name their child after the alleged Son of God,[1] nor for our Muslim brothers to opt for their great spiritual leader, Muhammad.

The British, however, seem to be more literal. If you call your child Jesus, it must be because you either think your child is the Son of God, or that he's jolly similar. Undoubtedly he will be teased and bullied by his child-hood peers, and his inability to turn water into wine will

---

1 How did *He* come up with his son's name?

be heavily criticised during his student years. Not only that, the poor lad will never know when people are calling to him or not. Every time someone stubs a toe and exclaims 'Jesus!', he will come running over, only to be sworn at and sent packing. Deep emotional scarring. Best not to deliver that to a child simply by the choice of a name. There are so many other ways of achieving the same results, so no need to rush it.

Foreign names are fun, but most are synonymous with a particularly famous film or pop star from that country. Or a mad politician or dictator. (The name Adolf really fell in the popularity stakes in the 1940s and '50s.) And then again, do we really want to be seen to be naming our child *after* someone?

I certainly wasn't going to suggest to Fran that we went down the route often taken by Americans (one that they shamelessly stole from our royal families), of giving the child the same name as the father and then slapping a number at the end.

Oscar Hammerstein II

Loudon Wainwright III

Tony Hawks II

This name says more about the father than the mother. Presumably she has played little part in the name-choosing process. She may, at some early stage, have whimpered that she quite liked 'Daniel' or 'Sam', only to be shouted down by the tyrannical father, desperate to have his name and specialness prolonged on this earth. Another similar trick, and one that the kings and queens of England rejected, is just to whack a 'junior' at the end.

Sammy Davis Jr

George Bush Jr[2]

It says a lot about the male domination of society that this kind of thing is acceptable. The poor woman has already been asked to surrender her family name, but now she has been trounced again. 'Look, darling,' explains the father, 'never mind that you've carried this thing around in your belly for nine months and heroically endured the physical challenges of childbirth, we're giving it *my* name, OK? Good. Thought you wouldn't mind.'

Our former Chancellor of the Exchequer Nigel Lawson must have been tempted to run with Nigel Lawson II for his first son, but I imagine he recognised this as an American fad with which he wasn't comfortable. The perfectly acceptable name of Dominic was picked. However, he rather let himself down when his first daughter was born two years later. The name Nigella was chosen. *Nigella* is a genus of about fourteen species of annual plants in the buttercup family Ranunculaceae, native to southern Europe, north Africa, and south and south-west Asia. It's not a recognised girls' name. OK, Daisy, Rose, Lily, Iris and Jasmine are all names derived from flowers – but they are flowers with which we are familiar. Did Nigel really name his daughter Nigella because he loved the flower and thought she was just as pretty? Or did he go for it because it sounded quite like Nigel? Which just happened to be his name. I don't know. But given that I've never liked his politics, or his quite

---

2   Rather disappointingly Brunel went for this, too, calling his first born Isambard Brunel Junior. (Were the son still alive he could claim that Isambard Brunel Junior School in Portsmouth was named after him and not his dad. If he could be arsed.)

irresponsible climate change scepticism, I'm quite prepared
to hazard an ungenerous guess.

Fran and I developed a new game of batting names
around over dinner every evening. We came up with very
few that were acceptable to both of us. One of the main
problems seemed to be that the name, however much we
both liked it, nearly always had some unpleasant connotation for one of us. It had been either the name of a rotten
teacher, a child who had once bullied us, or someone who
had jilted me or made fun of Fran's dresses. So few names
were free of a negative connection to the past. Even if they
were the names of people you liked, there could be a
problem, too, as the unreasonable thought popped into
your head – what if they became too opinionated?

'Ah, Fran and Tony must think so much of me to name
their child after *me*.'

Of course, there was the option of avoiding this pitfall
by just making a name up. Names, well they are only
sounds, after all. 'Mark' is a sound. Why not reverse the
sound and call your child 'Kram'. Mitt Romney's parents
did that with 'Tim'. Or what about simply rearranging the
letters of the existing name that seems to most suit your
child, thus preserving a notion of individuality?

So 'Simon' becomes 'Somin' or 'Smoin', and 'Jane'
becomes 'Jena' or 'Naje'.

No doubt this method was what resulted in the invention
of the name Cnut. Presumably by some parents who didn't
exactly think the world of their new offspring.

The idea of inventing a name did appeal. The problem
was the kind of names I kept making up. They just didn't
sound right:

Spettle
Ignomia
Egremont
Egremona
Earnley
Thelft
Scarnley
Higlia
Groil
Prinkear
Grindel
Trime

The most frustrating thing is that even though these names are patently ridiculous, there will always be someone who'll like one of them.

'Skedge? What a nice name.'

'Fleem? Lovely. So imaginative.'

* * *

Relatives aren't helpful during the naming process either, and soliciting their help is unadvisable, because it will give them early grounds for feeling rejected. Given how often one is politely going to rebuff their child-rearing sugges-tions in the future, there's no point in getting the ball rolling before the little thing has even popped out. Fran's relatives, on the male side, seemed to be drawn to rather grand names with connections to greatness. Horatio and Spartacus were suggested. Thankfully, no ideas for girls' names were forth-coming. Fran's mum did suggest 'Organia', but we think this was more of a dig at our penchant for buying organic food, rather than a real suggestion.

'Organia? Nice name,' said someone, though, I forget who.

A name, no matter what it is, will always be liked by someone. One of Fran's friends even liked 'Isambard'.

Separating ego from the naming process is impossible. When we name our child, we make a statement about ourselves, just as we do when we decide on our haircut, what clothes we pull on, and which car we drive. What do all these things *say* about us? And why do we *care*? And even if we don't care, what does *that* say about us?

Put simply, naming your child is a nightmare. Such a nightmare, in fact, that there was a part of me that just wanted to call the baby *Child One*. The Spanish name 'Juan' almost allows you to get away with this.

Juan.

If you don't go for the ridiculous guttural, gobbing sound that the Spanish employ with Js (just showing off), then it's near as dammit 'One'. If it turned out to be a boy, then that was my current favourite. If we ever have a second, then we'd have to call it Two, but we'd need to be innovative with the spelling. We'd need to make stuff up, claiming that it was the Vietnamese name 'Tooh', meaning 'beautiful waterfall' (who is going to check?); or spell it 'Tout', the French word for everything – because our child means everything to us. We could provide sick bags for people when we explained it to them.

Florence Nightingale's parents had an interesting system. They named their children after the places where they were born. Florence was named after the great Tuscan city of her birth. Her sister wasn't so lucky – she was named Parthenope, after Parthenopolis, the Greek settlement in Naples where she popped out. Their brother got the really raw deal though, born in a little village in Worcestershire. I guess that's why we hear so little about poor Bell End Nightingale.[3]

* * *

Preparation for birth became more of a talking point in our house, partly because my publishers had sent me every book that they'd ever printed on the subject. Certainly for something that ought to be as natural as natural things come (I mean hadn't we been giving birth for tens of thousands of years?[4]), there seemed to be a lot of varying methodologies on offer.

The approach that we were to end up following turned out to be governed by Fran's decision to attend 'pregnancy yoga' classes, and it was through conversations with her teachers that she began to learn about 'natural childbirth'.

Natural childbirth. It's odd that such a name should even exist, implying as it does that childbirth could be *un*natural. However, exist it does, and it advocates that an adequately prepared woman can give birth at home, without routine medical interventions.

---

3   One of those three facts was made up. Can you guess which one?
4   Far fewer years than this, if you happen to be a creationist. According to Genesis (the book, not the band), Man popped up much later than this – after Adam and Eve had done some top-drawer sinning. Quite how the rest of us were 'begot' without some serious incest going on, is not explained. However, given that we're also told that Adam lived for 930 years, we may have some grounds to question the scientific credulity of these details anyway.

'What is "adequately prepared"?' I asked Fran, as we discussed the matter over dinner one night.

'I'm not certain, but we'll both find out at the birthing class I've booked us on.'

'Ah yes. Forgot about that,' I said. 'Perhaps I'll read around the subject a bit before we go. Don't want to show myself up.'

So it was that I started to read fervently about childbirth. My father's generation would have frowned upon this interfering approach. Birthing was ladies' business and men should stay out of it. Indeed, that used to be the way in years gone by. Men didn't really start to get in on the birthing act until religion urged them to do so. According to many a scholar who has done far more research on the subject than I have, in the Middle Ages midwives were singled out as witches by the patriarchal society and Roman Catholic Church, because these women had immense influence in the community. Influence that they wanted to usurp.

This was exactly what happened to those poor lasses in Bideford in 1682. They'd been delivering babies using natural remedies, and without any help from men, so they'd had to pay for it. The priests wanted to be around at births, in order to be on hand to nab the souls of the newborns before anyone else got in there. Slowly, a naturally female domain was permeated.[5]

The infiltration continued with the medicalisation of

5   The fact that religious men could quote the following from Genesis 3:16 can't have helped the women's cause: 'To the woman He said, "I will greatly increase your pains in childbearing; with pain you will give birth to children. Your desire will be for your husband, and he will rule over you."'

birth. Medical technology has moved on greatly, and let's face it, for the most part this has been a good thing. Maternal mortality fell substantially during the twentieth century. However, obstetricians have increasingly taken over responsibility for normal births, in addition to their involvement in complicated births, especially in parts of the world with thriving private practice. (Surely they're not intervening because this is where greater profit lies?) Intervention has become the norm, and there is increasing evidence that each intervention, though solving one problem, actually *causes* another.

The fear factor plays a big role in this, too. The NHS in the United Kingdom faces such a huge bill each year for medical negligence that it is reasonable to ask whether professionals are encouraged to act 'defensively' (particularly as 70 per cent of litigation is involved with obstetrics). Most obstetric cases are connected with labour-ward practice, and 99 per cent of these relate to 'failure to intervene' or 'delay in intervention'. The Scandinavian countries and the Netherlands, who did not follow the trend towards steep increases in Caesarean sections during the 1990s, have a tradition of perceiving birth, above all, as a normal physiological process, and of valuing low intervention rates.

Ah, the Dutch and the Scandinavians. They're so cool. So often do I end up citing their practices when arguing for a sensible, calm, and yet still courageous approach to social policy. They don't overreact. They look at the facts, and they decide on the best thing to do. Then they *trust* in it. One wonders if the *Daily Mail* were on sale in Scandinavia whether it would sell any copies.

At the end of my period of extensive reading on the subject, I offered my conclusion to Fran.

'I think *trust* is the issue.'

'How do you mean?'

'We need to trust in your body and in our baby's ability to negotiate his or her way out of it.'

Clearly, I had become a complete hippy. I could imagine the peels of deriding laughter were I ever to express these views in any public forum. For now, however, this was my position. Perhaps I'd change my mind after Karin's home birth preparation course, and after I'd been made familiar with every last detail of what was involved in getting the baby from womb to world.

Things kicked off with everyone introducing themselves and outlining why they were there. An awkwardness permeated the air, but a certain amount of ice was being broken. The other two couples did a pretty good job of explaining how they'd learned that a home birth can make for a very positive start to a child's life, and why they wanted to learn more today. I was last to go, just after Fran, so I had a bit of time to think about what I was going to say.

'There's been some terrible mistake,' I said, when it was finally my go. 'I thought this was going to be a discussion about football.'

It had been a risk – attempting to inject some humour into proceedings, but there was just enough laughter, albeit of the nervous variety, for it not to have been an embarrassing blunder.

'No, seriously,' I continued, 'I'm here with Fran for us to find out whether a home birth will be right for us.'

The use of 'No, seriously' is rarely a sign of supreme

confidence in either oneself, or one's audience. It marks a belief that the listener is so out of touch with your humour that they need instruction as to when it is being implemented, otherwise how will they know that everything you say isn't an attempt at being funny? Thus, your serious comments need flagging up. Another example of this is the expression, 'Just kidding', which I've noticed Americans like to use a lot. Instead of saying, 'Just kidding', I think it would be more honest if people said, 'I've misjudged my attempt at a witty quip so badly, it's not clear that what I said was meant in jest, unless I immediately identify it as such with a short statement herewith.' It's not as punchy, granted, but it's somehow more honourable. Americans are also big fans of declaring, 'That's funny!' at great volume. What I don't understand is why, instead of doing this, they don't just *laugh*. I think you'll find that's the correct procedure.

If this had been the Middle Ages, then Karin – our delightful and gentle teacher of this active birthing class – would have been rounded up and floated or drowned until either her guilt or death was established. During the course of the day, she talked us through what happens when a woman gives birth. Doesn't sound very heretical, does it? We were shown how the baby navigates its way out of the body, going into clever little turns at opportune moments, to accommodate the fact that its head is rather large for the task in hand.[6]

We learned about the different stages of labour, nature's

---

6   If at any point I get too technical for you, just stop reading and have a bit of a lie-down.

way of pushing the baby down through the cervix and deeper into the pelvis. We discovered that oxytocin and endorphins are produced by the body to ease this process, and how adrenalin – the body's chemical that puts us in fight or flight mode – can be an enemy of the process, if it arrives too early on the scene. The adrenalin is required for the final stages, when the body needs to be readying for birth. Until that stage, being relaxed and calm is what really helps the process along.

A thought occurred to me. When does being relaxed and calm *not* help us? Well, maybe when we're in extreme danger, which is exactly the time that the adrenalin in our bodies kicks in naturally and shuts down the thought processes, leaving us to work on instinct. It overrides our other feelings. (No one is depressed when they are running away from a bear. Although I am not advocating this as a form of treatment. Tempting though it might be in some cases.)

But how often in our life are we in extreme danger? And how often are we calm and relaxed? In one of the tea breaks, I took a moment to wander away from the others and ponder this subject. For just how much of my life was I relaxed and calm? Was I actually relaxed and calm at this moment, here at this class, drinking this nice cup of tea? Probably not. All this information about what Fran would soon have to go through was challenging. If it was challenging for me, then what would it feel like for her?

How calm and relaxed am I now as I write these words? I suspect not as calm and relaxed as I could be. Maybe there's some anxiety about whether I'll deliver the book on time. Some concern about whether people will like it. Perhaps I'm anxious that there will shortly be some spelling mistakes and that the proofreader of the book won't spit them?

I decided, as I washed up my cup and then headed back into the class, that it's the mind – the great controller – that we need to master, whether we're rewiring a plug, commanding an army, or giving birth. The mind controls the body, and the body, most of the time, does as it's told. Except now, when for no reason it has typed the words tit and cock.[7]

It became clear that I was to be Fran's birthing partner in all this. This meant that I would be on hand to provide water, snacks, massages, and loving encouragement during the labour. One particularly tricky point was going to be 'transition'. This is the point when the adrenalin kicks in for the expectant mother. By all accounts, it's a frightening time for her and she commonly announces that she 'cannot do this anymore', or that she needs painkillers. She'd need helping though this challenging stage. In order to do this, I'd been given a very complex brief, the gist of which seemed to be:

When 'transition' happens, try to find the right words to comfort and soothe your partner even though with every word you utter, she will try to kill you.

Hmm. That was going to be fun.

'I'd like to try hypnobirthing,' said Fran as we drove home, our heads brimming with birth info.

'Really. What's that?'

'I heard about it at pregnancy yoga class. It teaches you

---

7 It could have been worse, it could have been in capitals. That will only happen when, for some reason, I'm anything but calm and relaxed.

techniques that can help you through the challenging stages of labour.'

'Sounds great.'

I was up for anything that would protect me from having a knife driven through my chest during the birthing process.

'You'll be fine,' I added. 'I'm completely relaxed about this "transition" business. Together we'll crack it, no worries.'

TIT AND COCK.

15

All the Sixes, 666

'I'm going down to Reg's in the tractor, wanna come?' asked Ken, after I'd popped round to borrow a tool and ask for some advice.

I did this on an impertinently regular basis, knowing that nine times out of ten, Ken would simply come round and do the job himself, rather than allow me to flail around with dangerous devices or utensils.

'Reg wants to see my Massey[1],' he continued, 'and it's a lovely day, so I thought I'd take it down there.'

It was indeed a wonderful spring day, the kind where you dared to tempt fate and announce that the winter was behind you. Too many times had I done this over the years, only to be battered by hail and sleet at Easter.

'Yes, I'm up for that,' I replied keenly. 'I've never been on a tractor before.'

Up until this point in my life, tractors had simply been annoying things encountered on country roads that you didn't want to get stuck behind. They were slow and noisy

---

1 Massey Ferguson. Ken was lucky enough to be on first-name terms.

vehicles that needlessly moved hay around the place, depositing a good proportion of it on the road around them as they dawdled along. The tractor was a vehicle I had come to associate with a sigh. Perhaps this morning would provide an opportunity for me to change this not-altogether rounded view of them.

It was a tight squeeze in the cab. It had not been designed for two people and I had to wedge myself in behind Ken's seat in an uncomfortable compromise between squatting and standing. Ken fired up the engine and smiled in satisfaction in a way that could only be done by a man who had rebuilt that very same engine. I smiled too. The engine sounded good to me. Well, loud. It sounded loud to me, and I figured that had to be good. You don't want a tractor with a quiet engine. You're not going to win anyone's respect that way.

Reg lived about a mile and a half away, at the bottom of a hill on the other side of the village. The advantage of being up in the tractor's cab was that as we slowly progressed down the road, I could now see over the hedgerows and, for the first time, I was seeing into the land of properties that I'd never noticed before. Ken gave me the full history of who lived where, and who had been their various colourful predecessors. I was surprised to learn that he had an elder brother who lived alone in a cabin, recluse-like, on a plot of land less than half a mile from Ken's.

'Brother Tom keeps himself to himself,' said Ken. 'We don't see him much, but when we do we get on well enough.'

'Did Brother Tom ever marry?'

'No.'

A beat.

'He's got a son though.'

We arrived at Reg's before I had time to ask further questions about Brother Tom's backstory and he looked set to remain the mystery figure who lived at the end of a narrow trail, in a cabin overrun by shrubbery. The type who might fascinate and frighten children in equal measure.

Reg waved us into his farm and indicated to Ken where to park. I struggled out of the tractor cab as Reg admired the Massey. There followed some lengthy conversation between the two enthusiasts about the gearbox and the steering console, in which I chose not to participate. A similar pattern followed as we moved into Reg's barn-cum-workshop and began to study his four-wheel-drive Zetor. This was not my domain. I felt as 'at home' here, surrounded by machinery and farm paraphernalia, as Ken and Reg would have been in a voice-over booth in a Soho recording studio. (Indeed, Reg would have damaged the eardrums of the sound engineer bellowing into the microphone.)

I made a mental note that most of this equipment around me ran on oil. Most of that oil came from the Middle East, certainly not locally. It was transported in tankers that used oil. All of it coughed carbon into the atmosphere. All of us, like it or not, are caught in a carbon trap. Unless we live like a hermit and don't engage in society we pretty much have to emit it.[2]

'YOU'RE GOING TO DRIVE THIS TRACTOR FROM JOHN O'GROATS TO LANDS END!' Reg bellowed to me from a few feet away, pointing to his beloved Zetor.

---

2   Maybe this guy has the right idea: http://opensourceecology.org/wiki/TED_Talk

'We'll see about that,' I replied, careful not to commit. 'What's that attached to the back of your tractor?'

'IT'S A WELDER.'

My brief inclusion in the conversation was abruptly halted as the discussion turned to whether the MIG welders were better than this one. Holding no strong views on this, I slipped away and studied the hens – the ones who had provided Fran and me with many a boiled egg and omelette. They strutted confidently around the place, pecking, clucking and generally fidgeting. Only one of them looked up at me.

'Thanks for all the eggs,' I said.

The hen looked back at me with an expression as blank as mine had been during the MIG welder dialogue.

I made a quiet note to myself to stop talking to hens.

* * *

'See that cottage there?' Ken announced, as we headed back up the hill, the tractor 'love-in' now a thing of the recent past. 'That's where we used to live. I lived there until I was eight years old.'

'Were you born there?'

'Yes, I was. It was a cold February day. Snow was on the ground when my mother went into labour and my father had to walk to the next village to get the nurse. By the time he and the nurse made it back, my mother had given birth to me.'

'Wow. No help?'

'No help at all. Not unless you count my three-year-old brother.'

This was rather encouraging. Perhaps it was something I could throw back at future dissenters when we explained about our plans for a home birth. So often, the explanation of our birth plan had elicited a sharp intake of breath and a slow deliberate shaking of the head, as if to indicate that this choice was equivalent to driving a car without brakes. The prevailing opinion seemed to require thousands of years of history to stand aside and make way for the careering juggernaut of medical intervention. Ken, how-ever, had made it into the world without an obstetrician, a doctor, a midwife, or even a plumber.[3] And he'd come out all right. He'd even gone on to rebuild a tractor engine.

'That cottage had no electricity or mains water,' said Ken, almost with pride.

'How did you manage?'

'We got our water from a well, and we used a Tilley par-affin gas lamp.'

'How was it?'

'It was absolutely fine. It was all we knew, so we just got on with it.'

I considered all the devices we had in our kitchen. A few hours without the power that we took for granted and our world would begin to fall apart.

It was quite possible that in the future we humans might need to live by a new slogan. Tragically, it currently didn't sound like one that would win any general elections.

Have a little bit less and enjoy it a whole lot more.

* * *

3   They're always late.

'The trouble is that George doesn't want to do the calling anymore,' Rose explained. 'He says he's too old.'

The occasion was our third village hall committee meeting. We'd already sorted out some pressing bureaucratic matters regarding the shift in power from the old committee to this one, and the new committee's feet were very much under the trestle table. We were discussing item four on the agenda, the idea of reintroducing an event that had previously been a success – Meat Bingo. At first, I'd heard 'Meet Bingo' and I'd begun to wonder if this was a kind of dating night where people could be paired off according to what numbers coincided on their cards. But no, it turned out that it was simply bingo in which you could win a joint of meat instead of other prizes. My thought was, if we're going to have bingo evenings where the prize is specific, then why stop at Meat Bingo? We could have Petrol Bingo. Salt Bingo. Insulating Tape Bingo. But all in good time. These would have to be suggestions that I'd propose when my stranglehold on power was more complete.

'Oh. That's a shame to lose George,' said Mary. 'He was a good caller. We'll need to find someone else.'

There followed a hideous silence where I felt the weight of expectation around the table. I held off for as long as I could. Finally, it all proved too much for me.

'Well, I suppose I could do it,' I said, begrudgingly.

I am not a big fan of bingo. I'd played it once before in France, and even with a different language and the challenges which that brought, I'd still found it to be an incredibly tedious evening. Perhaps, I mused as the discussions turned to finalising the arrangements, that actually *calling* the bingo would make it a more enjoyable evening all round. A chance for the performer in me to shine.

'OK. Item five,' I announced in my best Mr Chairman voice. 'Trying to get more people up to the village hall who never normally come to events.'

'Could we distribute leaflets letting them all know what's on?' suggested Brenda.

'Good idea.'

It was decided that we would share the task and each committee member would leaflet different areas of the village. I figured that this would be a good way to get to know new people, because as well as passing on the information about the village hall, it could be a kind of cold calling for friendship. Facebook on foot.

In reality, I didn't do most of it on foot. I decided to do the more remote houses by car, after I'd delivered to my immediate neighbours. Two doors along, I met Alf. Actually I didn't meet him, we'd met briefly once before, as he reminded me, when he'd delivered the local parish magazine to our door. His recollection of this, and my failure to do so, might have been easier to bear if Alf had not been ninety-three years old. Like a lot of very old people do, he dropped the revelation of his age quite early on in our conversation.

'Wow, you look fantastic on it,' I said.

This was not a routine, sycophantic remark. I really meant it. Alf was the finest example of a 93-year-old man that I had ever laid eyes on. In conversation, too, he proved that his faculties were all there, and we'd already established that his memory was working better than mine. He attributed his good health to country air, nice views, and not getting too worked up about anything.

'Regarding the bingo,' he said, 'Vera and I don't get out as much as we used to, but I applaud what you're doing at the village hall and we'll try and get up there.'

Impressive stuff. Now I had something to which I could aspire. Given that I was about to enter fatherhood at a more senior age than most, it would be my duty to try and emulate Alf. So, encouraged by the uplifting chat with my Peter Pan neighbour, I jumped in the car in order to reach the houses that were located at the end of a long, bumpy lane. Everything started well enough. Nobody was in at the first two houses, so I stuffed the leaflets in the front doors. At the next two stops, people were at home and I was able to introduce myself as a neighbour, explain my new role, and engage in a positive conversation about the village hall and its potential to bring people together. I felt rather buoyed by the positive responses. The bumpy road then became ridden with potholes, and the required driving was suddenly a far cry from the city action for which my car was designed.

I pulled into the drive of a farm, parked up, and saw Sam – the guy who'd had a cup of tea with us after the 'sheep in the garden' incident. He immediately came over and invited me in for a reciprocal cup. I said yes, partly because I didn't want to say no, and partly because I was due a break, having been on this arduous task now for a full ten minutes.

When I got out of the car, I noticed that the front right tyre was flat. Oh dear, how foolish of me to think that the Smart car, the city runaround, could cope with these stony, unkept-up country lanes. Yes, I was in a Smart car. You know – those piddly little things that look as if the back has been cut off? Silly looking, but good for the environment.

That had been our thinking anyway and we'd bought a second-hand one a month previously. However, bringing the Smart car up this particular lane had not been so smart.

Sam jumped immediately into crisis-assistance mode and he and I began looking for the spare tyre. The Smart car is anything but conventional, and my embarrassing ignorance about it was soon exposed. Was the boot at the front? I didn't know. How did you open the bonnet? I didn't know. Did it even have a bonnet? I didn't know. Was that where the spare tyre was? I didn't know.

'Do you have the manual?' asked Sam.

'I don't know,' I replied.

Encyclopedic ignorance. If there was something that anyone needed *not to know* about this vehicle, then I was there with all the lack of knowledge at my fingertips.

A search in the car (struggling first to find compartments, and then open them) revealed no manual.

'Come in, have a cup of tea, and we can search the internet,' suggested Sam.

If you ever get bored, you can do exactly what I did next. Simply type the following into Google.

Where is the spare tyre on a Smart car?

It takes you to a forum. The first answer is: 'There is no spare tyre, so remove the steering wheel and get out and push the thing like the shopping trolley that it is.'

Yeah, yeah, very funny. Internet wise guy.

The trouble was that all the other answers confirmed that the Smart car has no spare tyre. How could that be? Surely it was illegal? No, some further research revealed the awful truth is that they do it to save weight. It seemed that my environmentally friendly miles per gallon were coming at the expense of leaving me stranded if I ever got a puncture.

I followed the course of action that was fast becoming a default position when anything went wrong. I called Ken.

Quite irresponsibly – and worse still, without informing me – Ken had gone out. His position as best neighbour in the world was suddenly questionable. I'm not sure that he could be allowed to have a life. How dare he not remain on 24-hour call?

It was decided that I should leave the car and walk home. I would have to order the new tyre from the local garage, nip down with Ken to collect it, before whizzing back up the lane to fit it. All very inconvenient and time consuming. Never mind, I'd delivered a tremendous six of the eighty-five leaflets I'd been given, so I could go on a tour of Sam's farm without any guilt.

It was impressive. Without the use of any pesticides, Sam, Lucy, Kate, Becky and Joe, who'd met each other on a co-operative farm where they'd been volunteering, were growing a vast range of vegetables, some that I'd never heard of. According to Sam, livestock were to follow, but only in a way that would help create a sustainable farm. (He explained briefly that keeping a few pigs meant you could get land turned over that would otherwise have required a tractor and fuel.) I admired the way five 'thirty-somethings' had upped and left city life to follow a dream – to live and work on a sustainable farm.

They were doing something that most people in society would describe as 'mad'. Not least because the chances of economic success were so slim. Margins were tight for this kind of farming, and myriad things could go wrong. Theirs was certainly not the kind of risk-taking whereby, if they were successful, they would become extremely rich. The most optimistic prognosis was that they would tick along nicely. But surely that's the point? Wasn't that why Fran and I had been drawn to this place? So we could tick along nicely? London had taught us that life was a competition, and the prizes were property and lifestyle. We were rejecting that, trusting that a simpler life could offer different, but ultimately more fulfilling rewards.

'All of us have got part-time jobs, so we've got income outside the farm,' said Sam.

Very wise. Not a good idea to have all your eggs in one basket – at least until you have ensured that the basket doesn't have holes in it.

'I think it's brilliant what you're doing,' I said. 'I hope you guys are successful.'

This wasn't just polite conversation. I really meant it.

***

'Do you think we should hire a doula?' asked Fran.

Fran was now nicely rotund, but she still maintained her petite grace. Hers had not been a troublesome pregnancy, and the general consensus amongst friends and neighbours was that she had blossomed during it.

'A what?'

'A doula.'

'What's a doula?'

'She supports us through the whole birthing process. Physically and emotionally, before and after. She's kind of like a coach.'

280

'Like a tennis coach?'

Fran looked at me blankly.

'But with no need to explain topspin,' I added.

Fran ignored my frivolous remarks and went on to explain that a doula would try to guide her through labour without recourse to painkillers. She would be our 'representative' for the natural-birthing approach, in the event that the midwife was putting us under pressure to go down a route that involved medical intervention.

'Do you have anyone in mind?' I asked.

'Well, Patricia, my pregnancy yoga teacher, is a doula.'

'And do you like her?'

'Yes.'

'OK, let's hire her.'

What was happening to us? Were we becoming New Age, home-birth junkies? As well as having booked ourselves on a hypnobirthing course, we'd now also taken the decision to hire a doula. What next? Were we getting carried away? Perhaps we needed something to bring us back down to earth. Something like a good old-fashioned night of bingo.

***

I arrived to find a packed house of all ages. It seemed that the prospect of winning some food items that were readily available on supermarket shelves was enough of a draw to lure people away from their television sets. (TV is OK up to a point, but let's face it, an evening's viewing will win you very little meat.) The prizes – neat little supermarket cartons of packaged meat cuts – were laid out on trestle tables, in an alarming number of rows. My initial thought was, my word, we're going to play an awful lot of bingo here tonight. Claire, the evening's organiser, and a genteel lady of an age consistent with those who seemed to volunteer to help with the village hall, took me through the rules. She explained that each game had three prizes – minced beef when one line was filled, chicken thighs for two lines, and a rib of beef for three lines. I was also reminded of a couple of the stylistic tricks of the trade for the caller – '88' as two fat ladies, and the like.

'You turn the wheel,' explained Claire, 'then you take out a numbered ball, read it out and place it in the numbered grid. When someone calls "House!", I'll bring their cards up for you to check off, and then we crack on.'

'That's all there is to it?'

'That's it, in a nutshell.'

'And how many games are we playing?'

'Eleven. Ten normal games and one Golden Game at the end for the big prize of the full meal – a complete chicken with all the accompanying veg.'

My heart sank at the prospect of eleven games. It did seem an awful lot. Still, perhaps the time flew by once you got started.

I sat at my table and watched as the clock ticked round to 7.30 p.m., and I was given the nod to start proceedings. The gentle murmur of conversation died away as I explained the format of the evening, and a feeling of great expectancy filled the room.

'OK. Eyes down!' I announced, with as much passion as I could muster. 'If the numerical gods shine on you tonight, then some of you could walk away with chicken thighs.'

Several titters, and one comment about someone nearby

having pig's thighs already. Good, I thought, we're off to a very good start.

Unfortunately, the lyricists of 'Things Can Only Get Better' and 'The Only Way Is Up' were once again going to be exposed as fantasists.

I cannot think of a better way of enabling you, dear reader, to empathise with the experience of what followed, other than to ask a small favour of you. Could you please read the next paragraph out loud? Thanks.

Two and four, twenty-four. Seven and nine, seventy-nine. On its own, five. Four and three, forty-three. One and six, sixteen. All the fives, fifty-five. Eight and five, eighty-five. Two and nine, twenty-nine. All the fours, forty-four. Nine and zero, ninety. Three and eight, thirty-eight. Two fat ladies, eighty-eight. On its own, nine. Five and nine, fifty-nine. Seven and six, seventy-six. Three and one, thirty-one. (*Are you still doing this?*)

OK. Now imagine doing that for two hours.

By my calculations, I must have read out around seven hundred numbers in all the eleven games. No excitement. No variation. The only momentary respite from the tedium came in the form of the numbers eleven and twenty-two. For the first of these numbers, convention has it that the caller announces 'Legs eleven', after which the bingo players, should they so choose, offer up a wolf whistle. For twenty-two, the caller adds the wildly creative description of 'Two little ducks' into his patter, which is enough to cause a voluntary response from some players of 'Quack, quack', such are the levels of euphoria now being reached. I cannot tell you how welcome these sounds are when you have just read out 640 numbers back to back. They are the audio equivalent of visits from loved ones for prisoners with long sentences. They sustain you. They give you hope. Without them, you wither, you suffer, you decay.

'Two little ducks, twenty-two.'

'Quack! Quack!'

A feeling of hope. I can get through this.

I am now of the opinion that bingo is evil. The thought that up and down the country theatres and cinemas have been converted into bingo halls simply appals me. Once there was entertainment that challenged, titillated, amused, inspired, moved or scandalised. Now there's some poor sap reading out hundreds of numbers, one after the other, so that a room full of administrators (that's right – they're not players, they're administrators) can stand a reasonable chance of winning some soulless prize. There may be something wrong with me, but I just cannot see the point of it.

Why not shorten the whole procedure and reduce the suffering? If the 'players' are up for winning prizes based on the random drawing of numbered balls, then why not pare down the misery by having one ball in a sack for each player present, and draw out one ball to provide a winner? OK, I know that makes it just a raffle, but it's fundamentally the same as bingo in *spirit*, only so much quicker. And better. And more *humane*. It spares condemning a human being to a life of misery as a bingo caller.

The evening drew to a close at around 9.30 p.m. I was truly exhausted. Chicken thighs and ribs of beef had been redistributed amongst 'lucky' members of our community, and the ritual (what would anthropologists make of this?) had ground its way to a routine and inevitable halt, leaving people to make their way home with deadened senses and the sound of my monotone voice ready to haunt them in their sleep.

A word of advice. If anyone asks you to call bingo – say anything to get out of it. If you have never called bingo in your life, then you are very lucky. You have something over me, and you should do everything in your power to preserve that advantage. I will bear the scars forever. Any situation where I have to read out numbers, for any reason, will bring me out in a cold sweat. Never again will I be able to pass chicken thighs in a supermarket without breaking into a run. And if I happen upon two fat ladies, then I might need to be restrained from attacking them with a rib of beef.

No wonder George had said he was too old. He was probably only twenty-two.[4]

* * *

'You should come with us on a tractor run one day,' said Ken.

'What's a tractor run?' I replied.

'We raise money for the Devon Air Ambulance by a load of us all taking our tractors out on a road run, and then parking up somewhere and having a good natter.'

Ken's suggestion had been raised at one of my many morning visits to his workshop to ask either:

(1) How something worked in the house that I ought to have known already.

(2) To ask how to fix something that I ought to have known how to fix already.

---

4   Two little ducks. Quack, quack.

(3) To ask Ken to fix something for me that I ought to have known how to fix already.

Ken had been busily working on the Massey Ferguson, replacing a sprocket or adjusting a back axle, or doing something equally abstruse.

'When is the next tractor run?' I asked.

'Sunday. You could join us if we could find a tractor for you to drive.'

'I could borrow Reg's,' I suggested.

'What? His Zetor? Do you think he'd lend it to you?'

'No harm in asking.'

So it was that I found myself in Reg and Ann's kitchen – on the pretext of buying eggs – raising the subject of borrowing a 46-year-old Czechoslovakian tractor.

'I need a run out in it, before I take it from Lands End to John O'Groats,' I said, dangling the carrot of a trip in which Reg's tractor could achieve greatness by featuring in a one-minute segment on a regional news programme.

'HOW LONG WOULD YOU WANT IT FOR?' bellowed Reg, as if I was at the other end of an extremely long corridor.

'Just a day.'

'WELL, I DON'T SEE WHY NOT, AS LONG AS YOU LOOK AFTER IT.'

Ken was most surprised that Reg had agreed to this, but seemed delighted that his incompetent townie neighbour was going to join in with a traditional rural pastime.

'Trouble is, I don't think he's got insurance for his Zetor,' said Ken, ever the pragmatist.

'Ah,' I replied. 'Leave it with me.'

Another visit and twelve eggs later, Reg had agreed to

insure the tractor, provided that I sorted out all the paperwork on his behalf. I took the tractor's registration details and diligently completed my homework after a half-hour phone call to the broker which, once my life is completed, will not rank as one of its more exciting highlights.

'I thought he'd back out at that point,' said Ken, when I reported the news of the successful insuring of the tractor.

'No, he's on for it. He just wants me to come down in the morning and give it a little run, so he can see that I'll know what I'm doing on the day.'

'That's a good idea. Do you want me to come with you?'

'Yes. I'll pop round in the morning and we'll head down together.'

* * *

Reg may have been eighty-six years old, but he was eighty-six going on thirty-six. He always seemed to be pottering with farm machinery whenever I went round, just as he was on this occasion when we pulled up in Ken's pick-up truck. He moseyed out of his workshop and glared at us. No hint of a smile. His was a face with a default setting of grumpy, but there was usually a distant twinkle in his eye that seemed missing this morning. I countered with an ebulliently cheerful tone.

'I'm here to put the tractor through its paces.'

'YOU'D BETTER BE BLOODY CAREFUL WITH IT. IT'S VINTAGE, YOU KNOW. FORTY-SIX YEARS OLD. I DON'T WANT YOU RUINING IT.'

'I won't ruin it.'

'YOU'D BETTER BLOODY NOT. I LENT THAT SAM MY HAY BAILER AND HE BUGGERED IT UP.'

'I won't bugger it up.'

'YOU'D BETTER BLOODY NOT.'

I figured that Reg had read very little Jane Austen. For him, no doff of his cap followed by:

Ah, good morning, Master Hawks. 'Tis indeed a fine morning for you to be embarking on your maiden journey upon my trusty four-wheeled companion. May I wish thee the finest of journeys, albeit only brief and primarily educative in nature.

'I'LL GET THE BLOODY THING STARTED. BUT DON'T BUGGER IT UP. YOU'D BETTER NOT BURN THAT CLUTCH OUT.'

Reg climbed onto the tractor and started it up, sending a plume of filthy smoke into the air, filling the workshop, and causing him and his precious machine to become lost in a black cloud, one that matched his current mood. Seconds later, he and his machine emerged from the workshop and pulled up alongside me and Ken.

'OK. GIVE IT A RUN ROUND THE FARM,' he said, dismounting, 'AND DON'T BURN THAT BLOODY CLUTCH OUT.'

'Does it work the same way as a car?' I asked, innocently enough.

'JUST STICK IT INTO GEAR AND GET GOING,' came Reg's response.

Compassionate Ken stepped in and told me the basics, but he didn't know how the gearbox worked, as each tractor tends to be quite different to another – and foolishly he'd not familiarised himself with how the Czechs arranged their gearboxes.

'Reg, how does the gearbox work? Where are all the gears?' I asked.

Instead of offering me a verbal reply, he stepped up and shoved the thing into gear himself.

'TAKE IT ROUND THE FIELD,' he bossed.

I looked at Ken, who raised his eyebrows and shrugged. I released the clutch and I was off. All went well for the first twenty-five yards, as I and the tractor chugged along nicely. Time to stick it into second gear, I thought. I pushed down on the clutch with my left foot and started grappling with the mysterious gear arrangement. I pulled, twisted, pushed and wiggled, but to no avail, I just didn't seem to be able to get this gear stick to engage in any other position than the one it was already in. My foot remained on the clutch, something that didn't seem to please Reg altogether.

'TAKE YOUR FOOT OFF THE BLOODY CLUTCH OR YOU'LL BURN IT OUT!'

'If I do that, I'm not sure what'll happen,' I called back, 'as I don't know what gear I'm in.'

'TAKE YOUR FOOT OFF THE BLOODY CLUTCH OR YOU'LL BURN IT OUT!'

I imagined an exchange that might take place at home between Reg and Ann.

REG: 'ANN, PASS THE SALT, THESE POTATOES NEED MORE SALT.'

ANN (from the cooker): 'In a minute, Reg, the chip pan is on fire so I'm just putting it out.'

REG: 'ANN, PASS THE SALT, THESE POTATOES NEED MORE SALT.'

ANN: 'It's spreading through the kitchen. The whole house could go up in flames.'

REG: 'ANN, JUST PASS ME THE BLOODY SALT, THESE POTATOES NEED MORE SALT.'

Reg didn't need salt now. All the evidence suggested that he needed me to take my foot off the clutch. The last scintilla of doubt was removed as he screamed at me once more.

'TAKE YOUR FOOT OFF THE BLOODY CLUTCH!'

I took my foot off the clutch. The tractor started going backwards.

'IT'S IN REVERSE, YOU BLOODY FOOL!'

Thanks, Reg, I never would have guessed that.

I grappled with the gear stick. I pulled, twisted, pushed and wiggled, desperately trying to get it out of reverse. Within moments, somewhat unwillingly, I drew up alongside Ken and Reg.

'TAKE YOUR FOOT OFF THE BLOODY ACCELERATOR,' said Reg.

Ah, good, something else for me to take my foot off. I was getting the hang of this now. Driving a tractor was all about taking your foot off things. Compassionate Ken stepped in.

'Tony, a tractor's not like a car. You don't need to go through the gears. Just stay in the gear that you set off in. That's why you don't need to use the clutch.'

'HE'S BURNING MY BLOODY CLUTCH OUT.'

'Let me try again,' I said, realising that the best way to deal with Reg when he was in this mood was to imagine that he wasn't there.

I tried again. I did much better. I circled the field displaying, if not competence and confidence, then persistence and pluck. A few minutes later, I pulled the tractor up before the two men who had been observing me like examiners.

'That was good,' said Ken.

'I'M NOT GOING TO LET YOU TAKE HER,' said Reg.

'What?' I said, somewhat in disbelief.

'I'M NOT GOING TO LET YOU TAKE HER. YOU'LL BURN THAT BLOODY CLUTCH OUT.'

And that was pretty much it. I knew there was little point in reasoning with Reg. Reason was to Reg, what subtlety is to Lady Gaga. Ken knew it too.

'Never mind, Tony. Thanks anyway, Reg,' he said.

I looked at Reg. I wondered for a moment if all his posturing obstinacy masked a sadness.

'I'll pop down with the insurance policy soon,' I said.

And with those profound words, Ken and I slowly climbed back into his pick-up truck and drove away.

'Actually, I thought you did quite well on that thing,' said Ken. 'I think he'd decided he didn't want you to take it before we got there.'

'Really? Why?'

'I don't know. Maybe he didn't want to risk it getting damaged. He's very fond of that Zetor.'

And so it was that the Zetor remained in Reg's workshop. The only difference was that now it would sit there with third-party insurance cover. So if Reg's tractor managed to inflict any damage, without actually moving, on any other vehicle, then Reg would be fully covered.

It was nice to know that something good had come out of all our efforts.

16

The Finger

One of the many benefits of living in an old democ-
racy like Britain is that justice – whilst subject to
occasional miscarriages – is often seen to be done. One
case I can cite as an example was when the government
inspector ruled in our favour against the Dartmoor
National Park Authority. To our delight, our appeal was
upheld, which meant that we would now be free to do
what any sensible couple does when they are faced with
the challenges surrounding the arrival of a new baby, and
that is to add builders into the mix. It makes perfect
sense.

The baby, of course, was going to grow up into a country
kid, distinct from its parents in this regard.

'You do realise that our child will be Devonian?' I said to
Fran over breakfast, as the spring sunshine threatened to
soothe and transform a chilly night into a mild and pleasant
day.

'Of course.'

'Well . . .'

'Well, what?'

'Well, I was wondering if we've really got to know the real Devon.'

'How do you mean?'

'Well, beyond our immediate neighbours, so much of our contact seems to be with incomers.'

'That's true, but I don't see what we can do about it.'

'I have an idea.'

'Oh dear.'

'It's OK. It doesn't involve you.'

'That's a relief.'

* * *

I wanted to move slowly, just like they would have done in days gone by. I wanted to experience the raw countryside and turn something that would normally take an hour into a whole morning's activity. I wanted to be as green as I could, and not rely on fossil fuels every time I needed to get something done. I wanted to meet a real Devonian at work, as part of a genuine commercial transaction.

I was going to cycle to town and get my hair cut.

It was an ambitious plan, I'll admit, but the week previously I'd spotted an authentic-looking barbershop in a neighbouring village and it looked like a piece of old Devon. The real thing. A tiny establishment with only one seat and with the red-and-white spirally sign outside. It was the first of its kind I'd seen since our move, such is the current trend towards unisex salons and so called 'stylists'. I prefer the brutal honesty of a place that tells you straight: 'We won't wash your hair and blow-dry it later, and we won't offer you a cup of coffee. We won't guarantee a trendy look.

Here's the deal – you give us a few quid and we'll cut some of your hair off.'

These establishments don't advertise themselves as hairdressers, because they won't dress your hair. They're barbers, so what they will do with your hair is cut it – and it's a service they offer exclusively to men. Well, boys, too, but only for those whose parents aren't bothered whether their child has a few cuts on his neck, or gets teased at school for having naff hair. Actually, at school I recall that a modicum of teasing happened after a barber visit, regardless of the quality of the cut. You knew that the moment you walked in to the playground, another child would approach you, point to your hair, and declare:

'HAIRCUT!'

Others would then join in. Nothing particularly derogatory was being said, but nonetheless it felt like something one should feel embarrassed about. You'd had a haircut and it had been spotted. Shame on you. Never mind, this kind of stuff is character-building and has enabled us all to grow into the balanced, neurosis-free and self-assured individuals who have helped to create the near-perfect society that is all around us.

I have a good bike. It's sleek, light, it makes other cyclists look across at me admiringly, and it cost me £700 secondhand. However, it just wasn't good enough. One of the reasons we had been drawn to this area of Devon was the presence of the rolling hills that lead you gently into the more austere terrain of Dartmoor. These hills, as I was now discovering, were deceptively steep, and no matter from which direction they were tackled on a bicycle, they were unreasonably demanding.

Attempting to cycle up them tested the thighs and calf muscles to breaking point, and freewheeling down them made the wrists ache, whilst the brakes were squeezed as tightly as possible to avoid joining this year's road accident statistics. I'd figured that this seven-mile cycle would not be too much for me – lithe picture of fitness that I was – so I had set off in earnest, only now viewing it as extremely daunting. However, the sensible option of turning back and getting the car would have involved swallowing too much pride, so I elected to battle on.

In one sense, I was greatly rewarded for my stubbornness. The scenery was delightful. Although the rising hedgerows blocked many a spectacular view, the gaps created by farm gates afforded occasional glimpses that made it more of a treat. For a while, I freewheeled alongside a gently flowing stream and into dense woodland. The soft autumn sun streaked through the trees like rock-concert spotlights, picking out ferns and wild flowers instead of writhing pop stars. When the stream veered away from the narrow lane and left me facing a forbidding incline, I dismounted and pushed the bike up the hill. This gave me all the more time to appreciate the nature that was around me. The birds chattered away, providing a chorus of sound that was contradictory – random and yet seemingly orchestrated.

From time to time I would attempt to cycle up one of the hills, wanting to rise to the challenge, and to try and convince myself that I was a proper cyclist. The gears didn't seem to go low enough for what was required, but I did my best. Cycling uphill in low gears requires a significant loss of dignity. I always snigger at the sight of cyclists pedalling furiously, so fast that it looks as if their Lycra leggings will catch fire from the friction, the bike inching forwards as nearby pedestrians pass them, sneering as they go.

Currently that undignified cyclist was me, but I was spared the humiliation of an audience – unless you counted cattle and sheep. They might have been sneering, but it was impossible to be sure. What animals actually think about has always been a mystery to me. Once I compiled a little list of the possible thoughts that some animals might have.

* * *

A horse: 'When humans break *their* legs, how come they just put it in plaster?'

A fish, swimming in waters where fishermen are active: 'I wonder what happened to Ian?'

A sheep: 'Don't tell me, it's just grass on the menu again? Ho, hum.'

A whale: 'How come when *they* lie on the beach, everyone leaves them alone?'

* * *

Finally, I encountered another human being. Two, in fact. A Land Rover containing a farmer and his wife who, in their mud-stained overalls and ruffled hair, could have been dressed by a film's costume designer briefed to create two rustic figures. They had to slow down to a halt to allow me to pass, so slender was the lane. We exchanged good mornings and I enquired of the farmer if I was heading the right way for my designated village.[1]

'Keep on this road, don't turn right or left,' he said, the second part of his sentence suggesting that he didn't believe I'd listened to the first part.

I followed his instructions, shunning all the tempting lanes on either side of me and, at last, after a total of fifty minutes of walking a bike up hills and freewheeling down them almost out of control, I could see my destination in the valley below. In this case, the hill that led to it was actually too steep to go *down*. Not convinced that my brakes could handle it, I dismounted. I figured that of all the ways to pass away, being found headfirst in a Devon ditch was not glamorous enough.

When I reached the bottom of the hill, I was greeted by a High Street full of villagers going happily about their daily business. I was enjoying this picture of rural Britain so much that I chose not to remount the bike, but to keep pushing it so that I could absorb all that was around me. By the time I reached the barbershop, a warm, contented smile had broken out upon my face. It soon disappeared. There, in the window of the barbershop, were the words:

CLOSED ALL DAY WEDNESDAY

Profound irritation replaced the warm feelings. It was difficult to know what was more annoying – today being Wednesday, or the proprietor of the shop electing to make Wednesdays the day he closed. I stared in disbelief at the

---

1   This is far better than using a sat nav, as local farmers probably make fewer mistakes, even though most of them aren't linked up to satellites.

sign. I now faced the seven-mile journey home, the only difference being that this time I would experience the pain of the undulating hills from the opposing direction.

I heaved, sighed, dismounted, trudged uphill, remounted, flew down hills barely in control, did some more heaving, threw in a touch more sighing, and eventually made it home – rouge, damp, exhausted. Fran looked at my hair.

'Blimey, he hasn't taken much off,' said Fran.

It was a full minute before I had the breath or the motivation to explain.

* * *

I'm not proud of it. I should have cycled back there the next morning. But I didn't. I jumped in the car. It still took close to twenty minutes, given that the top speed I attained was probably not much more than ten miles an hour. In spite of the aches from the previous day's exertions, I strode down the High Street with a confident swagger. Today was Thursday, and Thursday was a cracking good day to get your hair cut in rural Devon.

The High Street was busy, but in a small-village kind of way, rather than an Oxford Street kind of way. Everything is relative. Pleasingly, an emerging car provided the perfect parking place in front of the barbershop. As I got out of the car, I noticed a distinct improvement on the previous day. No 'closed' sign. I looked inside. No one was to be seen. The barber would be out the back, I hoped. I pushed open the door and a bell rang. My mind darted back to my youth. Ah, that bell ringing above the door. That familiar sound I'd heard as a small child, as my mother lugged me and my brother on shopping expeditions from one small independent trader to another. At that time, the large supermarket was still only a fledgling concept, and mothers walked to the shops with their unruly offspring in tow, before staggering home laden with the week's shopping in bulging, burdensome bags. These mothers were unsung heroines.

A man appeared. He was younger than I'd hoped. He was in his forties. I guessed that the son had taken over the business. It was good to see that it was staying in the family and that there would be continuity.

'Morning. What can I do for you then?' asked the barber, in an accent that was not instantly recognisable as Devonian.

I wonder if he noticed the disappointment on my face. This man was supposed to be a genuine local, and here he was addressing me in an accent that was – well, northern, I think. Was it Yorkshire?

'Don't I recognise you?' he said. 'Have you been in here before?'

Regrettably, this is not an uncommon thing for me to be asked. As someone whose TV appearances are few and far between, I may have made the odd, fleeting appearance in people's front rooms, but I've never stayed long enough or visited on enough occasions to have made a lasting impression. Consequently I'm not a well-known face, but I do look vaguely familiar to quite a reasonable tranche of the UK population. As a result, I have quite a lot of awkward conversations. This is one that I once had with a uniformed airline pilot whilst waiting in the lounge at Gatwick Airport.

PILOT (*Approaching Tony, who is looking at the departures screen and seeing that his flight requires him to 'Board now at Gate 14'*): 'Excuse me, but haven't we met before?'

TONY (*Looking the pilot up and down*): 'I don't think so.'

PILOT: 'No, we've definitely met before. Do you live in Southampton?'

TONY: 'No.'

PILOT: 'Are you near Southampton, in Hampshire?'

TONY: 'No, I don't live in Hampshire.'

PILOT: 'Do you spend much time in Southampton?'

TONY: 'No.'

PILOT: 'We have definitely met, though, I remember your face.'

TONY: 'It may be that you have seen me once or twice on the TV. I used to appear reasonably regularly on shows like *Have I Got News for You* and more recently *Grumpy Old Men*.'

This is the point where usually the questioner is greatly relieved and needs suffer no more of the agonising discomfort caused by not being quite sure why I look so familiar. In the case of the airline pilot, however, he was not having any of it. He declared that he didn't watch TV and that he definitely knew me from somewhere else. He continued to pose a string of irritating and pointless questions: 'Had I played table tennis as a junior in the national leagues?' 'Did I holiday in Crete?' 'Did I sail?' 'Had I ever worked in the airline industry?'

Five minutes into this tiresome exchange, I wanted to say one of two things – either:

'Look, I'm your brother, you idiot, don't you remember?'
Or:

'Look, I don't know you. Nor do I want to know you.
Even if I did know you, which I don't, you have demon-
strated in this short and yet excruciatingly dull and pointless
exchange, that you would be the type of person that I would
want to avoid. Now sod off to Southampton, a city I shall
take great care not to visit in the future for fear of bumping
into you again.'

Of course, being the cowardly Englishman that I am, I
just alerted him to the imminent departure of my flight and
beat a hasty retreat.

As it turned out, this barber happened to be one of the
more unusual cases who actually *knew* who I was.

'Wait a minute, you're Tony Hawks, aren't you?' he said,
his accent sounding distinctly northern now.

It turned out that the barber had read a few of my books
and enjoyed listening to me on the radio. It also became clear
that my suspicions about his accent were not unfounded.

'I'm from Stoke,' he explained, perhaps sensing that I
needed clarification.

Though geographically disappointing, Mark the barber
was a nice guy. He explained how he and his family had
moved down this way when his wife had got a job in
Torquay, and he'd since bought the barbershop and was
slowly building it up. We engaged in an agreeable conversation about the beauty of Devon and how much we were
enjoying being 'incomers'. Had we found our spiritual
home here? We both hoped so.

I paid for the cut and Mark asked if he could take my
photo, just to prove to people that I'd been into the shop. I

was getting the star treatment. As I posed, an old man entered and greeted us both, his vowels flattened by a pleasing Devonian twang. He was bald. The kind of bald that made one wonder why he had come into a barbershop. He observed our short photographic session with interest. Slightly embarrassed, I joked that I was modelling my haircut for one of those pictures in the window.

'Right,' said the old man, 'I bet he won't be taking my photo!'

* * *

One bright, late-February morning, with just under a month to go to Fran's due date, I did something that I'm told is not typically male. I made a doctor's appointment that was cautionary in nature. Just recently, my urination had begun to concern me a little. I was getting up at least once in the night, and sometimes I wasn't emptying my bladder completely after each urination. In short, my pissing was pissing me off. Given that I now had to pay attention to the R word, as outlined in Chapter 6, I felt it wise to check that this wasn't the beginnings of a prostate problem, which could have more serious implications.

In the doctor's bland and sparse waiting room I bumped into Brenda – my fellow village hall committee member. A little embarrassed by the location of our encounter, we still exchanged a polite 'How are you?' This is not a thing to do in a doctor's surgery, given that the answer ought probably to be:

'Well, I'm crap, obviously, otherwise I wouldn't be here, would I?'

However, Brenda and I responded to each other's polite but meaningless questions with polite but meaningless answers. We then had a short discussion about some village hall business, which no doubt made the others in the waiting room even more eager to be called in to see the doctor.

'Mr Hawks. Dr Shadley. Room four,' announced the receptionist.

I stood up.

'He's in room four, you say?'

'Yes.'

Phew, that was a relief. No correction on my question *'He's* in room four, you say?' Thankfully, I wouldn't have to go through the uncomfortable process of specifically requesting a male doctor, thus giving clues to Brenda and the others that my reason for being there was probably not a blocked ear. It's hard to say which would have been more awkward for me – having a female doctor delve around inside my pants, or announcing to a roomful of strangers and one village hall committee member that I didn't want a female doctor delving around inside my pants. Rocks and hard places.[2]

Dr Shadley did not look unlike the kind of man with whom I might be sharing a pint in the pub. He was close in age to me, well-kempt, and with a pleasant, engaging manner.

'How can I help?' he enquired.

Displaying anything but eloquence, I offered my explanation.

---

2   Certainly no hard places in my pants. This whole experience was as far from arousing as it could get.

'I see,' he said, in a way that made me a little nervous. 'Well, of course the easiest way to proceed at this point would be for me to examine you. Are you happy for me to do this?'

'Well,' I said, cautiously, 'what would that involve?'

'I'll have to put my finger up your bottom.'

Momentary disbelief. Did he just say that? If I had just taken a sip of tea, then surely I would have spat it out, such was the shock.

Dr Shadley could see that I looked shaken.

'I insert one finger in your anus and I can reach your prostate from there and have a good feel.'

This wasn't making things any easier. This was new territory for me. I'd never met a man before who had wanted to shove his finger up my arse. Or at least who had admitted it. Especially this quickly. I mean, we hardly knew each other.

I suppose if I take a moment to reflect here, it can't have been that nice for him either. I guess, like most doctors, he must sit in his room of a morning secretly hoping that everyone will have earache or a slight cough, rather than a string of complaints that require him to stick his finger up their arses.

The mind boggles as to why so many young people want to be doctors, if this is the kind of thing that they're going to end up doing after all those years of study. According to UCAS figures for 2012 entry, there were 82,489 applications to medical courses for only 7,805 places. This means there were 10.6 applicants for every place. Surely they could get that number down dramatically if they started mocking up my current situation at the interview stage?

Thank you for applying to Bristol University's medical school. Now, if you'd just like to bend over, I'm going to shove my finger up your arse to see if you're the type we're looking for. And after I've finished, I'd really appreciate it if you'd do the same to me.

Err . . . maybe I'll do geography after all.

'How does this work, doctor?' I asked, realising what a dumb question this was.

'If you just take your trousers and pants down and lie on the couch, I'll have a quick feel around and check on everything.'

'I see. And how long does it take?'

'Just a minute.'

I was tempted to ask him if he could do it without hesitation, repetition and *especially* deviation, but the time didn't seem right.[3]

I pulled myself up onto the couch, slid my trousers and pants down, and rolled onto my side – offering the doctor my bare arse. This was not something that came easily to me. It seemed to be either extremely rude or unreasonably forward.

I braced myself. Having been someone who had enjoyed routine heterosexuality enough not to have felt the need to indulge in extensive experimentation, this was all new. I decided to adopt a tactic I use when I'm at the dentist and he is hovering over me with a pulsating drill. I try to imagine the worst pain that one could experience, and then ready myself for that. The thinking is that any discomfort then

---

3   This comment only makes sense if you are familiar with this: http://en.wikipedia.org/wiki/Just_a_Minute

felt will be mild in comparison, and therefore much easier to bear.

In this situation there was no pain. It was an odd feeling, though, and not one that felt comfortable. It was certainly not pleasurable, as some claim to find it, perhaps because I was not relaxed enough. As the doctor's digit probed, I became more anxious. What would he find up there? The keys to the garden shed? They had been missing for over a month now and Fran had repeatedly said, 'Well, they must be somewhere.'

Oddly, when the sixty seconds was up, there was no whistle. Just a feeling of immense relief as the finger was removed and my sphincter snapped back into its favourite position. Closed.

'I'm pleased to say that there's nothing to worry about,' said the doctor. The doctor that I hardly knew.

This was an immense relief. I can't pretend that in the few seconds the examination had taken, I hadn't allowed my mind to run wild with dark thoughts concerning my own mortality.

'Just keep a close eye on things and if the symptoms continue or get worse, we'll take another look,' he continued.

That would be fun.

'Thank you, doctor.'

'No problem. It was nice to meet you.'

'It was nice to meet you, too.'

I would have to manage my social life such that I didn't meet anyone in that manner again.

* * *

The month of March announced itself with a crisp, bright morning. A few weeks remained for us to cram ourselves full of as much information on childbirth as we possibly could. Our hypnobirthing classes doubled up on much of what we'd already learned in our active birth classes. We shared the sessions with another couple who, like us, seemed open to new ideas but weren't your typical New Agey, hippy types that you might expect to find on this kind of 'alternative' course. Far from it, Jim was a plumber and his wife Sarah, a hairdresser.

The main difference between this and the previous course we'd attended was that Fran learned some self-hypnosis techniques, as well as a couple of variations on the breathing exercises. Our teacher, Trina, displayed the customary bubbly vivaciousness that I now considered must be compulsory for anyone working in anything connected with childbirth. She was keen to have us be careful what language we used. Instead of 'contraction' we were asked to use the word 'surge', as it has a more positive connotation. I was taught massages I could give to Fran, and we learned how to block out any negative-speak we might hear that could cause us to be fearful going into the birth. Over three sessions, we took in a lot of information and consumed a lot of biscuits. (These also seem to be compulsory at any birth-related gathering.)

We were brimming over with information and different techniques. What we really needed now was for labour to begin so we could put them into practice before we forgot them all, but instead life went on as usual. Sometimes it felt as if we were in a kind of suspended reality. Everything was still going on around us, but somehow it was of diminished importance. Even the village hall committee meetings lost their edge. The exhilaration of discussions about the intro-duction of a new cleaning rota, or finding dates for the next skittles evening, were tempered by the knowledge that a rather more sensational event was on the horizon. We were even able to handle the successful outcome of the debate about whether to replace the padlocks on the store cup-board without euphoria. No highs and lows for us right now. Just a clock ticking.

'Enjoy your last days of freedom,' was the common refrain we heard when we chatted to our fellow villagers. 'Get some sleep in now, because soon you won't get any.'

I was reminded of how it felt when I was a twenty-year-old and I was told that I should enjoy myself now, because life was going to get a lot harder. I couldn't understand the logic of this because at twenty, a human being is a pretty confused entity. We're struggling to come to terms with adulthood, the opposite sex, and the perceived need to find a career. Telling you that those days ought to be the hap-piest days of your life wasn't terribly helpful. Neither was what we were hearing now, which seemed to be something of this order:

'Congratulations. You are about to have the most won-derful thing happen to you. Well done. Small thing, though – this wonderful thing that is about to happen to you will have a small by-product. It will totally ruin your life.'

Anyway, the final days of 'freedom' didn't feel very free at all. There was too much uncertainty. At any given moment, we were only hours away from having our lives changed forever. That's the deal. Unless you book in for a Caesarean section, you don't know when you're going to have your baby. It can come early, like that unwanted big bill, or late, like a parcel you've waited in for. Babies come when they're ready, I guess, and it is most unreasonable of them. In the meantime we wait, and we tread carefully.

This must be what it feels like when two countries have declared war on each other but no hostilities have yet begun. It's confusing. Unsettling. Disconcerting. Looking at the distant horizon, knowing that at any moment enemy bombers might appear, can take the edge off the nice sunny day. Thankfully for us it would be labour and a newborn baby, rather than air strikes or invading armies. Not unless NATO had overreacted to our decision to appeal against Dartmoor National Park Authority's refusal of our planning application.

Fran and I spent our evenings either reading – our heads buried in books about childbirth – or doing some rather odd things. Having kept healthily open minds about most of the 'New Agey' writings about childbirth, we had decided to encourage our baby to get itself into the right position for its birth. We talked to it, and I'd even written a little song[4] that we would sing to it regularly of an evening. I can remember when it first hit the headlines that Prince Charles talked to his plants and he was considered a 'loony' by the mainstream press. No doubt there is now evidence proving that plants respond well to posh people addressing them in aristocratic accents, saying: 'Very nice to meet you – and what exactly do you do?' Soon a scientific paper would

4   Listen here: www.tony-hawks.com and click on Once Upon A Time in the West Country.

emerge detailing how singing instructions to a foetus assists birth.

> Head down, chin to chest
> You know that this is best
> Back to belly, hands to heart
> All on the left now
> You're ready to start
>
> 'Cos baby knows best
> Baby knows best
> *(Repeat and fade)*

Fran had even picked a date for the birth.

'It's going to come on Thursday the twentieth,' she declared.

This was good, positive thinking, but it wasn't exactly based on any scientific or biological evidence. Nevertheless, we kept the day clear.

17

Braking Bad

'It doesn't matter about Reg and his Zetor,' said Ken.

He'd popped over especially to deliver the news and he was standing in the porch smiling as I answered the door.

'Andrew is going to lend you his Massey 35.'

'Andrew?'

'My son Andrew. He's finished doing it up – but he's going to take his Fordson Super Major to the tractor run so the Massey's spare and you can drive it next Sunday.'

'Really?'

'Yes. Pop over tomorrow and I'll give you a lesson.'

'Great. Are you not worried that I'll burn the bloody clutch out?'

'You'll manage.'

* * *

As expected, Ken's teaching style was less radical than Reg's. I was given a clear and detailed explanation of how everything worked and I felt reasonably confident as I climbed aboard. The tractor was beautiful – well, insofar as a tractor can be beautiful, I suppose. Its pristine red paintwork glistened in the spring sunshine and it looked brand new, so lovingly had it been restored. After twenty minutes of driving around a neighbouring field with Ken perched behind me providing instructions, I figured that I knew pretty much all I was required to know. I only needed to use three gears – second, third and reverse; the accelerator was where the indicator is on a car; and using the brake involved standing upright because the tractor would only stop if one's entire body weight was applied to it.

'It seems fairly straightforward,' I said to Ken, as we pulled into his drive.

'Yes. The main thing to remember is to keep over to the side so that cars can get past you.'

'OK. What time is it all happening?'

'Come round to mine at nine-thirty a.m. on Sunday.'

'Will do. How long does it last?'

'Allow all day.'

Ah. All day with a tractor. A little longer than I was expecting. I did my best to keep a neutral expression.

'That OK?' checked Ken.

'Fine. Just fine.'

* * *

Sunday morning was dry and cloudy and thankfully no rain had been forecast. This was excellent news given that the tractor I would be driving had no cab, and sitting all day on a slow-moving vehicle whilst cold water tipped out of the sky would bring little pleasure. Actually it was difficult to assess quite what pleasure I was expecting to get from the day. As I walked round to Ken's I began to wonder why I was going on this tractor run. Perhaps I was expecting a rural experience that would bond me with my environment? Or maybe I was just curious? Yes, that was it. I wanted to know what it was about men and tractors that had made them decide to hang out socially.

Ken and Andrew were tinkering with the three vintage tractors that were now parked on the drive. To an aficionado the sight would have brought great pleasure and a wealth of conversational possibilities. All I saw were three tractors. Two red ones and a blue one. One very big one (Ken's), one slightly smaller one (Andrew's) and a little one (mine). I suddenly realised that the paucity of my tractor vocabulary was going to be sorely exposed today. Sitting astride this tractor all day, I would be like a non-swimmer wading out to sea without armbands, but wearing a very nice vintage pair of trunks.

Everything began smoothly enough. The younger version of Ken, Andrew, started up my Massey, nodded to me to jump aboard, and the three of us headed off in convoy to the field that had been assigned for mass tractor rendezvous, which was about a mile away. We stopped only once to pick up a man who resembled Father Christmas, and who climbed into the back of the trailer that Ken was pulling behind his tractor. I called to Andrew, who was behind me.

'Who's that?'

'Tom, Ken's brother.'

Ah, so this was Brother Tom. The recluse. Well, he certainly looked the part. White hair and beard, blue dungarees, a hat that wouldn't look amiss on a skier, and a shepherd's wooden stick. He settled neatly into the metal container that he had seemingly elected to spend a large proportion of his day in, and off we all set.

There were a dozen or so tractors parked in the field when we arrived, flanked by the kind of men who you might expect to see flanking tractors. They had the look of men who toiled the land; rugged, hardy, dishevelled. Today was a big day out for them and their machines. After we'd all parked up Ken introduced me to his brother only to become surrounded by a cluster of welcoming mates. Finding myself isolated somewhat, I chatted with Brother Tom.

'Do you know much about tractors?' he asked.

'No. This is the first time I've driven one any distance.'

'You did well. I'm going to look at that McCormick Super over there. Want to come?'

'Yes please.'

It was either that or stand around looking a bit lost. So I looked at a McCormick Super.

Brother Tom turned out to be a most engaging companion for tractor perusal. His enthusiasm, which occasionally bordered on excitement, was infectious. He spouted all sorts of information about each tractor he examined – and examine them he did – over the next half hour.

'How do you know so much about tractors?' I asked him, as he bent down to study the rear of a yellow one.[1]

* * *

---

[1] That's how I describe it. Brother Tom would have supplied a tad more detail.

'Because I read *Tractor and Machinery* magazine. It's full of stuff about vintage tractors. Mind if I smoke?'

'Not at all.'

I'd expected him to light up a cigarette but instead he produced a vintage pipe and lit it. Perhaps he subscribed to *Pipe and Machinery* magazine too.

The owner of the yellow tractor then appeared and talked us through each stage of his loving restoration of the machine that glistened before us. Two and a half years he'd worked on it. Brother Tom nodded his head in deference. I had to stop myself from shaking mine in disbelief. The restorer smiled proudly, revealing a set of teeth that suggested he had prioritised tractor restoration over visits for dental work.

I looked up to see that whilst Brother Tom and I had been burying our heads into the arse ends of ageing farm machinery, the field had filled with tractors. And families. Kids pointed excitedly and clambered aboard to sit at the wheel. Mums nattered with mums. The atmosphere was like that of a fairground, but there was only one ride in town, and that was about to begin.

'We're all off now Tony,' said Andrew. 'You go second to last so that Ken can bring up the rear and keep an eye on you.'

'OK,' I said, cheerfully jumping aboard the Massey.

Perched on my tractor, I watched as Brother Tom climbed back into his pen at the rear of Ken's tractor like an obedient pet. The 'run' part of the tractor run was about to begin. Suddenly the neighbouring hills echoed to the sounds of forty-six tractors all starting up. A bit of a din to me, but music to the ears of nearly everyone else in attendance.

'JUST FOLLOW THE TRACTOR IN FRONT!' shouted Ken from the cab of his large Massey, 'OR IF YOU LOSE THEM, FOLLOW THE BLUE ARROWS. I'LL BE RIGHT BEHIND.'

And off we set. In single file, down Dartmoor's narrow lanes, this impressive cavalcade of vintage tractors making its cacophonous way through the peaceful countryside. Occasionally we would meet a poor driver who had pulled to one side to allow what they believed to be one tractor to pass. By the time I dawdled past them, and they'd watched more than forty tractors go by, their faces bore an expression that seemed to combine despair and resignation. Their wave and weak smile suggested that they knew they would be late and that there was no point in fighting it.

My Massey performed well, but driving it was far from relaxing. Gear changes, especially on hills, were not easy and usually involved a noisy clunking, and the brakes demanded most of my body weight to be effective. We wound our way through narrow lanes gift-wrapped with hedgerows beyond which lay dramatic moorland. At the helm of a smooth-running saloon car this would have been an enjoyable drive, instead it was ninety minutes of quite intense concentration. I was greatly relieved when the tractor ahead of me turned into a large field and there, mirage-like, a row of tents awaited us manned by wives and teenage children. Like tank-driving military personnel, we all happily dismounted and headed off to queue for our rations. I felt a little like a soldier who might have come through a minor skirmish – relieved to be in one piece. I didn't know where I was, currently having the geographical sense of someone who'd been blindfolded and spun around in circles. Never mind, the forty-five other tractor drivers knew exactly where we were, and that was good enough for me.

As I stood in the food line, the conversation and banter continued all around me. Alas, I had little to offer and no one asked me about the vehicle I was driving. Perhaps they sensed that I was not a serious tractor man. They might have a name for my type – the ones who drop in, piss around on someone else's tractor, and then bugger off never to drive a tractor again in their lives. Or maybe not. They seemed a friendly enough crowd. It was more likely that I just looked hopelessly out of place, and there seemed no easy route into any banter.

When I reached the head of the queue it was nice to see the warm, comforting face of Lin, who plied me with tea, quiche, a pasty, and pointed out another tent where cakes were there for the taking.

'How are you getting on, Tony?' she asked.

'Just fine. This tractor driving is a breeze.'

These were the words of someone who thought the rest of the day would be plain, albeit noisy, sailing. Well, why not? I'd clearly got the hang of this tractor-driving business and from now on it would just be more of the same.

'We just head home after this?' I said to Andrew, when he found me perched on a dry-stone wall consuming my fourth cup of tea and second piece of cake.

'A couple more hours, I'd say,' he replied.

I tried not to sigh.

'You've got the hang of that tractor, so you can head off with the lead tractors if you like,' he added.

'Righto,' I said, suddenly sensing that 'righto' was

something that Devonian tractor drivers didn't say to each other that much.

* * *

Andrew led the way and I joined the bustle of machines becoming about tenth in the line for the afternoon part of the run, just behind yellow tractor man – meaning that I could admire his impressive restoration work as well as the countryside, which happened to be even more beautiful than what we'd witnessed in the morning. Breathtaking views of the moor enabled me to relax and forget what I was sitting on. Here, on top of the moor, vistas opened up that stretched for miles all around us. No motorways or cities in view, not even an aeroplane criss-crossing the horizon. Total peace, but for the blasting engines of forty-six tractors.

Around four o'clock – the time that should have been teatime – we began to head down the steep winding lane to the valley road that would eventually lead us home. Like the experienced tractor operator that I now was, I ensured that the Massey was in low gear and was crawling along with the engine effectively acting as the main brake. Just as I turned a corner and entered a particularly steep section I could see that yellow-tractor man had made an unscheduled stop. Odd. Why wasn't he moving? Ahead of him I could see that tractors were also at a standstill. Something was clearly blocking the road ahead and causing a tractor tailback. Routinely, I lifted myself into the standing position that was needed to get the tractor to stop, and I applied my full body weight to the brake.

Nothing.

It made no difference whatsoever.

Panic. Adrenalin pumped. Suddenly my body was in full 'fight or flight' mode – which was useless, given that I was stuck on a moving tractor and could do neither. My tractor that wasn't careering out of control, but was gently crawling in low gear towards . . . well, towards a vintage gem. A lovingly restored yellow tractor.

'COME ON!' I shouted as I continued to try and get the brakes to work.

I now lifted my left foot from the clutch and put both feet on the brake. I jumped. Still nothing. With each passing second, the beautiful yellow tractor was becoming closer and closer. The lane was too narrow for me to pass. This was it! There was no choice, I was simply going to ram the tractor in front of me, undoing thirty months of one poor man's painstaking restoration work. He'd brought it here in good faith to show it off to his mates, one of whom would soon tow it home in another vintage tractor that had been lucky enough not to have been travelling directly in front of me.

'COME ON! COME ON!'

Just a few more seconds available to plead with the brakes to co-operate. But co-operate they would not. I braced myself for the inevitable collision. For a split second the irony of the situation was not lost on me. Here I was taking part in a tractor run to raise money for the Devon Air Ambulance service and any moment now we would be calling out the Devon Air Ambulance service to come and demonstrate whether or not they were worthy of our charitable donations.

One last jump on the brakes. Nothing. With the yellow tractor now just a few feet away, its driver blissfully unaware of what was happening behind him, I braced myself for the impending collision. Then, in the very last dying moment before impact, something flipped in me. I realised that I couldn't do it. I simply couldn't allow my tractor to drive straight into the one before me and I span the wheel round to the left, and directed the tractor into the hedgerow beside the road. Anything could be waiting for me and the Massey. If the hedge wasn't strong enough to hold us, we could pile right through it and plunge down the hill that might be awaiting the other side. My action was not one of a man who had weighed up the risks or all the options. It was an instinctive decision probably based on some recent evolutionary development in Man that meant he could recognise that hedges were softer than yellow tractors.

THUD.

The Massey crashed into the hedgerow, and – to my immense relief – it stopped. Through the shrubbery, now pushed apart by the recent insertion of a red vintage Massey Ferguson, I could see a gradient ahead of me that would have meant the end of Andrew's tractor if the hedge hadn't stopped us. It would have been the end of me too, had I not have been able to throw myself off in time.

The feeling of intense relief was short-lived and was now replaced by acute embarrassment. Yellow-tractor man had remained unaware of the near miss that had taken place just behind him – his engine ticking over and drowning out any sense that another tractor was about to drive into his rear end – but I was only too aware though that the tractor driver behind me, and the one behind him, had just watched me steer my tractor into the hedge, seemingly for no reason other than on a whim. I would need to explain myself.

Sheepishly,[2] I lowered myself from the stalled Massey that was now at a forty-five-degree angle to the lane.

***

Slowly I walked back towards the strong-jawed, stoic-looking driver in the tractor behind me.

'Sorry about that,' I called up to him, raising my voice to be heard above the engine that he had optimistically left running. 'The brakes wouldn't stop the tractor. I had no choice but to drive into the hedge.'

A pause. Then the driver smiled and nodded. That was it? A smile and a nod? Had he any idea what I had just gone through? I didn't know what it was worthy of, except that it was worthy of more than a smile and a nod.

'What shall I do?' I now asked.

A shrug.

Just a shrug. That was it? What was it with this bloke? Was he related to Dr Spock? What did one have to do to elicit any emotion from him? I looked back at the unimpressive configuration of hedge and tractor that was a few yards below us and tried to figure it out for myself. There was no shortage of tractors that could tow me out of the hedge, but the lane was so narrow that there probably wasn't room for the required manoeuvres. It looked just possible that I might be able to reverse the tractor back

---

2   Actually it wasn't sheepishly. Sheep have the good sense not to drive tractors. It's about the only sensible thing they do. Or rather don't do.

onto the lane. That would be much simpler. I suggested this to the man who, perhaps in more ways than one, was now looking down on me.

He nodded.

I could have guessed as much.

'If I manage to reverse it out, you don't mind waiting for the other tractors to get a safe distance away from me – perhaps even to the bottom of the hill?'

He shrugged and shook his head.

Sometimes out of adversity positive things can come. OK, this hedge collision may have represented a disappointing and complicated development in my brief flirtation with tractors, but here was the foundation for a new and great friendship. This experience, and our ability to share it in the way we had, would surely lead to a great bond between us; afternoon walks, evening drinks, late-night suppers together, during which he could smile, nod and shrug, and then smile, nod and shrug again until there was no more smiling, nodding and shrugging to be done.

When the tractors ahead of me began moving again, I remounted my tractor, scrunched the Massey into reverse gear and released the clutch. I was more than a little nervous. Would I be able to reverse us out of the hedge – or would I block the thirty-six tractors behind me? Would I ruin the tractor run, and mess up the afternoon for the half-dozen other vehicles that were possibly going to use this road in the next few hours? To my intense relief, I felt the tractor edging backwards and back onto the lane. A huge embarrassment had been averted.

The road ahead of me was clear and that made it safe for me to continue, but I was fully aware that the tractors ahead might have to stop again for some reason. If this happened whilst I was facing down a hill then I'd be faced once again with the unpalatable choice of driving into a yellow tractor or the hedgerow. The hedgerow might not be so kind to me next time. That's why when the road levelled out and a small clearing appeared just around a bend, I decided to pull over and stop. I would wait for all the tractors behind me to pass, and discuss the options with Ken. He'd know how best to get this vehicle home.

Emotional man smiled and nodded as he drove by, as did the driver on the tractor behind him. However, the next tractor stopped and the driver called across to me.

'Need a tow?' he asked.

I declined the kind offer and went on to explain what had happened and how I was waiting for Ken.

Off he went. The next tractor that came along stopped. The driver called across.

'Do you need any help?'

Once again I explained the situation.

When the next tractor stopped, the terrible truth dawned on me. Being positioned as I was in a small clearing that was just around a bend, none of the tractors that were passing could see the short conversations I was having with the drivers ahead of them. I now realised that every remaining driver on the run would stop and offer to help me, and that there was nothing I could do about it. About thirty consecutive explanations as to why I didn't need their help would be needed. This was going to be exhausting.

Ten tractors and explanations later, I considered the option of hanging a sign around my neck saying:

'THE ANSWER IS NO. PISS OFF AND LEAVE ME ALONE.'

But I had no felt pen. Or card. Instead I tried to look at ease. Like I didn't need help. Like I was on top of things.

'Do you need a tow?' the next driver asked.

Oh dear.

Twenty-six detailed explanations later, Ken arrived – the tractor driver whose help I actually did need. Brother Tom was still sitting in the trailer, being pulled along behind like livestock on the way to the abattoir. Both men looked at me, seeking an explanation. The required words left my tongue with consummate ease. I'd had a good thirty rehearsals for this and I'd honed the simplest way of getting the message across in the shortest time.

Ken's solution was simple.

'You just come down the hill behind me. If we have to stop and the brakes won't hold you, just come into the back of me. That'll be fine.'

I saw a flicker of anxiety cross Brother Tom's face. Had Ken forgotten that he was towing his brother in a trailer? Or was he confident that the trailer was tough enough to withstand the impact of another tractor? I hoped so. I liked Brother Tom, and I didn't want him to be on the front page of *Tractor and Machinery* magazine for all the wrong reasons. Ken set off before there was time for debate, and Brother Tom seemed content enough to have a tractor with no brakes follow him down a hill. These country folk were a hardy bunch.

I began to enjoy the scenery again for the rest of the journey. With Ken ahead of me I felt safe. This final leg of the tractor run was serving as a metaphor for what had happened to me since I'd arrived in the West Country. Whenever I was in trouble then Ken was there to sort me out. Be it lending tools, fixing washing machines, towing cars, felling trees, shifting pianos and now chaperoning tractors, he was always the saviour – just as he had been again today. Long may that continue . . .

* * *

Patricia, the doula, seemed to be a good call. Yoga teachers tend not to be a stressed-out bunch and Patricia was no exception. She'd had a ton of experience of delivering babies, and she'd even had a couple herself, so she knew the score. She made several visits to the house to see how we were feeling, and to gauge how our preparations were going. On one of these occasions she recommended we try an exercise that many expecting couples found very helpful.

'We're going to use visualisation to take you both on a journey,' she said. 'But before we do that, can you share with me one of the fears that you might have around the birth?'

I sat back in my chair for a moment and wondered how it had all come to this? Not that long ago I had been living the London life, pursuing a career and going to dinner parties where we discussed our favourite restaurants. Now I was being asked to embark on visualisations by a lady in loose-fitting purple clothes. What's more, I was paying her. Was I a different person? Could I have changed that quickly? If so, had I instigated the change or was it a natural by-product of simple living. Had rural Devon weaved its spell on me?

Fran certainly embraced this visualisation stuff more readily than I did, and she answered Patricia's question about our fears.

'We're concerned that we'll get unsympathetic midwives who will bully us and try to force us into interventions that I don't want.'

'OK, close your eyes both of you,' said Patricia. 'Now picture the scene where this conflict is manifesting itself.'

Obediently I closed my eyes. I tried to imagine the scene, but I failed. Why I failed, I don't know. Whether I was trying to process too much information – to see it like one might watch a scene from a movie – I don't know, but I simply didn't see the pictures. Patricia was quickly off onto the next part of the visualisation though. She now asked me to imagine what I was saying to the people who were there at this scene, and how they were reacting. This was difficult since there was no one there yet. But Patricia continued.

'Imagine that these people are now gone. How do you feel?'

Well, I was doing better now because there was nobody there. But how did I feel? Well, the truth was that I felt confused, and a little concerned about what I was going to say at the end of this exercise.

This concern now dominated my thought processes. Patricia's instructions faded into the background and I no longer focused on them. They had no relevance to me since they required me to imagine dialogue and interaction with people and things that I had been unable to imagine in the first place. I was in an imagination cul-de-sac. As the time passed, my mind started to wander. I began to consider whether we needed to buy bananas, or if we should take the car into the garage for a service. After a few minutes of this I heard Patricia's voice again.

'Now I want you to open your eyes and draw a picture. Make the picture represent what you were feeling at the end of this journey that you've just been on. Off you go.'

What? Draw a picture? Draw a picture of what? How could I draw a picture of what I'd been thinking about? A banana in a garage? I looked at Fran. She was off – happily scribbling away. This was because she'd paid attention and I hadn't. I felt like I was at school. I had two options. I could tell the truth and explain that I'd failed at the very first hurdle and that my mind had wandered off – or I could bluff it out. The first option shouldn't have been a problem. It was not like school, after all. I had hired Patricia and so effectively I was the boss. There was absolutely no reason why I shouldn't have just explained what had happened.

Instead I began drawing. I heard a football result in my head.

Bluff It Out United 3, Integrity Albion 0.

Patricia went upstairs to the loo and I anxiously scribbled away, keen to draw something that would get me out of this hole.

'So Tony, what have you drawn?' asked Patricia when she returned, full of eager anticipation.

'I've drawn some mountains.'

'Great. Why?'

'Because they represent strength. They tower above situations, looking down on them, but without being drawn into them. They are nature. They change and adapt with the seasons, but they are immovable.'

'Superb,' said Patricia.

'And such a great drawing,' said Fran, 'I'm going to put that on the wall in the room where I give birth.'

I was a natural. I was going to be one hell of a birthing partner.

18

A Distinguished Guest

The date that Fran had allocated for the birth of our child passed without incident. It seemed that the power of the mind has its limitations. Perhaps the baby's mind was stronger than Fran's and that he or she had another day assigned in their womb diary: *Tuesday – Be born*.

I doubt it works like that though.

In fairness, Fran had picked a date that was four days before the date we'd been given by the midwife, so the lack of arrival was no cause for concern. However, when the due date itself arrived and passed without Fran showing the remotest hint of being about to give birth, some little alarm bells began to ring. I remembered Ken and Lin telling us how their son had arrived two weeks after the due date. Wow. Fourteen days waiting. That must have been tough. I wasn't sure if I could face that long in limbo-land.

That evening over dinner, I looked at Fran and I simply couldn't see a woman who would be a mother any time soon. I felt that, like Ken and Lin, we were in for a long wait, too.

'Baby will come when it's ready,' Fran pointed out.

'Yes, baby knows best,' I replied, without conviction.

* * *

The following morning, Fran woke me at 5.30 a.m. announcing that she'd been up for a few hours.

'What have you been doing?' I asked.

'Getting ready for having a baby.'

'What do you mean?'

'I mean that labour has started.'

I jumped out of bed, asked a string of useless questions and tried hard to mask the blind panic and turmoil within. Strangely, this moment had unearthed a kind of ludicrous denial within me. Although Fran had been evidently growing in size, and although we'd seen scans of the baby with our own eyes – I still didn't actually think it was going to happen. The actual baby bit. Not really. Not to us. Not to me.

However, now it seemed that it *was* going to happen. And it seemed like it was going to happen *today*. That wasn't fair. I wasn't ready. Fran's body, though – or the little mite inside it – had decided otherwise, and the contractions or surges were well under way. Fran climbed back into bed with me and we discussed the day ahead. OK, there weren't that many options on the table – a day trip to Alton Towers or a visit to a National Trust property were ill-advised – and we would be mostly responding to the events that came to pass inside Fran's body. Fran was certain that she wanted to have this baby at home, and that she wanted to do it without any drugs or medical interventions. As natural a birth as would be possible.

I held Fran close to me, as she bore with great fortitude the surges of these initial contractions, and tried to recall all the information that I'd been taught in the run-up to this momentous event. I drew a blank. How long and close together should contractions be before we were supposed to call the midwife? I couldn't remember. Neither could Fran. I called and woke Patricia, our doula, and told her that the contractions seemed to be coming every three minutes and they were about forty-five seconds long. She said she'd be straight over to assess the situation.

The bedroom was organised just how Fran wanted it for the birth, with drawings, photos and goodwill messages on the walls, and the sound system set up to play the hypnobirthing CD. The contractions were strong, but Fran was bearing them, soothed by the gentle voice in the speakers urging and encouraging her with positive affirmations, and reminding her to breathe herself into a relaxing place. In the meantime, nature was moving the baby ever closer to the world outside the womb.

When Patricia arrived — cool, calm, collected as ever — she immediately commented on how relaxed Fran looked.

'Looks like the hypnobirthing is working,' she said.

'When shall we call the midwife?' I asked.

'What do you think, Fran?' Patricia said.

'Can we leave it as late as possible?' replied Fran.

'Sure.'

And so we returned to the job in hand, a trio now, rather than a duo. Fran announced that she wanted to throw up but couldn't, I held her hand, and Patricia pulled out some knitting. We'd chosen well, I thought. If anything went wrong during the home birth, then we had someone on hand who could knit a hospital. Patricia was simply preparing for what could be many hours of waiting, but her first instinct was to be active. She went across to Fran and began massaging her back, the results of which could be read immediately on Fran's face.

I continued in a more administrative role, timing and making a note of the frequency of Fran's contractions – doing it all on my mobile phone. Initially, I felt this was an action that would be applauded, but then I became a little concerned as to how it looked to Patricia. Did she think that I was leaving my partner to battle her way through these challenging contractions whilst I sent texts to my mates?

BIRTH GOING OK, BUT BOY, DOES IT DRAG! YOU STILL OK FOR A PINT LATER? THEY'LL HAVE LIVERPOOL v UNITED ON THE BIG SCREEN

'At eight thirty, she had a 45-second contraction, and at eight thirty-four, a 40-second one,' I blurted out, anxious to reveal that I was on the case.

'Thanks, Tony,' said Patricia.

In the background, we could all hear the looping CD reminding Fran of what she wanted.

My birth will be easy because I am calm and relaxed
My baby is moving down gently

I wondered if this stuff actually *did* anything? Anybody's guess. It certainly didn't seem to be doing any harm. I'm not sure that the same could be said about many of the drugs that the pharmaceutical giants produce. A calm voice, set against a background of soothing music, *does* actually help you to relax, and it's beautiful in its simplicity. It was certainly working for Fran, almost certainly better than it would have done for me in the same situation. I've come to resent the tone of the voice adopted by the narrators on these relaxation CDs. They're too earnest. Too laden with implied meaning and depth. Then there's that music. Pan pipes. Why pan pipes all the time? Instead of visualising a deserted beach with waves gently lapping at the shore, I'm picturing myself snatching the pan pipes off the bearded, cross-legged musician and chucking them in the recycling bin.[1]

***

Time passed. Fran managed her body's recurring bouts of cramping, or whatever it was that was happening to her, with an admirable dignity and strength. As she had been coached to do, she seemed to be shutting the world out and going *into* her body, greeting each surge in the knowledge that it was bringing her closer to her new baby. How wonderful, I thought, that we were able to do this in the peace of our own bedroom, and away from the challenging atmosphere of a hospital. For us, no resuscitation machinery was standing by – instead, a framed portrait of a pig. Yes, Titch was looking on. Fran had been advised to surround herself with warm and loving images to help release the oxytocin that would aid the birthing process, and Titch had made it to the bedside table.[2]

'Any new feelings, Fran?' asked Patricia, as her knitting

1 Always thinking of the environment. It's well-known that pan pipes can be recycled into . . . well, more pan pipes.
2 There was a picture of me, too. It was slightly behind Titch's, because it must have got knocked.

needles clicked gently together, sounding like a metronome that had rebelled against the straitjacket of uniformity.

'Yes,' replied a composed Fran, 'it feels like I want to have a poo.'

Patricia put down her knitting needles.

'Tony, I think you should call the midwife. This means things are moving on.'[3]

Patricia glanced across at me and raised her eyebrows, a look which I took to mean, 'Get a move on.'

Forty-five minutes later, I was welcoming the midwives Odette and Fiona into our house. They were affable, composed, and although I couldn't speak for Fran, if you had to have two strangers help extricate a living being from inside your tummy, then they seemed like the sort you'd want on your team. I offered them tea, which they declined, and asked them to have a quick read of our birth plan. In this we had outlined Fran's desire for a natural birth with as little intervention as possible. They read it politely and promised that they would do all they could to follow it. I knew the form, though, and as much as any NHS midwife might want to leave a birthing mother alone to let events unfold as naturally and as peacefully as possible, they still had to follow protocol. These were the rules, and if they didn't heed them they got into trouble. It was as simple as that.

Once the midwives made it upstairs to Fran, Odette

---

3   This is because the baby is pressing down on the bowels. It's worth noting that, generally speaking, wanting a poo is not a sign that significant events are about to take place. (Although I believe Neville Chamberlain wanted a poo when he declared war on Germany.)

immediately began asking the questions that we knew would have to come. When did your contractions start? How long between them? When did you have your last pee? The estuaries of which two Devon rivers join to the north of Bideford and west of Barnstaple to empty into the Bristol Channel?

Fran did her best to answer without breaking the magical aura of calm that now surrounded her. I thought that she did particularly well with the last question, and ought to have been awarded extra birthing points for a correct answer. However, in spite of the plethora of paperwork that was now laid out on the floor around Odette, there seemed to be no scorecard included. One for the regulatory authority Ofbabe to look into.

Examinations followed, all offered and delivered as unobtrusively and as delicately as possible. Blood pressures and temperatures were taken, and then the dreaded 'internal'. Fran had not relished the prospect of this type of inspection, but it would enable the midwives to establish just how far into the birthing process she had progressed. As I looked at Fran lying there waiting whilst the midwife was pulling on a rubber glove, I recalled my own 'internal', as administered by Dr Shadley. At least when that had been done to me, three other people hadn't also been in the room, with one furiously writing up notes on the state of my arse. Childbirth for the mother, it seemed, required a comprehensive farewell to bashfulness. Let's just say that the birthing mother is unlikely to reach for the make-up mirror to check how the mascara is looking.

'Wow!' said Fiona, upon completing the examination. 'That's amazing. I can feel the baby's head. It's about an inch away.'

'Fran, you may well be having this baby before lunch,' said Odette.

Perhaps all that work had paid off in the preceding months. Fran's pregnancy yoga, the hypnobirthing meditations, the active birthing exercises – maybe even the song that we'd sung – had prompted the baby to get itself into the right position to be delivered. Everyone smiled at the news of the baby's possible imminent arrival, except Fran, who was still so focused on the job in hand that she wasn't hearing the conversations around her. Yes, at 11 a.m. we were all feeling extremely optimistic.

At 2 p.m. it was a totally different story. I could tell from the whispered conversations of the midwives that all was not well. For some reason, Fran's progress had completely stalled over the preceding few hours. Patricia had tried a few massage techniques, and yes, the contractions had continued, but the fact remained that Fran hadn't really entered the transition stage, and she'd had no urges to bear down and deliver the baby. Odette went out to make a phone call and I had a strong suspicion that she was calling her supervisor to see how much leeway we could be allowed. Time had clearly now become a factor.

'Do you have a mirror?' asked Fiona.

What a time to worry about your appearance, I thought.

'If we can hold the mirror below Fran, we can see what's going on down there when she has her contractions.'

'Down there' was an expression that I was hearing quite a lot. In spite of the raw and uncompromising nature of birth, I'd noted that people were still rather squeamish about using explicit language. It was a little odd, but now I think about it, maybe 'down there' was preferable to 'up your vaj'. That is what you'd hear if, owing to NHS staff shortages, you'd been sent a scaffolder instead of a midwife.

I set off on a mission to find a suitable mirror and scoured the bathroom with no success. Fran never bothered with make-up and thus no pocket mirror was to be found. I lifted the mirror off its hinges on the wall and carried it through to the bedroom. It was greeted with hoots of laughter.

'Way too big!' said Fiona.

'That's all I can find,' I replied.

'How about the one in the porch? That one looks to be smaller,' suggested Patricia.

'Right.'

Off I set, with a growing suspicion that the mirror I'd been sent to fetch was not significantly smaller than the previous one. And I was right. Nevertheless, I took it off the wall and brought it up to the midwives for their perusal. Somehow I figured that it might be a better shape for what they had in mind. Simply coming back and explaining that we had no suitable mirrors in the house might look like I hadn't really been trying.

Of course, the response was as before – with the addition of a hint of disbelief. Did this guy just bring in an identically sized mirror? How bright is he? What kind of a father is he going to make?

I set it down with the other mirror and rushed to assist Fran in another contraction. As I held her, frustratingly powerless to help beyond this simple act of compassion, the two mirrors were propped against the wall behind her, directly in my eyeline. I looked at myself. I didn't look well at all. It looked like it was me, not Fran, who had gone into the transition stage.

Odette returned from her phone call and asked if they could try some things to get the labour moving again. There was some concern that, in spite of all the water that Fran had been drinking, she'd not passed any urine. Perhaps the baby was in such a position that a blockage had been created. They wanted to use a urinary catheter to drain the bladder, and then for Fran to really try and consciously push the baby out, as they orchestrated some coached pushing.

'What do you think, Fran?' asked a concerned Odette.

'Can we talk it though?' replied an even more concerned Fran.

My heart sank. This had been one of my fears – that we would come into conflict with the approach of the midwives, and the natural birth that Fran so desperately wanted would be thwarted.

'Of course, you talk it through,' said Odette. 'We'll wait outside.'

What followed bordered on conspiratorial. Here we were – me, Fran and Patricia – huddled and whispering on the floor, like plotters against a government. Outside the door, our two house guests were probably trying to second-guess what we would say and were readying their arguments. These felt more like scenes from a Second World War spy drama than a Devon home birth. In hushed tones, the plotters discussed their options. Patricia felt that given enough time this baby would arrive naturally, but she also knew that something was amiss, and that the midwives' supervisor was almost certainly placing them under huge pressure to intervene in order to kick-start this stalled labour.

'Once they start the coached pushing,' explained Patricia,

'it really does become a race against the clock. If the baby doesn't come within a certain period, then they'll want to take you into hospital.'

'I don't want to have this baby in hospital,' announced Fran, whose position could not be clearer.

'But then the same applies if we don't do any of the things they're suggesting, right?' I asked. 'They'll still be pressing for us to go into hospital, if the baby doesn't arrive soon?'

'Yes. The only reason they haven't pressed for a hospital transfer already is because they've taken readings and checked that the baby's heartbeat is still fine, and there's no foetal distress. Basically, they see Fran's second stage of labour as having stalled and, according to protocol, they have to be seen to be doing something about that.'

'Shall I have a go at the pushing?' said Fran. 'I think I can get this baby out.'

'I think they will be very pleased if you say that,' said Patricia.

'OK. Let's do it.'

It was very generous of Fran to have used the term 'let's'. There was no 'let's' about this at all. It was very much 'her' that was going to do this pushing.

When I broke the news to Fiona and Odette, they seemed relieved. They wanted this home birth to happen, too, but their jobs were on the line if they didn't follow the codes of practice expected of them.

The fresh approach coincided with a change in the team, as Odette's shift finished and a new midwife arrived. Gwyneth. She was a no-nonsense woman whose direct and honest approach would prove invaluable in the next hour or so.

Odette slipped away, and with her so did the period of about two hours of relative calm – a calm, perversely, that had not been calming. Quietly, tension had been building in the room. There was a release now, as once again the bedroom became a place of action. The new team of Fiona and Gwyneth were able to use the catheter to extract a good amount of urine from Fran's bladder, confirming the theory about the blockage. Fran underwent an internal examination one more time, just to check that the baby was in the right position. Everything seemed fine.

No whistle was blown and there were no formal announcements, like 'Let pushing begin', but it felt as though there might have been. Everyone got ready and Fran took up a new position, whereby gravity could help bring the baby closer to taking a peek at the world outside the womb. Patricia sat on the birthing ball, with Fran squatting in front of her and facing away. She then hooked her arms under Fran's armpits and supported her. Meanwhile Fiona crouched on the floor before her, waiting to do what was necessary 'down there'. Gwyneth hovered over a seemingly ever-growing pile of paperwork on the bedroom floor.

Quite why a birth needs to be so admin-heavy remains a mystery to me. I can only assume that it stems from the lack of trust we have in our work culture. The assumption is that something hasn't been done, unless it's written down. Never mind that the act of writing it down means that some other important assistance in the birth cannot be given; everyone knows that during the act of childbirth, the most important thing is to end up with a decent set of graphs, and a comprehensive list of what happened and when. You don't want an unhappy boss back at the hospital.

Yes, I know it looks like a photo of a happy mother and her baby, but I'm not sure I can believe you until I see the facts and figures. Go away and come back when you can tell me how much urine was passed.

I crouched to the side of Fran, held her hand, and waited for the first 'coached' contraction to begin. The moment Fran tensed up and her breathing intensified, raised voices filled the once meditative space.

'PUSH, FRAN, PUSH!'

'COME ON, FRAN, YOU CAN DO IT!'

'THAT'S IT, THAT'S IT, FRAN. GIVE ME ANOTHER PUSH LIKE THAT!'

'WELL DONE, FRAN! YES! YES! ONE MORE!'

And then I heard something odd. In a momentary lull in the cacophonous support, I could hear the soft-voiced lady on the hypnobirthing CD gently advising Fran to 'relax', because her birth was going to be 'easy'. Almost immediately she was drowned out again as the shouted instructions kicked back in. Frankly her message was too quiet, too repetitive, and currently, too downright fallacious. What Fran was going through now was anything but easy. As these coached contractions continued, I could only imagine that it was Fran's fierce determination that was keeping her going, along with the spoon-fed dollops of manuka honey that I was providing. She did *not* want to be transferred to hospital, and that was giving her the strength for each extra push.

For me, the experience was both distressing and bewildering. It was hard to see someone you love in such a challenging situation, but I was also struggling to come to terms with whether this was *actually* happening. It all seemed too significant, too important, and too vital to be real. Outside the window, I could hear the occasional van or tractor pass by and I knew that Tuesday afternoon was carrying on as normal. Deliveries (of an altogether different nature) were being made, children were being collected from school and farmers were tending to their crops. Nobody knew what was happening in our bedroom, except those who were currently in it, and somehow that made it feel less real and more like a dream.

'COME ON, FRAN, ONE MORE PUSH! YOU CAN DO IT!'

Try to think of a hundred variations on this theme and I'm pretty certain that they were said in that room over the next ninety minutes or so.

Yes, ninety minutes. More probably. Fran gave it her absolute all every few minutes for over an hour and a half, and, despite the manuka honey refuelling, the poor girl was close to exhaustion.

The baby was close to arriving. 'Down there' was opening up and we could now see the hair on the baby's head, but Fran was just not quite able to force the head out.

'One more go,' said Fiona.

The contraction began, as did the accompanying chorus of encouragement – sounds not dissimilar in nature to those that might emanate from the stands at some great sporting spectacle:

'GO, FRAN, PUSH!'

'COME ON, FRAN, YOU CAN DO IT!'

'THAT'S IT, THAT'S IT, FRAN. GIVE ME ANOTHER PUSH LIKE THAT!'

'YES! YES! ONE MORE!'

My heart sank as I could see that this last push from Fran

didn't make a significant difference in the movement of the baby. I began to fear the worst; that the transfer to hospital Fran so wanted to avoid was now going to happen. Fiona had other ideas.

'Fran, how do you feel about us making a cut?'

'What?' managed a shattered Fran.

Fiona explained that they could perform an episiotomy – a small, diagonal cut in the vagina that would increase the exit route for the baby.

'We'll give you a local anaesthetic[4], so you won't feel anything.'

To my surprise, Fran agreed immediately. She was clearly at a point where she had very little left in the tank and needed to give birth soon.

Knives appeared. A small kit of sharp instruments was passed to Fiona, along with a needle and syringe. The anaesthetic was injected, and the cutting began. I looked away. Fran didn't even wince. The wonder of modern medicine. This would have been the point in years gone by when the mother would have been in absolute agony, and when the lives of both mother and baby would have been at risk. Gwyneth was able to step in and check the heartbeat of the baby and, to our great relief, reveal that it was still healthy.

When the next contraction arrived, the coaching recommenced and Fran pushed for all her worth. Baby's head was nearly there.

'Next time, you'll have your baby, Fran. Hang in there.'

---

4   I've had these at the dentist and I'm a fan of anaesthetics that are administered locally. They're so much better than the ones that are administered twenty miles away.

These words seemed to inspire Fran and when the next contraction arrived, she found one more reserve of energy and produced a push – at least for Fran and me – of historical proportions. Something extraordinary happened. In what seemed like a fraction of a second, out whizzed the baby, like it had been fired from a piece of industrial machinery. It plopped into Fiona's waiting hands, umbilical cord wrapped around it. It was crying. It was covered in gunge. It was an unbelievable sight. And it had a cock and balls. Probably a boy then.[5] In only a second, our lives had changed forever.

Fiona handed the baby boy to Fran, who clutched it to her chest. Hers and the baby's eyes met. Love at first sight. Pure joy. Nine months of preparation for this moment. Mother meets baby. The enigmatic lodger has shown his face at last. Exhaustion and love mixed on Fran's face to create the warmest smile I had ever seen.

And me? Well, I had been busy filming these first precious moments on my phone, conscious of activity around me, the midwives doing what midwives do at this point, the joyous sounds, a crying baby. I waited for my own emotional release – the tears of joy – and yet they didn't come. I still felt like an observer, oddly distanced. I stroked Fran's hair and congratulated her. I looked down and saw that the baby was already on Fran's breast. A very English lad. It was nearly four o'clock, so he knew it was teatime.

I was offered the opportunity to cut the umbilical cord, which had now stopped pulsating and was ready to be clamped. I declined the offer politely, because for me this

---

5 All that research hadn't been wasted.

was no big deal. I would sooner have someone do it who had done it before. *My* special moment was still to come.

'Are you ready now for the third stage, Fran?' asked Gwyneth.

Ah, yes – the third stage. I'd forgotten about that. As if the rigmarole of birth had not been testing enough, the mother now had to go through the further duty of birthing the placenta. Once again, Fran turned down the offer of the drugs that could facilitate this process, and she opted for a physiological third stage. Gwyneth suggested that they all went off to do this in the bathroom, and I was told to take my shirt off and to lie down with the baby and get some 'skin to skin' time. The baby was passed to me and I took it in my hands. Immediately I felt the fear that I have always felt when handling a baby – what if I drop it? I was expecting the fear to be diminished by the fact that, for the first time, this would actually be *my own* baby I would be dropping, but in reality the fear was more intense. Dropping somebody else's baby was stupid and careless, but dropping your own made you an abuser, and it probably had an accompanying prison sentence. I held on tight as I lifted the baby towards me and laid him across my chest, his little eyes looking up at me.

This was the moment. I became lost in his features, all-consumed by his presence. Here was the tiniest human being I had ever seen, who until a few minutes ago had been inside my partner's belly. Now he was beginning a life, and I was one of his protectors; I was to be his guide, his mentor. In this moment, the enormity of the task didn't overwhelm me – rather it filled me with pride. I would give my all and I would rise to the task. I had a strong sense that the past counted for nought. This was the real beginning. This was life's remaining challenge – to welcome this distinguished guest, to entertain him, to keep him peaceful and happy.

My eyes focused in on the baby's mouth and I could see that it looked like mine. Confirmation, if I needed it, that I was truly holding my genetic offspring. In some primal part of me connections were made, and whatever these connections were, they led to my tear duct. Slowly I wiped away the tear of joy. My first real tear of joy? Maybe. Our lives are full of firsts. The first time we walk, the first time we talk, the first time we dance, the first time we drink alcohol, the first time we make love. This was the first time I had ever stared at someone for forty minutes. This minuscule being had me transfixed. I barely noticed the sound emanating from the bathroom, where brave Fran was completing the placenta birthing procedure. A midwife appeared and assured me that all was well and that Fran would soon return to put the baby to her breast. Then we would begin family life together.

I hadn't looked once at the midwife during this last exchange. I was still caught in the headlights of the reclining life form before me, the beautiful, perfectly formed baby boy. Our Devonian son.

What now? I thought.

A split second of sheer panic. Aaaaaaaah! I had no idea.

Then I calmed down.

It was OK. I'd ask Ken.

Epilogue

The baby – we still didn't have a name[1] – slept on my chest for that first night, because Fran was so exhausted that she was out for the count, and nothing, but nothing, would wake her. A simple thing, you'd imagine, sleeping with a tiny, little human being on your chest, but it was both exciting and terrifying in equal measure. Each time he went quiet, I needed to check his breathing. My night sleeping with Titch in Tavistock hadn't prepared me adequately for confident fatherhood, and somehow I couldn't yet trust that this baby was built to keep on going.

In the morning I arose, convinced that I had bonded with my boy, and punch drunk with weariness, I began to ready myself for my role in these next few weeks.

House nurse.

Whilst Fran recovered, I would attempt to run the house. Such a task was daunting for a fresh and vibrant version of me, but the sleep-deprived idiot who was attempting to navigate his way around the kitchen

---

1 We'll have that sorted by the time of the sequel.

cupboards felt overwhelmed. It was shaming. Fran had gone through this extraordinary physical feat of carrying a baby and giving birth, and yet I was struggling with the fear of making breakfast, lunch and dinner, and operating the washing machine, dishwasher and vacuum cleaner. Putting off a start on the housework, I took five minutes to text friends and family with news of the birth. Then I picked up the phone.

'Ken?'

'Yes?'

'It's Tony. We've had a little baby boy.'

'That's marvellous news. You wait till I tell Lin. She'll be thrilled. Well done.'

Ten minutes later, I looked out of the window. There were blue balloons all the way along our front fence. A car went by and beeped its horn. The village had now been informed. Forget all the modern technology. Sod email, Facebook and Twitter, the balloons were up and the message was clear. A little baby boy.

The phone rang. More congratulations? No, it was Fran, using her mobile from upstairs. I didn't know it yet, but this method of communication would mimic the old-fashioned bells that rang when the aristocracy wanted something from the staff below stairs. Could I bring Fran a drink? You bet. I rushed up with a cup of tea (not before knocking several things over first) to see my heroine proudly holding our new baby. Taking care not to crush baby, we managed our first family group hug. Wow.

Later that day, Lin popped round and took all the linen, sheets and general detritus of the birth and shoved it all through her washing machine. I'm not sure what model it is, but it must be a good one, because everything returned looking spotless.

Throughout the day cards dropped in through the letterbox and presents appeared in the porch. All were resolutely blue.[2] Fran and I were touched by just how many people in the village cared about us. If we needed confirmation that we had made the right call moving here, then here it was – in blue and white. The offers of help that accompanied the best wishes were tempting. When I read 'Let us know if there's anything we can do to help', I wanted to reply, 'Yes, come and cook every meal for us, change the nappies, do the washing and sort out all the shopping. Take Saturday mornings off.'

The R word more than ever loomed large at the start of every day; confirmation that our lives had changed forever. It occurred to me that becoming a parent is a great leveller. Never mind the career or life achievements you may have notched up so far in your life, from now on it was all about how loving you could be. You may have been a brilliant scholar or virtuoso musician; you may have made a fortune as an astute, hard-working entrepreneur; you may have even written a bestselling book involving eccentric journeys with white goods – but all that would count for nothing in your parenting henceforth.

All that mattered now was how much love you had left for those around you, and especially this brand-spanking-new, little human being. It was as if somebody had taken all

2 It seems we live in a culture that supports the notion that boys like blue and girls like pink. If you don't believe me, go out and try to buy a pink card for a male newborn. If you're lucky, you might find one in Brighton.

the values you'd held until this point in your life, and tossed them up into the sky. You could reach out for them as they fell back down through the air, and you might catch one or two on the way down, but ultimately you were starting again.

* * *

Fran and I handled those early weeks as best we could, given that we had read the equivalent of a small library's worth of books on childbirth, but nothing at all on what to do with the thing once it had 'popped' out.[3] Armed with a valiant ignorance, we bumbled and dithered our way through with a touching clumsiness – at least, we hoped that young Hawks would have found it so, had he been able to recognise what was going on. One day I'll attempt to tell him, and he'll show as much interest as I did when my parents attempted to do the same.

We found ourselves following our instincts, whilst at the same time trying to filter the diverse and contradictory advice that was constantly on offer from those who had walked this road before us. I can't remember the number of times we were warned against doing something, because we would be making 'a rod for our own backs'.

Don't feed them when they're hungry, otherwise they'll keep expecting food when they're hungry.

Yes, well, that's just inconsiderate and we'd definitely need to stamp out that kind of behaviour.

A few times, we were told that we would have to be

---

3   Yes, I know – only a man could describe birth thus.

careful, otherwise our baby would 'manipulate' us. Yes, and there's some sound reasoning behind that theory, too. Everyone knows that the main reason why babies can't stop the poo coming out of their arses is because all their attention is going on spinning an elaborate web of schemes and stratagems that will enable them to get what they want. We would have to be vigilant. We wouldn't want to offer our baby comfort when he was crying, if actually what lay behind his tears was a desire to get the bedroom painted a colour that better matched his favourite Babygro. Yes, we'd be on the lookout for that.

All that we were sure of was that almost everything that had ever been written about parenting seemed to be the polar opposite of something that had been written elsewhere. The only thing on which there appeared to be general agreement was that babies shouldn't be dropped on their heads – although someone somewhere will no doubt have a theory that this strengthens their necks, and prepares them for the hard knocks of life that are still to come. All we could hang on to was the fact that we had the two most important resources available to our child – time and love.

On top of that, we could sprinkle the extra ingredients of a delightful environment in which to live, and a good bunch of caring, attentive neighbours. And how our neighbours shared in the excitement of a new baby in the village. Each time we'd bump into somebody – on the few occasions when we had the time or inclination to venture outside – an excited yelp would be followed by delighted fussing and extensive questioning. Most commonly we heard:

'Is he good?'

At first this confused me. What *did* they mean? *Is he good?*

Were they asking if he did much voluntary work, ran errands for the elderly, or raised money for charitable causes? If so, then he wasn't *good*, because he did none of those things. But if he wasn't good, then did this make him bad? But how could he be bad? He'd hardly burgled any houses, put anyone to death, or claimed for expenses on a second home in his constituency that he didn't use. I assume that what was really being asked in this question was 'How badly had he disrupted our lives?' *Is he good?* means 'Does he cry much?' or 'Does he sleep through the night?' Dangerous criteria for judging goodness, in my book. Hitler, Pol Pot, Stalin, and Saddam Hussein were all good sleepers and, as far as I know, they only cried when they stubbed their toes.

In spite of the odd unwelcome tip on parenting, we were generally delighted to be in a community where who we were, and what we were doing, mattered to those around us. Most of the time we were too sleep-deprived, vague and dazed to notice it, but we had definitely gone from being anonymous Londoners to part of a community, and this community was helping us to fumble through our first fortnight of parenthood, a period that we were coming to view as a state of joyous upheaval.

We had a vision for the future, too, just like those early pilgrims on the *Mayflower* who, like us, had headed West to start a new life. We wanted to raise our child learning to grow food; to be conscious of, and responsible with, the energy that he would use; to learn to love others, but above all himself; and to sit in on village hall meetings to make sure that we bought in toilet paper before it ran out.

And one day maybe, just maybe, he'd get to drive Reg's Zetor tractor.

From: Tony Hawks
Sent: Wednesday, 2 April 2014, 12:58 p.m.
To: Ian Hislop
Subject: this is all your fault

Ian
This is all your fault.
If you hadn't saved my seat next to Fran at the
Samuel Johnson Prize then none of this would have
happened.

Tony and Fran x

From: Ian Hislop
Subject: Re: this is all your fault
Date: 3 April 2014, 09:05:42 GMT+01:00
To: Hawks Tony

Amazing ! Congratulations to you both ! What a wonderful result from such a small act – we have done something useful with our lives after all! Ian and Victoria x

Acknowledgements

I'd like to say a big thank you to all the characters who appear in this book. Without you there is no story and you are what makes it fun. I hope I have done you justice and please forgive me for not spending more time describing how beautiful/handsome you are. I wanted to – honestly – but those bastard editors at the publishers wouldn't have it. I'd also like to say thank you to those bastard editors at the publishers.